PINCHED

PINCHED

HOW THE **GREAT RECESSION** HAS

NARROWED OUR FUTURES

and WHAT WE CAN

DO ABOUT

IT

DON PECK

CROWN PUBLISHERS

New York

Copyright © 2011 by Don Peck

All rights reserved.
Published in the United States by Crown Publishers, an imprint of the
Crown Publishing Group, a division of Random House, Inc., New York.
www.crownpublishing.com

CROWN and the Crown colophon are registered trademarks of
Random House, Inc.

Library of Congress Cataloging-in-Publication Data is available upon request.

ISBN 978-0-307-88652-1
eISBN 978-0-307-88654-5

Printed in the United States of America

Book design by Lauren Dong
Jacket design by W. G. Cookman
Jacket illustration by Kevin Orvidas/Getty Images

10   9   8   7   6   5   4   3   2   1

First Edition

"We are unsettled to the very roots of our being. There isn't a human relation, whether of parent and child, husband and wife, worker and employer, that doesn't move in a strange situation. . . . There are no precedents to guide us, no wisdom that wasn't made for a simpler age. We have changed our environment more quickly than we know how to change ourselves."

—WALTER LIPPMANN,
*Drift and Mastery: An Attempt to Diagnose the
Current Unrest,* 1914

CONTENTS

INTRODUCTION

WHAT LIES ON THE OTHER SIDE OF THE GREAT RECESSION?
Nearly three years after the crash of 2008, the American
economy has partly recovered, the market has long since rallied, and
Wall Street is back from the dead and newly flush. In many of the
nation's most affluent suburbs and in the centers of its most dynamic
cities, life has gone back to something like normal. Yet outside these
islands of affluence, jobs remain scarce and the housing market dev-
astated. Millions of families have fallen out of the middle class, and
millions of young adults have found themselves unable to climb up
into it. Throughout much of the country, debilitating weakness lingers on.

This book is about the enduring impact that the Great Recession
will have on American life. What we know from three comparable
economic calamities—the panic of the 1890s, the Great Depression,
and the oil-shock recessions of the 1970s—is that periods like this
one deepen society's fissures and eventually transform the culture.
The social changes that occurred in the midst of these other major
downturns lasted decades beyond the end of the crises themselves.
The Great Recession will prove no different. The crash has already
shifted the course of the U.S. economy, and its continuing reverbera-
tions have changed the places we live, the work we do, our family
ties, and even who we are. But the recession's most significant and
far-reaching ramifications still lie in the future.

"If something cannot go on forever," the late economist Herbert
Stein famously said, "it will stop." The Great Recession put an end
to many unsustainable habits, most notably a decade-long mania for

credit spending, fueled by a national housing bubble of epic proportions. But by deflating that bubble—and halting all the optimistic spending that had gone along with it—the recession also laid bare other, much deeper economic trends: the growing concentration of wealth among a tiny sliver of Americans; the thinning of the middle class; the diverging fortunes of different regions, cities, and communities. Indeed, as periods like this one usually do, the recession has accelerated these trends.

When, and for that matter *how*, will the United States fully recover? These are urgent and complex questions, and in this book I will do my best to answer them. But in truth, societies never just "recover" from downturns this severe. They emerge from them different than they were before—stronger in some ways, weaker in others, and in many respects simply transformed.

Across American society, old, familiar patterns of work, family, and everyday life have been disrupted and remade since the crash. Intense economic forces are remolding the American experience and redefining the American Dream.

• The economic rift between rich Americans and all other Americans is gaping wider as the former recover and the latter do not. And in the recession's aftermath, a cultural rift has grown, too: for the very rich, in particular, global affinities and global ambitions are quickly supplanting national ties and national concerns. Increasingly, the very rich see themselves as members of a global elite with whom they have more in common than with other classes of Americans. Politically influential and economically powerful, they are becoming a separate nation with its own distinct goals.

• The fortunes of different places also are diverging quickly. High-powered areas like New York, Silicon Valley, and Washington, DC, are putting the recession behind them. Former oases for aspiring middle-class Americans—Phoenix, Tampa, Las Vegas—have been exposed as mirages. Nationwide, newer suburbs on the exurban fringe appear to be in irreversible decline, and the families living in them are stuck and struggling. As a result, middle-class mores and lifestyles are being transformed—and so are the futures of middle-class children.

• Women are fast becoming the essential breadwinners and authority figures in many working-class families—a historic role reversal that is fundamentally changing the nature of marriage, sex, and parenthood. Working-class men, meanwhile, are losing their careers, their families, and their way. A large, white underclass, predominantly male, is forming—along with a new politics of grievance. Both will shape the nation's character long after the recession is fully over.

• The Millennial Generation, the largest generation in American history and perhaps the most audacious, is sinking. Many twenty-somethings will emerge from the Great Recession with their earning power permanently reduced, their confidence dimmed, and their ideals profoundly changed.

Some of the transformations under way are direct results of the recession's severity. When jobs are scarce, incomes flat, and debts heavy for protracted periods, people, communities, and even whole generations can be left permanently scarred. And some of these changes are products of economic forces that predate the recession but have been strengthened by it. In the end, the crisis cannot be separated from the technological revolution that was under way in the United States for years beforehand: it was in some respects the denouement of that revolution, and the related revolution in global trade. The global economy is evolving at an unprecedented pace, and while some Americans and many U.S. businesses have adapted well, the country as a whole has not. It will remain economically vulnerable and socially divided until it does.

Pinched begins with some history, explaining why the Great Recession stands apart from the downturns that immediately preceded it, and detailing what we can learn from the aftermath of other crashes, further back in America's history, that more closely recall this one. The heart of the book describes how this period has changed the character and future prospects of different people and communities throughout the country: striving middle-class families, inner-city youth, newly minted college graduates, blue-collar men, affluent professionals, elite financiers. When they linger long enough, hard times and deep uncertainty can greatly alter people's values, social relationships, and even personal identity. Around the nation, some of those changes are just now becoming visible.

The final section of the book describes how our politics and national character are changing as a result of economic weakness—and how we can recover from this period and build a stronger, more resilient economy and society. Part of the answer lies in smarter, more creative, and more decisive government actions. And part lies in a renewed private commitment to civic responsibility and community life. This period of globalization and disruptive technological change, distilled and made toxic by the Great Recession, has left our social fabric tattered. We can restore it, both through public action and through our own daily choices.

We sit today between two eras, buffeted, anxious, and uncertain of the future. But the United States has endured periods like this in the past, and has emerged from them all the stronger. Indeed, America's capacity for adaptation and reinvention is perhaps the country's best historic trait. The time is ripe for another such reinvention. I hope that this book, by describing and connecting the problems our society faces and by suggesting some potential remedies, might help inform the pressing question of how we can pull it off.

1

NOT YOUR FATHER'S
RECESSION

THE GREAT RECESSION ENDED, ANY STUDENT OF THE BUSINESS cycle will tell you, in June 2009, a year and a half after it began. It was the decade's second and more severe recession; the economy shrank by more than 4 percent and more than 8 million people lost their job. The average house fell 30 percent in value, and the typical household lost roughly a quarter of its net worth. The Dow, from peak to trough, shed more than 7,000 points. One hundred and sixty-five commercial banks failed in 2008 and 2009, and the investment banks Bear Stearns and Lehman Brothers ceased to exist.

Even these summary figures are bracing. But this clinical accounting does not capture the recession's impact on American society—a heavy trauma that has changed the culture and altered the course of innumerable people's lives. And of course, for many Americans, the recession has not really ended. As of this writing, while parts of the economy are recovering, the unemployment rate is still nearly twice its pre-recession level, housing values are still testing new lows, and millions of families who'd thought of themselves as upwardly mobile or comfortably middle-class are struggling with a new and bitter reality.

The Great Recession will not be remembered as a mere turning of the business cycle. "I think the unemployment rate will be permanently higher, or at least higher for the foreseeable future," said Mark Zandi, the chief economist at Moody's Analytics, in 2009. "The collective psyche has changed as a result of what we've been through. And we're going to be different as a result." By early 2011, mass layoffs had ceased, by and large, but job growth remained anemic. What few jobs have been created since the recession ended pay much less, on average, than those that were destroyed.

In its origins, its severity, its breadth, and its social consequences, the current period resembles only a few others in American history—the 1890s, the 1930s, and in more limited respects the 1970s. As with each of those historic downturns, the Great Recession and its aftermath will ultimately be remembered as a time of both economic disruption and cultural flux—and as the marker between the end of one chapter in American life and the beginning of another.

Inevitably, the rhythm of life changes in countless ways during economic downturns. People drive less, and as a result, both traffic fatalities and total mortality usually decline. They also date less, sleep more, and spend more time at home. Pop songs become more earnest, complex, and romantic. In nearly all aspects of life, even those unrelated to budgets and paychecks, caution prevails.

Some of these changes are mere curiosities, and most are ephemeral, vanishing as soon as boom times return and the national mood brightens. But extended downturns yield larger and more long-lasting changes as well, ones that can be felt for decades. Fewer weddings have been celebrated since the crash, and fewer babies born. More young children have spent formative years in material poverty, and a greater number still in a state of emotional impoverishment brought on by the stresses and distractions of parental unemployment or household foreclosure. Many young adults have found themselves unable to step onto a good career track, and are slowly acquiring a stigma of underachievement that will be hard to shed. Many communities, haunted by foreclosure, have tipped into decline.

Bewilderment—and, increasingly, a sense of permanent loss—has filled the pages of the nation's newspapers. "I never thought I'd be in the position where I had to go to a food bank," said Jean Eisen, a 57-year-old former salesperson in Southern California, to the *New York Times*. But there she was, two years after she'd lost her job, waiting for the Bread of Life food pantry to open its doors. "I never imagined I'd be unmarried at 37," wrote one anonymous professional to the advice columnist Emily Yoffe at *Slate*. He'd been jobless for three years and was living with his parents. "I used to think I was a catch," he wrote. "Every passing month makes me less of one."

"There's no end to this," said Kevin Jarret, a real-estate agent in Cape Coral, Florida, to the *Times*. His investment properties were long gone, lost in foreclosure, and so were his wife and daughter; hardship is "trying on a relationship," he said. His house was mostly empty; he'd sold most of his furniture to put food on the table. He'd kept a statuette of Don Quixote, in an irony that did not escape him. "You know, dream the impossible dream."

Nearly four years after it began, the Great Recession is still reshaping the character and future prospects of a generation of young adults—and those of the children behind them as well. It is leaving an indelible imprint on many blue-collar men—and on blue-collar culture. It is changing the nature of modern marriage, and, in some communities, crippling marriage as an institution. It is plunging many inner cities into a kind of despair and dysfunction not seen for decades.

Not every community or family has been hurt by the Great Recession, of course. Although there are many exceptions, the people and places that were affluent and well established before the crash have for the most part shrugged off hard times; it's the rest of America that is still suffering. That, too, will be a legacy of this period: by and large, it has widened the class divide in the United States, and increased cultural tensions. In countless ways, we will be living in the recession's shadow for years to come.

WHY HAS THE Great Recession been so severe? And why has its grip on the country proved so stubborn?

Part of the answer stems from the nature of the crash itself. Major financial crises nearly always leave wounds that take many years to heal. Sickly banks lend sparingly and consumers, poorer, keep their wallets closed, making a strong and rapid rebound all but impossible. One study of more than a dozen severe financial crises worldwide since World War II, published in 2009 by the economists Carmen Reinhart and Kenneth Rogoff, found that on average, the unemployment rate rose for four full years following a crisis (by about seven percentage points in total). Housing values fell for six straight years (by 35 percent). Real government debt rose by an average of 86 percent, fueled by tax shortfalls and stimulative measures. And yet, absent quick and aggressive government action, the pain sometimes lingered longer—as Japan's "lost decade" in the 1990s and the Great Depression both attest.

The crisis had many culprits, not least among them a financial industry that casually took vast gambles, in the belief (largely correct) that in the event of catastrophic losses, the government would pick up the tab. Yet for more than a decade before the crash actually happened, Wall Street's actions were well aligned with Main Street America's dreams and desires. Finance nourished a growing American appetite for debt and fed a way of life that had long since become unsustainable. For a generation or more before the crash, Americans' spending was untethered from their pay. Two great asset bubbles—the tech bubble of the late 1990s, followed almost immediately by the housing bubble of the past decade—encouraged people to routinely outspend their income, secure in the belief that their ever-rising wealth could make up the growing difference.

Knowingly or not, the Federal Reserve encouraged this practice (and the bubbles themselves) by keeping interest rates low in good times as well as bad, and some economists celebrated a "great moderation" in the business cycle—the success the Fed had in keeping recessions rare, short, and mild over the previous thirty years. But in some respects the Fed was merely delaying the pain of adjustment, and setting up consumers and the economy for a much larger fall.

It is hard to overstate the extent to which the housing bubble distorted and weakened the U.S. economy. For years and years, too much money was sunk into houses and too little into productive investments (from 1999 to 2009, according to the economist Michael Mandel, housing accounted for more than half the growth in private fixed assets nationwide; by comparison, business software and IT equipment made up just 14 percent of that growth). The construction, real-estate, and finance industries, increasingly reliant on one another as the years went by, became grossly bloated, making up almost a quarter of U.S. output in 2006 (up from about a fifth in 1995). Too many high-school students forswore college for construction, and too many top college graduates went to Wall Street. And, of course, too many families bought houses in boomtowns like Phoenix and Las Vegas, and are now stuck in place.

While it was still rising, the housing bubble masked many problems. Most people's incomes did not grow throughout the aughts (indeed, the ten years prior to 2009 marked the first full decade since at least the 1930s in which the median household income declined) and employment growth was historically low as well. Housing provided the sense of upward mobility that paychecks did not. That's one reason the recession has felt even worse than the usual statistics indicate: many Americans, even those who didn't lose their jobs, lost a decade's sense of progress. Long deferred, a decade's disappointment has been concentrated in the past three years.

Housing is by far the largest asset held by most American families, and also their most leveraged investment. Since the market peaked, more families have lost more of their wealth than at any time since the Great Depression. Nationwide, nearly one in four houses was underwater at the start of 2011. Nearly one in seven mortgages was in arrears or foreclosure, almost double the rate before the recession began. And it is by no means clear that housing values have yet hit bottom; near the end of 2010, some analysts believed housing was still as much as 20 percent overvalued nationwide.

Most recessions end when people start spending freely again, and consumer spending has risen since the depths of the crisis. But given the size of the bust, a large, sustained consumer boom seems unlikely in the near future. The ratio of household debt to disposable income, about 85 percent in the mid-1990s, was almost 120 percent near the end of 2010, down just a little from its 130 percent peak. It is not merely animal spirits that are keeping people from spending freely (though those spirits are dour). Heavy debt and large losses of wealth have forced spending onto a lower path. Household "deleveraging" is likely to take years to complete.

In the long run, the prescription for the U.S. economy is clear: exports need to grow and consumer spending needs to shift from America to Asia, where savings and surpluses are high. If Asian consumers can be persuaded to save less and spend more, exports can power U.S. growth and job creation while American consumers rebuild their finances and settle into sustainable lifestyles. That transition is essential not just for the health of the U.S. economy, but for the sustainability of global economic growth.

But as Raghuram Rajan, an economist at the University of Chicago and the former chief economist of the International Monetary Fund, wrote in his recent book about the crisis, *Fault Lines: How Hidden Fractures Still Threaten the World Economy*, the cultural and institutional barriers to spending in Asia are exceedingly high. China's resistance in 2010 to measures that might substantially depreciate the dollar (making U.S. exports more competitive and Chinese imports less attractive) underscores that point. Meanwhile, Europe and Japan—both major markets for U.S. exports—remain weak. And in any case, exports make up only about 13 percent of total U.S. production; even if they grow quickly, the base is so small that the overall impact will be muted for quite some time.

One big reason the economy stabilized in 2009 was the stimulus. The Congressional Budget Office estimates that even in the fourth quarter of 2010, the stimulus buoyed output by perhaps 2 percent and full-time equivalent employment by perhaps 3 million jobs, although its impact was by then declining. The stimulus will continue to trickle into the economy for the next year or so, but as a concentrated force, it's largely spent. The extension of the Bush tax cuts at the end of 2010 delayed fiscal contraction, and other measures in the bill provided some new stimulus for 2011. But with federal government debt nearing historic highs, the prospects for further action look limited today. The president's federal budget proposal for fiscal year 2012 projected a deficit of some $1.6 trillion in 2011. When fiscal contraction begins—as, sooner or later, it must—it will inevitably begin to drag growth down, rather than pump it up.

BY THE MIDDLE of 2010, according to one survey, 55 percent of American workers had experienced a job loss, a reduction in hours, an involuntary change to part-time status, or a pay cut since the recession began. In January 2011, almost 14 million people were unemployed, and the average duration of unemployment, more than nine months, was longer than it had ever been since the Bureau of Labor Statistics began tracking that figure in 1948. Unemployment benefits have been extended to ninety-nine weeks in many states, but even so, nearly 4 million people exhausted them in 2010. In February 2011, the percentage of the population that was employed was at its lowest point since the recession had begun; the apparent improvement in the unemployment rate in the months before that was the result of people leaving the workforce altogether, or deferring entry into it.

According to Andrew Oswald, an economist at the University of Warwick, in the United Kingdom, and a pioneer in the field of happiness studies, no other circumstance produces a larger decline in mental health and well-being than being involuntarily out of work for six months or more. It is the worst thing that can happen, he says, equivalent to the death of a spouse, and "a kind of bereavement" in its own right. Only a small fraction of the decline can be tied directly to losing a paycheck, Oswald notes; most of it appears to be the result of a tarnished identity and a loss of self-worth. Unemployment leaves psychological scars that remain even after work is found again. And because the happiness of family members is usually closely related, the misery spreads throughout the home.

Especially in middle-aged people, long accustomed to the routine of the office or factory, unemployment seems to produce a crippling disorientation. At a series of workshops for the unemployed that I attended around Philadelphia in late 2009, the participants—mostly men, and most of them older than forty—described the erosion of their identities, the isolation of being jobless, and the indignities of downward mobility. Over lunch I spoke with one attendee, Gus Poulos, a Vietnam-era veteran who had begun his career as a refrigeration mechanic before going to night school and becoming an accountant. He was trim and powerfully built, and looked much younger than his fifty-nine years. For seven years, until he was laid off in December 2008, he was a senior financial analyst for a local hospital.

Poulos said that his frustration had built and built over the past year. "You apply for so many jobs and just never hear anything," he told me. "You're one of my few interviews. I'm just glad to have an interview with anybody," even a reporter. Poulos said he was an optimist by nature, and had always believed that with preparation and steady effort, he could overcome whatever obstacles life put before him. But sometime in the past year, he'd lost that sense, and at times he felt aimless and adrift. "That's never been who I am," he said. "But now, it's who I am."

Recently he'd gotten a part-time job as a cashier at Walmart, for $8.50 an hour. "They say, 'Do you want it?' And in my head, I thought, 'No.' And I raised my hand and said, 'Yes.' " Poulos and his wife met when they were both working as supermarket cashiers, four decades earlier—it had been one of his first jobs. "Now, here I am again."

Poulos's wife was still working—as a quality-control analyst at a food company—and that had been a blessing. But both were feeling the strain, financial and emotional, of his situation. She commutes about a hundred miles every weekday, which makes for long days. His hours at Walmart were on weekends, so he didn't see her much anymore and didn't have much of a social life.

Some neighbors were at the Walmart a couple of weeks earlier, he said, and he rang up their purchase. "Maybe they were used to seeing me in a different setting," he said—in a suit as he left for work in the morning, or walking the dog in the neighborhood. Or "maybe they were daydreaming." But they didn't greet him, and he didn't say anything. He looked down at his soup, pushing it around the bowl with his spoon for a few seconds before looking back up at me. "I know they knew me," he said. "I've been in their home."

A 2010 study sponsored by Rutgers University found a host of social and psychological ailments among people who'd been unemployed for seven months or more: 63 percent were suffering from sleep loss, 46 percent said they'd become quick to anger, and 14 percent had developed a substance dependency. A majority were avoiding social encounters with friends and acquaintances, and 52 percent said relationships within their family had become strained. Like other studies of long-term unemployment, the report describes a growing isolation, a warping of family dynamics, and a slow separation from mainstream society.

There is unemployment, a brief and relatively routine transitional state that results from the rise and fall of companies in any economy, and there is *unemployment*—chronic, all-consuming. The former is a necessary lubricant in any engine of economic growth. The latter is a pestilence that slowly eats away at people, families, and, if it spreads widely enough, society itself. Indeed, history suggests that it is perhaps society's most noxious ill.

SINCE THE CRASH, periods of optimism have come and gone like the seasons—2009 gave us the "green shoots" of an economic spring, and 2010 a "recovery summer." And of course the economy has improved overall. Yet with each passing year, government and private forecasts have continued to push a full jobs recovery further and further into the future. In January 2009, a White House study predicted that, assuming the stimulus legislation passed, the unemployment rate would be about 7 percent by the end of 2010. As the end of 2010 approached, the Fed estimated that the unemployment rate would still be a full point higher than that when we ring in 2013. If the labor recovery follows the same basic path as it did in the previous two recessions, in 1991 and 2001, unemployment will still be nearly 8 percent in 2014. Even if jobs grow as fast and consistently as they did in the mid-1990s, it will not fall below 6 percent until 2016.

No one knows how fast jobs will come back—or where the unemployment rate will ultimately settle. The only theoretical limit on job growth is labor supply, and a lot more labor is sitting idle today than usual. Major technological breakthroughs—notoriously difficult to predict—could add speed and durability to the recovery. Smart government action or a rapid acceleration of global growth could do the same. Yet by many measures, the rate of innovation in the United States has been low for more than a decade—with the housing bubble, we simply didn't notice. And the trend following recent downturns has been toward slower recoveries, not faster ones. Jobs came back more slowly after the 1990 recession than they had in the previous recession in 1981, and more slowly after the recession of 2001 than they had in 1991. Indeed, American workers never fully recovered from the 2001 recession: the share of the population with a job never again reached its previous peak before this downturn began.

As of early 2011, the economy sits in a hole more than 11 million jobs deep—that's the number required to get back to 5 percent unemployment, the rate we had before the recession started, and one that's been more or less typical for a generation. And because the population is growing and new people are continually coming onto the job market, we need to produce roughly 1.5 million new jobs a year—about 125,000 a month—just to keep from sinking deeper.

Even as demand grows, the process of matching some workers with new jobs is likely to be slow and arduous. Over the past thirty years, temporary layoffs have gradually given way to the permanent elimination of jobs, the result of workforce restructuring. More than half of all the jobs lost in the Great Recession were lost forever. And while businesses are slowly creating new jobs as the economy grows, many have different skill requirements than the old ones. "In a sense," says Gary Burtless, a labor economist at the Brookings Institution, "every time someone's laid off now, they need to start all over. They don't even know what industry they'll be in next."

IN 2010, THE phone maker Sony Ericsson announced that it was looking to hire 180 new workers in the vicinity of Atlanta, Georgia. But the good news was tempered. An ad for one of the jobs, placed on the recruiting website the People Place, noted the following restriction, in all caps: "NO UNEMPLOYED CANDIDATES WILL BE CONSIDERED AT ALL."

Ads like this one have been popping up more frequently over the past year or so; CNN, the Huffington Post, and other news outlets have highlighted many examples, involving a wide range of jobs— tax managers, quality engineers, marketing professionals, grocery-store managers, restaurant staff. Sometimes the ads disappear once the media calls attention to them (a spokesperson for Sony Ericsson said its ad was a mistake). But new ones continue to appear. "I think it is more prevalent than it used to be," said Rich Thomson, a vice president at Adecco, the world's largest staffing firm, midway through 2010; several companies had recently told him they were restricting their candidate pools in a similar fashion.

To a certain extent, these restrictions are an unjust by-product of the desperation of many unemployed Americans, who have inundated companies with applications, sometimes indiscriminately. And of course, they also show the extent to which it is still a buyer's market, in which employers can afford to be extraordinarily

selective. But these restrictions may portend something more enduring, as well. Temporary unemployment can become permanent after
a time; companies sometimes ignore people who have been out of a
job for a year or two, and the economy—somewhat shrunken—just
moves on without them.

The economic term for this phenomenon is *hysteresis*, and it can
be one of the worst consequences of a very long recession. When
people are idle for long periods, their skills erode and their behavior
may change, making some of them unqualified even for work they
once did well. Their social networks shrink, eliminating word-of-
mouth recommendations. And employers, perhaps suspecting personal or professional dysfunction even where it is absent, may begin
to overlook them en masse, instead seeking to outbid one another
for current or recently unemployed workers once demand returns.
That can ultimately lead to higher inflation, until the central bank
takes steps to depress demand again. The economy is left with a
higher "natural" rate of unemployment, a smaller working population, and lower output potential for years to come.

The blight of high unemployment that afflicted much of Europe
in the 1980s and '90s is a case in point, and an important cautionary
tale. The persistence of high unemployment resulted from several
factors, including overly rigid labor markets in some countries and
welfare programs that dulled the incentive to find a job in many
others. But analysis by the Johns Hopkins economist Lawrence Ball
reveals that much of it was the result of hysteresis caused by a long
period of disinflation and weak demand in the early and mid-1980s.
In some countries, the natural rate of unemployment rose by five to
nine percentage points.

The scars from this period will be deepest for the unemployed,
but they will be felt by others as well. Communities marked by
high, persistent unemployment devolve over time; social institutions
wither, families disintegrate, and social problems multiply. Many
American inner cities still bear scars from the sudden loss of manufacturing, and the attendant rise in male unemployment, in the

1970s. Parts of Europe now struggle with a burgeoning underclass. When geographically concentrated, idleness and all its attendant problems are easily passed from one generation to the next.

American politics have grown meaner as economic anxiety has lingered. Anti-immigrant sentiment has risen, and support for the poor has fallen. By many measures, trust—which to a large degree separates successful societies from unsuccessful ones—has diminished. The number of active militias in the United States increased from 43 to 330 between 2007 and 2010. And while frustrations will ebb when the economy improves enough, ideas and attitudes carry their own momentum. Once they become sufficiently commonplace, they are never quickly vanquished.

One reason the problems ushered in by the Great Recession are so urgent is that once too much time passes, they no longer *can* be solved. Once the character of a generation is fully formed, it cannot be unformed; once reactionary sentiments come out of the bottle, they are hard to put back in. And once large numbers of people cross the Rubicon from temporary unemployment to chronic joblessness, they, their families, and their communities can be lost for good. Finding our way to a full recovery from this period, and soon, is not just a matter of alleviating temporary discomfort. By degrees, economic weakness is slowly narrowing the life opportunities of many millions of people, and leaving our national future pinched.

Economies do eventually mend, of course. But recoveries from deep downturns are commonly jagged, with several false starts before growth takes firm hold. One needn't look too far to find positive omens in the economy today. Business profits approached record levels in 2010, and it already seems to be morning in parts of America, particularly those parts in which the most influential Americans tend to reside. The million-dollar question is how quickly the dawn will come for the rest of the country—and how bright that dawn will be.

2

THE TWO-SPEED
SOCIETY

FOR MORE THAN TWO YEARS NOW, THE BLOGGER ANDREW SULLIVAN
has been regularly posting first-person accounts of the downturn,
e-mailed to him by his readers, under the rubric "The View from
Your Recession." Sullivan has a wide and varied readership, spanning generations and classes, and the posts collectively form a sort
of oral history of American life since the crash. Many of the stories
are heartbreaking—of lost jobs and lost houses; of failed family businesses and withered sex lives; of paychecks parsed and retirement
savings drawn down to support siblings or parents or grown children
who can no longer support themselves; of depression and drinking
and lives gone offtrack.

But some of the entries underscore the fact that the recession,
of course, hasn't hit everyone. "We are in our late 20s," wrote one
woman from New England in May 2009. "We bought a house last
summer, adopted a dog, and are enjoying our little life in our little
town." She and her husband had gotten their graduate degrees some
time ago, and she was working in university administration. "Everywhere I look," she wrote, "my life is unaffected by the recession.
Truthfully, if I did not watch the news or read your blog every day,
I would not believe that there is a serious economic crisis going on."

Another writer noted that while he felt for those who were suffering, his high-paying career as a software engineer was going like
gangbusters; the main impact the recession had had on him was to
reduce the price of fine wine, which he was buying in bulk. Yet an-

other, formerly in finance, had lost his young business (in wine distribution, as it happens) early in the recession, but a friend who had faith in him had invested $2 million in a new start-up he was running, which was growing quickly. (Among others writing in to say that business was booming, with varying degrees of chagrin, were the partner of a real-estate agent who'd had the vision to quickly specialize in foreclosed properties, a lawyer whose firm handled personal bankruptcies, and a freelance writer specializing in résumé-writing assistance.)

One unmistakable pattern is the upbeat tone of expatriate Americans writing in from China or India or Latin America to note how well they and nearly everyone around them seemed to be doing, making the stories they were hearing from the United States seem almost surreal. "I do feel for everyone back in the USA that [is] suffering now," wrote one reader from São Paulo, Brazil, where his U.S.-based company had sent him to open a low-cost office. "I do not know what to make of our case. It is what it is. I do not take it for granted. But 40 years from now, when we are sitting around with friends who talk about how bad things were back in 2008 and 2009, we won't have much to add to the conversation."

Even in the Great Depression, some people prospered. In the texture of the comments from Sullivan's readers—and in the stories I've heard in my reporting around the country—it's hard to miss just how unevenly this recession has affected different people in different places. In March 2011, the unemployment rate was 12.0 percent for people with only a high-school diploma, 4.5 percent for college grads, and 2.0 percent for those with a professional degree. In the Washington, DC, and San Jose (Silicon Valley) metro areas, job postings in February 2011 were almost as numerous as job candidates. In Miami and Detroit, by contrast, for every job opening, more than six people were unemployed. From 2009 to 2010, wages were essentially flat nationwide—but they grew by 11.9 percent in Manhattan and 8.7 percent in Silicon Valley.

Housing crashed hardest in the exurbs and in more-affordable, previously fast-growing areas like Phoenix, Las Vegas, and much of Florida—all meccas for aspiring middle-class families with limited savings and moderate education. The upper-middle class, most densely clustered in the closer suburbs of expensive but resilient cities like San Francisco, Seattle, Boston, and Chicago, has lost little in comparison. And indeed, because the stock market has rebounded while housing values have not, the middle class as a whole has seen more of its wealth erased than the rich, who hold more-diverse portfolios. A 2010 Pew Research Center study showed that the typical middle-class family had lost 23 percent of its wealth since the recession began; that figure was just 12 percent for the upper class.

The recession has even proved selective in its treatment of the sexes. Most downturns are harder on men than on women; male-dominated occupations like construction and manufacturing tend to be highly cyclical, unlike work in health care or education or other services, which is disproportionately performed by women. Three out of every four pink slips delivered during the recession were delivered to men. Among those who've kept their jobs, men have reported more pay cuts than women as well.

Why has this recession been so selective in the pain it has levied? And why are some people and places now coming back quickly, while most are not? In fact, all of these developments—the divergent fortunes of New York and Phoenix, of the rich and the rest, even of women and men—are related. Understanding them is essential to understanding the nature and meaning of the period through which we are now living.

ONE OF THE most salient features of severe downturns is that they tend to accelerate deep economic shifts that were already under way. Declining industries and companies fail, spurring workers and capital toward rising sectors; declining cities and regions shrink faster, leaving blight; workers whose roles have been partly usurped by technology are pushed out en masse and never asked to return.

Some economists have argued that in one sense, periods like these do nations a service by clearing the way for new innovation, more-efficient production, and faster growth. Whether or not that's true, they typically allow us to see, with rare and brutal clarity, exactly where society is heading—and what sorts of people and places it is leaving behind.

Arguably the most important economic trend in the United States over the past couple of generations has been the ever-more-distinct sorting of Americans into winners and losers, and the slow hollowing of the middle class. For most of the aughts, that sorting was masked by the housing bubble, which allowed working-class and middle-class families to raise their standard of living despite income stagnation or downward job mobility. But the crash blew away that fig leaf. And the recession has pressed down hard on the vast class of Americans with moderate education and moderate skills.

The rich and well educated, after experiencing a brief dip in their fortunes, are, for the most part, beginning to prosper again today. Much of the rest of America remains stuck in neutral or reverse. In perhaps the biggest picture, the Great Recession has exposed the United States as something that seems uncomfortably un-American: a two-speed society, with opportunities for some.

"The Great Recession has quantitatively but not qualitatively changed the trend toward employment polarization" in the United States, wrote the MIT economist David Autor in a 2010 white paper. Job losses have been "far more severe in middle-skilled white- and blue-collar jobs than in either high-skill, white-collar jobs or in low-skill service occupations." Indeed, from 2007 through 2009, total employment in professional, managerial, and highly skilled technical positions was essentially unchanged. Jobs in low-skill service occupations such as food preparation, personal care, and house cleaning were also fairly stable in aggregate. Overwhelmingly, the recession has destroyed the jobs in between. Almost one out of every twelve white-collar jobs in sales, administrative support, and nonmanagerial office work vanished in the first two years of the recession; one out of every six blue-collar jobs in production, craft, repair, and machine operation did the same.

Autor isolates the winnowing of middle-skill, middle-class jobs as one of several major labor-market developments that are profoundly reshaping U.S. society. The others are rising pay at the top of the socioeconomic pyramid, falling wages for the less educated, and "lagging labor market gains for males." "All," he writes, "predate the Great Recession. But the available data suggest that the Great Recession has reinforced these trends."

For more than thirty years, the American economy has been in the midst of a sea change, shifting from industry to services and information, and integrating itself far more tightly into a single global market for goods, labor, and capital. This transformation has felt disruptive all along. But the pace of the change has quickened since the turn of the millennium, and even more so since the crash. "Technology has changed the game in jobs," former GE CEO Jack Welch told CNBC in 2009. "We had technology bumping around for years in the '80s and '90s, and [we were] trying to make it work. And now it's working." Companies have figured out how to harness exponential increases in computing power better and faster, and to do so habitually; they've "learned to do more with less." Global supply chains, meanwhile, have grown both tighter and much more supple since the late 1990s—a result of improving IT and freer trade—making it easier to relocate routine work. And of course China, India, and other developing countries have fully emerged as economic powerhouses, capable of producing large volumes of high-value goods and services.

Some parts of America's transformation are now nearing completion. For decades, manufacturing has become continually less important to the economy as other business sectors have grown. But the popular narrative—rapid decline in the 1970s and '80s, followed by slow erosion thereafter—isn't quite right, at least as far as employment goes. In fact, the total number of people employed in industry remained quite stable from the late 1960s through about 2000, at about 17 million to 19 million. To be sure, manufacturing wasn't providing many new opportunities for a growing population, but for decades, rising output essentially offset the impact of labor-saving technology and offshoring.

But since 2000, U.S. manufacturing has shed about a third of its jobs, with the decline accelerating after 2007. Some of that decline surely reflects losses to China. Still, industry isn't about to vanish from America, any more than agriculture did as the number of farmworkers plummeted during the twentieth century. As of 2010, the United States was the second-largest manufacturer in the world, and the number three agricultural nation. But agriculture, of course, is now so highly mechanized that only about 2 percent of American workers make a living as farmers. American manufacturing looks to be heading quickly down the same path.

Meanwhile, another phase of the economy's transformation—one more squarely involving the white-collar workforce—is really just beginning. "The thing about information technology," Autor told me, "is that it's extremely broadly applicable, it's getting cheaper all the time, and we're getting better and better at it." Computer software can now do boilerplate legal work, for instance, and make a first pass at reading X-rays and other medical scans. Likewise, thanks to technology, it's now easy to have those scans read and interpreted by professionals half a world away.

In 2007, the economist and former vice chairman of the Federal Reserve Alan Blinder estimated that between 22 and 29 percent of all jobs in the United States would be potentially offshorable within the next couple of decades. Ultimately, this process may be more painful than the automation and offshoring of manufacturing, simply because it will leave more people exposed. And with the recession, it seems to have gained steam. The financial crisis of 2008 was global, but job losses hit America especially hard. According to the IMF, one out of every four jobs lost worldwide was lost in the United

States. And while unemployment remains high in America, it has come back down to (or below) pre-recession levels in countries like China and Brazil, which are growing quickly.

TECHNOLOGICAL ADVANCEMENT AND trade expansion offer large benefits to society, including better, cheaper goods and services. And over time, both trade and technology create new domestic jobs even as they destroy old ones. But major economic transformations like the one we're in the midst of today—Blinder once described it as a "third industrial revolution"—are inevitably wrenching. And during downturns, the forces behind them can be particularly vicious. Forced to cut costs aggressively (or given an excuse to do so), companies have pulled forward the difficult workplace restructuring and offshoring decisions that they otherwise would have made over many years, as natural attrition and retirement allowed. As a result, especially intense competition for limited job openings has forced many of the workers they've disgorged all the way down the ladder, or out of the workforce altogether. The downward mobility of these workers, meanwhile, has made life harder for high-school dropouts and others who've traditionally occupied the lowest rung of the jobs ladder, and who've fallen off it in large numbers since the recession began.

"I think [a middle-class life] is gone forever for a lot of people," said John Foss to the journalist Michael Luo in February 2009. Foss, a former stockroom clerk, had lost his job at Manchester Tool Company in New Franklin, Ohio, when its only plant had closed a year earlier. (The company's owner, Kennametal, was consolidating operations to improve efficiency.) Along with 85 percent of the plant's hourly workers, he'd been unable to find work since, and was searching for jobs in the $8- to $12-an-hour range, well below his previous wage of about $18 an hour. About a third of the plant's salaried workers—including engineers and accountants—had been asked by Kennametal to stay on, and salaried employees in general had fared better than their hourly coworkers after the plant's closure. As of December 2010, Foss was still jobless.

The recession has only sped the societal re-sorting that was already in motion. Both trade and technology have been quickly increasing the number of low-cost substitutes for American workers with only moderate cognitive or manual skills—people who perform routine tasks such as product assembly, process monitoring, record keeping, basic information brokering, simple software coding, and so on. As machines and low-paid foreign workers have taken on these functions, the skills associated with them have become less valuable, and workers lacking higher education have suffered.

For the most part, these same forces have been a boon, so far, to Americans who have a good education and exceptional creative talents or analytic skills. Information technology has complemented the work of people who do complex research, sophisticated analysis, professional persuasion, and many forms of design and artistic creation, rather than replacing that work. And global integration has meant wider markets for new American products and high-value services—and higher incomes for the people who create or provide them.

The return on education has risen in recent decades, producing more-severe income stratification by educational attainment. But even among the meritocratic elite, the economy's evolution has produced a startling divergence. Since 1993, *more than half* of the nation's income growth has been captured by the top 1 percent of earners, families who in 2008 made $368,000 or more. And in fact, incomes among the top 0.1 percent have grown even faster. Nearly 2 million people matriculated to college in 2002—1,630 of them to Harvard—but only Mark Zuckerberg is worth many billions of dollars today; the rise of the super-elite is not a product of educational differences. In part, it is a natural outcome of widening markets and technological revolution—a result that's not even close to being fully played out, and one reinforced strongly by the political influence that great wealth brings.

Recently, as technology has improved and emerging-markets countries have sent more people to college, economic pressures have been moving up the educational ladder in the United States. "It's useful to make a distinction between college and post-college," Autor told me. "Among people with professional and even doctoral [degrees], in general the job market has been very good for a very long time, including recently. The group of highly educated individuals who have not done so well recently would be people who have a four-year college degree but nothing beyond that. Opportunities have been less good, wage growth has been less good, the recession has been more damaging. They've been displaced from mid-managerial or organizational positions where they don't have extremely specialized, hard-to-find skills."

College graduates may be losing some of their luster for reasons beyond technology and trade. As more Americans have gone to college, Autor notes, the quality of college education has become arguably more inconsistent, and the signaling value of a degree from a nonselective school has perhaps diminished. Whatever the causes, "a college degree is not the kind of protection against job loss or wage loss that it used to be."

To be sure, it is vastly better to have a college degree than to lack one. Indeed, the return on a four-year degree is near its historic high. But that's largely because the prospects facing people without a college degree have been flat or falling. Throughout the aughts, incomes for college graduates barely budged. In a decade defined by setbacks, perhaps that should occasion a sort of wan celebration. "College graduates aren't doing *badly*," says Timothy Smeeding, an economist at the University of Wisconsin and an expert on inequality. But "all the action in earnings is above the B.A. level."

America's classes are separating and changing. A tiny elite continues to float up and away from everyone else. Meanwhile, as manufacturing jobs and semiskilled office positions disappear, much of what the United States has historically regarded as its middle class is in danger of drifting downward. Left in between is what might be thought of as the professional middle class—unexceptional college graduates, for whom the arrow of fortune points mostly sideways, and an upper tier of college graduates and postgraduates for whom it points progressively upward, but not spectacularly so.

If you live and work in the professional communities of Boston or Seattle or Silicon Valley or Washington, DC, it is easy to forget that even among people age twenty-five to thirty-four, college graduates make up only about 30 percent of the population. And it is also easy to forget that a family income of $113,000 in 2009 would have put you in the eightieth income percentile nationally, or that $200,000 would have put you in the ninety-fifth percentile. The professional middle class is too privileged for pity, but it has its own distinct worries and character, and its restlessness has shaped the political reaction to the crash.

THE SAME FORCES that have driven the separation of America's classes have also pushed men and women in different directions. As the middle class has hollowed over the past twenty years, both low-skill service jobs and high-skill, high-paying jobs have grown—and in roughly equal measure. But, as Autor notes, the sexes have not been equally affected: overwhelmingly, women have moved up from the dwindling middle. Men have been much more prone than women to move down, if not out.

Men still make more money than women on average, partly because of lingering discrimination. But the gap has been closing, in part because women have done so much better than men in the classroom in recent decades. The share of the male population receiving a college degree has been basically flat since 1980. In 2010, for every two men who graduated from college, three women did the same. Most managers in the United States are now women. And according to the research firm Reach Advisors, in 2008, among childless singles age twenty-two to thirty, women earned more than men in thirty-nine of the fifty largest cities in the country, largely because they were so much better educated.

In the long run, what is perhaps as significant as the trend in wages is the trend in work itself. Soon after the crash, women became a majority of workers for the first time in American history (though they've traded places with men several times in the months since then). That's not primarily because women have been streaming into the workforce; growth in women's employment has slowed in the past ten years, following rapid gains beginning in the 1970s. It's the opposite trend that is still going strong. Men have been gradually moving out of the workforce since the 1970s—not just in the United States, but in most rich nations. It's just happened faster since the crash. In 2009 and 2010, more than 18 percent of men in their prime working years were idle, the highest proportion since 1948, when the federal government began tracking that statistic.

Just as the housing bubble papered over the troubles of the middle class, it also hid, for a time, the declining prospects of many men. According to the Harvard economist Lawrence Katz, since the mid-1980s, the labor market has been placing a higher premium on creative, analytic, and interpersonal skills, and the wages of men without a college degree have been under particular pressure. And for whatever reason, in the lower tiers of the economy, men have had trouble finding and keeping work in the service sector. "And I think this downturn exacerbates" these problems, Katz told me. For a time, construction provided an outlet for the young men who would have gone into manufacturing a generation ago. By the middle of the aughts, manufacturing was hiring "very few" people in their twenties. Yet men without higher education "didn't do as badly as you might have expected, on long-run trends, because of the housing bubble and construction boom." It's hard to imagine that happening again. "We're not going to have the same sort of housing boom. It's just not going to be like 2002 through 2006. . . . There are long-run issues."

Women's growing success in the classroom and workforce is of course a cause for celebration. But the failure of many men to adapt to a postindustrial economy is worrying. The economy appears to be evolving in a way that is ill-suited to many men—at least outside the economy's upper echelons. Men's struggles are hardly evident in Silicon Valley or on Wall Street. But they're hard to miss in foundering blue-collar and low-end service communities across the country. In these less affluent places, gender roles, family dynamics, and community character are changing rapidly in the wake of the crash. And almost no one seems happy about it.

AS TRADE AND technology have re-sorted Americans economically, a geographic self-sorting has followed—and it is this sorting, along with its consequences, that the Great Recession has illuminated most starkly. In 2006, the urban theorist Richard Florida wrote that Americans were in the midst of a great migration—one perhaps as important economically and culturally as the westward march of pioneers in the early nineteenth century or the surge of immigrants and farmers into growing industrial cities toward that century's end. Society's meritocratic winners—including its billionaires and multimillionaires, but also much of the professional class—were physically separating themselves from the rest of the country. A "mass relocation of highly skilled, highly educated, and highly paid Americans to a relatively small number of metropolitan regions" was under way, and with it "a corresponding exodus of the traditional lower and middle classes from these same places. Such geographic sorting of people by economic potential, on this scale," Florida wrote, was "unprecedented."

In 1970, college graduates were dispersed relatively evenly throughout the United States. Eleven percent of the national population over the age of twenty-five held a bachelor's degree, and that figure stood at between 9 and 13 percent in half of the country's 318 metropolitan regions. Vastly more people hold a college degree now,

but a relatively small number of places have captured a dispropor-
tionate amount of the growth. In San Francisco and Washington,
DC, for instance, about half of all residents had at least a bachelor's
degree in 2004; in Cleveland and Detroit, just 14 and 11 percent
did, respectively. That same year, more than 20 percent of Seattle's
residents had an advanced degree, versus 2 percent in Newark, New
Jersey. A 2010 Brookings Institution report, "The State of Metropolitan America," concluded that during the past decade, the gaps
in both income and education between America's top metro regions
and those at the bottom had widened. "Gains in the 'war for talent'
among U.S. metro areas are accruing disproportionately to already
better-educated places," it said.

According to a preliminary examination of census data by the
urban analyst Aaron Renn, roughly as many college graduates moved
to Manhattan in the aughts as there are residents of Chattanooga,
Tennessee. In 2009, every one of the ten U.S. counties with the most
growth in college graduates per square mile were in or around New
York City, San Francisco, Boston, or Washington, DC. In most of
these counties, the inflow of college graduates and people with graduate degrees was substantially higher than the counties' total population growth: people with less education were on their way out.

Powerful economic forces have driven the country's best-educated
and most-skilled people toward one another. The Nobel Prize–
winning economist Robert Lucas argued that economic growth is
propelled, first and foremost, by spillovers in knowledge resulting
from the clustering of people rich in human capital. Physical proximity, and the constant networking it allows, enables smart, talented
people to generate ideas faster, hone them more sharply, and turn
them into products or services more quickly than they otherwise
could. From 1975 through 2001, patent production in San Francisco, Seattle, Atlanta, Austin, and Portland, Oregon, grew by more
than three times the national average, and skilled workers in these
and other highly educated cities saw their incomes rise rapidly. In

the 1990s, the ten metro areas with the most-educated residents saw personal incomes grow at nearly double the pace of the ten least-educated metro areas. Increasingly, in order to realize their full economic value, well-educated workers have needed to live in one of a handful of places. At the same time, because *routine* work can now be done from anywhere (or by machines), the physical presence of a nonprofessional middle class in these cities has become far less important to the growth and sustainability of their economies.

As high-income, high-potential workers have flooded dynamic cities and regions—dubbed "superstar cities" by the economist Joseph Gyourko—they have bid up housing prices and other costs, driving out the middle and lower classes. Some high-school graduates, and even college graduates from nonselective schools, have settled in the sprawling exurbs of these regions. Before the crash, more still had lit out for the suburbs of low-cost, fast-growing Sun Belt cities like Phoenix, Las Vegas, and Orlando. Meanwhile, Rust Belt cities like Buffalo and Youngstown, Ohio, have been slowly drained of their most talented young people, who've left for greener pastures.

The housing bust has revealed that many of these new middle-class magnets may have more in common with the cities of the Rust Belt than with city-regions like Boston or Austin or Minneapolis. Housing was the source of their growth, and also their primary product. With the construction boom over, many former boomtowns have few large, highly productive industries to sustain them, and a comparatively narrow base of human capital. In a Brookings Institution ranking of one hundred major American metro areas by the prevalence of college graduates in 2009, Phoenix ranked 66th, sandwiched between Akron and Cleveland. Tampa, Cape Coral, and Las Vegas were 84th, 85th, and 91st, respectively, in and among places like Dayton, Memphis, and Toledo. Little wonder, then, that some of the highest and most persistent unemployment rates in the country are to be found in these former boomtowns, along with long-struggling Rust Belt cities like Detroit. And little wonder that the most highly educated cities are showing signs of resiliency, despite experiencing much shallower losses in jobs and wealth to begin with.

TECTONIC SHIFTS IN the economy shake the culture as well. By temporarily accelerating some of those shifts, the recession has made them and their cultural consequences plainer, and given us a preview of what's in store for America in the coming decades—at least absent efforts to change the economic and social course the country now finds itself on. The fortunes of the rich are diverging from those of other Americans, as are the fortunes of Manhattan from those of Tampa. In less privileged parts of the country, a predominantly male underclass is forming, and that, in turn, is changing marriage, family, and community life in ways altogether foreign to the affluent nuclear families and young single professionals in and around Boston or Washington, DC.

These varied experiences may partly explain the ambivalence with which some policy makers, themselves members of the meritocratic elite, have responded to high unemployment and economic distress. And they clearly have fueled the rising popular discontent that can be seen in public discourse and at the ballot box. In the Great Depression, iconic images of bankers selling apples on street corners helped build a sense that everyone was suffering together. Patently, that is not the case today.

3

TWO DEPRESSIONS AND
A LONG MALAISE

A S OF THIS WRITING, IT'S BEEN ABOUT THREE YEARS SINCE THE financial markets crashed, and closer to four since the Great Recession officially began. More than two years have passed since President Barack Obama detected "glimmers of hope across the economy."

As noted earlier, at the current pace of the recovery, many more years will go by before unemployment rates again touch 5 percent, before most Americans pay down their debts, before housing values find their bottom and rise substantially again. Such a long recovery is not fated—technological breakthroughs, world events, and, not least, our own actions will all influence its pace. But it is possible that the economy won't be truly vibrant again for a long time.

Long, deep slumps are foreign to many Americans alive today, but of course they are not unknown in the nation's history. The final two decades of the nineteenth century saw steady deflation, hard times for typical workers, and great tumult. *The Great Depression* and *the 1930s* are now nearly synonymous. Most recently, from 1972 through the early 1980s, the United States endured economic stagnation, wage erosion, and a series of painful economic shocks; in some respects, the weakness lingered until the mid-1990s. If we align Wall Street's 2008 crash with the signal shocks of those periods—the panic of 1893, the crash of 1929, the oil shock of 1973—then we'd be sitting today in 1896 or 1932 or 1976.

The longer society stews in a deep slump, the more it is altered.

Changes to community character, generational ambition, and social harmony that are nearly imperceptible early in a downturn become suddenly overwhelming later. What follows is a pocket history of these three long downturns, with a focus on the enduring marks they left on America. Each delineates a major turn in the country's economic, political, and cultural history. And each holds lessons for us in the present day.

THE GILDED AGE AND THE DEPRESSION OF 1893

The last quarter of the nineteenth century was a period that in many ways recalls our own—a time of technological revolution, rapid global integration, vast economic change, rising inequality, market crashes, and long spells of disappointment and anxiety for many Americans. A series of financial panics rocked the country, culminating in the panic of 1893, a run on banks that crippled the financial system and ushered in a depression more severe than any the United States had yet seen.

From the 1870s through the turn of the century, "the public features of economic stagnation became more recognizable with each passing decade," wrote Alexander Keyssar in *Out of Work: The First Century of Unemployment in Massachusetts*. "Noisy plants grew silent for days, weeks, or months at a time. Adult men congregated on streets where adult men had been seen only on Sundays and after dusk. . . . Rumors of jobs brought hundreds of workers to the gates of individual factories. During the final decades of the nineteenth century, the recurrence of such scenes was for many Americans a source of anxiety and apocalyptic visions."

Dramatic changes swept the country throughout this period. The railroad, telegraph, and transoceanic steamer converted local and regional markets into national and global ones, exposing farmers and tradesmen to new competition. Likewise, transformational new industrial technologies—among them, the move from "batch" to "flow" processes in the making of many commercial and industrial goods—rewarded scale, punished small workshops, and left many workers with obsolete skills and careers.

Deflation was a fixture of the period; prices fell by nearly 40 percent between 1870 and the mid-1890s. As a result, debtors struggled terribly. Farmers, who typically carried debt from season to season, saw the price they could get for their crops fall year after year, a result of the opening of vast new swaths of land for cultivation. In many cities, meanwhile, the availability of jobs oscillated wildly. National unemployment rose above 16 percent in the depressions of 1873–77 and 1893–97.

The economy as a whole was by no means stagnant during the final decades of the nineteenth century. Fueled by new technologies, trade, and masses of immigrants to man new factories, it grew extremely quickly, and great fortunes were amassed by a new class of rising industrialists, whose ostentatious displays of wealth inspired Mark Twain to caustically name the period the Gilded Age.

But particularly after 1880, most people didn't share in this prosperity. Income inequality was likely higher near the end of the nineteenth century than at any other time in American history. In 1896, the social scientist Charles Spaur estimated that the richest 1 percent of the American population held more than half the nation's wealth; the poorest 44 percent, on the other hand, held 1.2 percent. According to the economic historian Benjamin Friedman, in 1895 perhaps half of America's families were making less than they had made in 1880, fifteen years earlier.

Unemployment became a widespread social problem for the first time during this period. Previously, most Americans had lived on farms. Paid work had come and gone, but home industry—farming, canning, clothes making, and so on—had made the notion of unemployment largely foreign. In the mid-nineteenth century, even the textile mills of New England had been staffed largely by young unmarried women, many of whom lived on local farms—not by a permanent labor force. But by the 1870s, these women had been supplanted by a permanent force of factory workers. As industry rose in scope and scale, cities grew larger and denser, and farm plots were squeezed out. Residents came to depend exclusively on wages to buy food and pay the rent. "For workers," Keyssar wrote, "the sting of joblessness became sharper and more penetrating. For middle-class critics, observers, and reformers, the phenomenon became more visible."

Some of these critics were struck, in particular, by the helplessness of the urban unemployed, who could not fall back on the more generalized skills of previous generations, and who sometimes seemed too dispirited to try. Wrote one observer in *The Atlantic Monthly* in 1878:

> I have been in scores of the homes of unemployed workingmen, in different parts of our country, during the last five years, where the chairs, tables, and bedsteads were all worn out and breaking down, so that in many instances there was not a safe or comfortable seat in the house. Yet the furniture had all been bought of dealers at high prices . . . and these workingmen were not able to repair it, or even to make new stools on which to sit while eating their food. They had been at work in shops, mills, or factories, and when these closed had so little power of self-help that months of idleness passed without anything being done to make their homes more comfortable. In such cases, everything that comes into the house, or that is used about it, must be bought, and requires money for its purchase.

Migration rose to unprecedented levels in the last quarter of the nineteenth century—the word *tramp* came into common usage—as masses of jobless men and families sought work. (Walking was the primary form of everyday transportation, so switching jobs usually meant changing residence too.) In the rootlessness and resettlement that characterized the period, one can find early glimmers of modern community life. Extended families split apart and never reunited;

communities became more transient, and the bonds within them weakened.

Both the economy and the material circumstances of American families have changed so much since those times that they are almost unrecognizable. (There was no government safety net to speak of then, and most families had meager savings at best. To feed themselves, the urban unemployed sometimes bought table scraps from local eateries for a few pennies a day.) But certain echoes from that time can be heard today. Then, as now, blue-collar workers were vastly more vulnerable than white-collar workers to job loss. (In 1885, among Massachusetts men, unemployment stood at 33 percent for longshoremen and at about 24 percent for general laborers, nail makers, lathers, masons, and ship carpenters. By contrast, it was just 3 percent for bookkeepers, clerks, and salesmen, and 2 percent for merchants and dealers.) Then, as now, job loss was hardest to overcome for older workers, who typically had great difficulty finding work again. (Seniority was seldom an effective ward against layoffs, except in small towns.)

And then, as now, some of the most intense worries among the struggling and unemployed involved the future of their children. "My oldest girl is fourteen and my boy twelve," wrote T. T. Pomeroy, a shoemaker living in Haverhill, Massachusetts, in the 1890s, "and my wife was telling at the breakfast table this morning what she was going to do with them. The girl is going through the high school, and she is going to teach school. The boy is going through high school and is then going to the school of technology." But this was just a fantasy, made bitter by its impending disintegration. "I was just thinking how hard it was that I couldn't do this for them," Pomeroy continued. "I have got to take my children out of school next year and hand them over to the task master."

IN HIS 2005 book, *The Moral Consequences of Economic Growth,* Friedman observed that as people struggled during the late nineteenth century, many of them came to resent the status, opportunities, and progress of others. Politics and, indeed, all aspects of public life became meaner and less inclusive. Job riots spread and anti-immigrant sentiment swelled. In 1882, Congress subjected new immigrants to a head tax and banned Chinese immigrants altogether. In 1887, a group of white nativists in Clinton, Iowa, founded the American Protective Association, an anti-immigrant group that also denounced Catholics; by 1894, its membership had swelled to 2.5 million people nationwide—or about one out of every fourteen adults.

Vigilante violence—lynching, beatings, arson, murder—rose sharply as the years went by. (According to one estimate, one person was lynched every two days, on average, between 1889 and 1898.) By the end of the 1890s, wrote C. Vann Woodward, a historian of the South, that region had become a "perfect cultural seedbed for aggression against the minority race," one nurtured by a long agricultural depression culminating in the acute distress that followed the panic of 1893.

The deterioration in race relations was not only the worst consequence of the period's economic weakness, but also its most enduring. "It is one of the most unfortunate coincidences of United States history," wrote Friedman, "that what was at the time the most pronounced period of economic stagnation since the founding of the republic set in just as Reconstruction ended and the federal government finally withdrew its troops from the defeated southern states. . . . No one will ever know whether the country's race relations, both in the South and elsewhere, would have taken a different course had economic times been better during this key period."

Like other forms of intolerance, racial discrimination and violence built slowly, reaching full flower only after years of economic anxiety and disappointment had passed. Reconstruction had ended in 1879, but it wasn't until the 1890s that most southern states began to enact the Jim Crow laws that would segregate society for generations, supported by a Supreme Court that had grown steadily less forceful in its support for equal rights. Demagogues gained traction; "Pitchfork" Ben Tillman, for example, won the governorship of South Carolina in 1890, and then a U.S. Senate seat. He called for the repeal of black voting rights and openly defended lynching.

In nearly every aspect, American politics and government became more reactionary. The Populist movement, a predominantly rural movement that is today identified mostly as an effort to abandon the gold standard, was also highly insular, xenophobic, and at times tinged by racism (although it solicited and received support from black farmers, particularly in its early days). "The populists sought to preserve the agrarian and small-town economy, and the way of life based on it, that had been America's past," wrote Friedman.

> They were angered by perceived exploitation, and emboldened by a sense of moral superiority. Populism was, correspondingly, an expression of resentment as well as resistance to the advance of the capitalist, industrialist, and therefore more urbanized economy that was to become America's future. . . . In their specific policy proposals and even more so in their broader social and cultural agenda, the populists represented a turning backward: a closing of American society, a rigidification, and in many ways a retreat from tolerance, in the face of continual economic disappointment.

The Populist movement was of course diffuse and dynamic, and reactionary thinking jostled with progressive ideas, support for women's suffrage being perhaps the most notable. But neither women's suffrage nor other policies that would have expanded individual rights actually advanced as long as hard times endured. Instead, many rights and freedoms were curtailed, and civic life diminished.

"THERE IS SCARCELY a workman, whatever the present comfort of his life, who is not oppressed by the horrible nightmare of a possible loss of his situation," reported the *Labor Leader* in 1893. "No faithfulness, no skill, no experience can protect him against the danger of being cast adrift with his family at the next shift of the market. He is part of the grist in the great mill of demand and supply, and when his time comes it remorselessly crushes him between its iron rollers."

The language of a budding labor movement was at times drenched in Marxism by the 1890s, prompting revolutionary fears among some members of the American elite. Other elites—troubled by society's unbridled greed; or by the dissipation that characterized city life in hard times; or even by the closing of the American frontier, and with it, the presumed loss of the pioneer spirit—feared the onset of American decline.

Of course, none of this came to pass. The discovery of new gold deposits and better mining techniques increased the gold supply and put an end to deflation. Bad harvests in Europe helped American farmers. And manufacturing technology continued to advance, providing new job opportunities and rising wages. What followed was nearly two decades of almost uninterrupted growth, the Progressive Era, which took some of the roughest edges off of laissez-faire capitalism, and the continued rise of America as the world's predominant power. Indeed, when we look back on the late nineteenth century today, what stands out is not the hardship and uncertainty of the period, but rather the utter transformation of the American economy—and of American life.

The United States emerged from the nineteenth century with an increasingly urban, industrial economy and a transient population, centered on immediate families, with weaker connections to extended family. It also emerged with an educated workforce that was the envy of the world (American farmers, cognizant of the decline of their profession, had pushed society to expand the education system, and had pushed their children through it). But this molting of the U.S. economy was disruptive, anxious, and, above all, bewildering to those who lived through it. It is only with the benefit of hindsight that we see it as a success.

THE GREAT DEPRESSION

Among all American economic calamities, the Great Depression of the 1930s stands alone in the pain that it levied, and it should be invoked cautiously as a comparison to our own times. From peak to trough, the nation's real output fell by 30 percent and the stock market lost nearly 90 percent of its value. Unemployment neared 25 percent in 1933, and didn't fall below 14 percent until World War II began. For more than a decade, until the war perversely lifted the U.S. economy, the economic environment was bleaker than any the country had experienced before or has experienced since. Still, the ways in which society changed in the '30s as initial panic gave way to years of grinding anxiety are in some respects instructive. In the Depression, one can see several of the same forces that are again reshaping the American family and culture today.

The Depression began with the stock-market crash of 1929, but the pattern of economic growth before the crash is telling. In the national memory, the 1920s stand out as a time of heady growth and dizzying gains in wealth, but in fact most Americans didn't experience the decade that way. Farmers still made up a quarter of the workforce in 1929, and they had missed out on the boom entirely; a crop glut following World War I had caused an agricultural depression. In America's towns and cities, unemployment was generally low, but in many industries, wages were stagnant or declining; along with agriculture, oil and textiles were known as "sick sectors." Even in heavy manufacturing, where wages for skilled workers grew quickly, the introduction of new, labor-saving technologies shrank the ranks of the workforce.

From 1920 to 1929, disposable per capita income grew by only about 1 percent a year, and even this low figure is misleading. Among the top 1 percent of earners, incomes rose 75 percent across the decade. A large proportion of families, however, saw scant income growth. Productivity gains showed up mostly in higher corporate profits, which rose 62 percent between 1923 and 1929. Dividends rose by roughly the same amount, but only a tiny fraction of Americans had any money in the stock market.

One thing that made the twenties roar—in addition to the conspicuous consumption of the moneyed—was the willingness of ordinary people to outspend their incomes, taking on debt to do so. The installment plan became a fixture of society in the latter part of the 1920s. By the end of the decade, 60 percent of all cars and 80 percent of all radios were being purchased on installment. Many Americans shared an infectious optimism, born of strong growth, even though most of that growth wasn't actually making its way into their paychecks. In his classic history of the era, *The Great Depression: America, 1929–1941*, Robert McElvaine wrote, "[A] growing number of people accepted the proposition that 'God intended the American middle class to be rich.' "

In Florida, land speculation was rampant in the mid-1920s, and buyers, attracted by the state's weather and potential as a winter haven, swarmed in; nine in ten never planned to occupy their property. The real-estate mania may have been most intense in Florida, but it was hardly unique to the state. "It was our fault," said one midwestern real-estate agent at the time, "for overselling [houses], and the banks' fault for overlending." In the go-go years of the 1920s, "everybody was buying a better home than he could afford." Stories of homeowners who'd seen their house appreciate "tenfold in value over the past ten years" had fed a frenzy.

Many factors caused the Depression—too much leverage in the equity market; too much inventory in U.S. factories; Germany's difficulty paying back war debt, and the cascade of problems that caused for the international financial system. Weak government response in the immediate wake of the crash—a failure to aggressively loosen either monetary or fiscal policy—contributed mightily to the catastrophe. And premature fiscal tightening in 1937 extended it.

But the Depression was also the result of a debt-and-consumption binge, and it unfolded, in part, as a real-estate crisis. Residential construction imploded in the 1930s, and foreclosures multiplied manyfold. By 1933, local newspapers were filled with ads for distressed-property sales. To ward off foreclosure, families began "doubling up," renting out rooms or portions of the house to lodgers. Many houses, vacant or inhabited by residents who could barely put food on the table, slowly fell into disorder and disrepair.

THE ECONOMIC CONDITIONS of the 1930s deeply influenced every facet of life. Skirts famously lengthened, and many boys, fearful of the consequences of an unintended pregnancy, came to regard girls as "booby traps." Marriage rates dropped sharply, but so did divorces; divorce was expensive, and government relief was easier to come by for families than for individuals.

In her classic sociology of the Depression, *The Unemployed Man and His Family*, Mirra Komarovsky vividly describes how joblessness strained—and in many cases fundamentally altered—family relationships in the 1930s. During 1935 and '36, Komarovsky and her research team interviewed the members of fifty-nine white middle-class families in which the husband and father had been out of work for at least a year. Her research revealed deep psychological wounds. "It is awful to be old and discarded at 40," said one father. "A man is not a man without work." Another said plainly, "During the depression I lost something. Maybe you call it self-respect, but in losing it I also lost the respect of my children, and I am afraid I am losing my wife." Noted one woman of her husband, "I still love him, but he doesn't seem as 'big' a man."

Taken together, the stories paint a picture of diminished men, bereft of familial authority. Household power—over children, spending, and daily decisions of all types—generally shifted to wives over time (and some women were happier overall as a result). Amid general anxiety and men's loss of self-worth and loss of respect from their wives, sex lives withered. Socializing all but ceased as well, a casualty of poverty and embarrassment. Although some men embraced family life, most became distant. Children described their father as "mean," "nasty," or "bossy," and didn't want to bring friends around, for fear of what he might say. "There was less physical violence and aggression towards the wife than towards the child," Komarovsky wrote.

Of course, even in the 1930s, most people kept their jobs, and the period's impact on family life varied greatly. "Many families have drawn closer and 'found' themselves in the depression," wrote the sociologists Robert Lynd and Helen Merrell Lynd in *Middletown in Transition*, their 1937 study of everyday life in Muncie, Indiana. With social options limited by thin wallets, some husbands, wives, and children gardened together and used their yards more in summer, and at night played cards or listened to the radio. Yet the Lynds acknowledged that in other families, the Depression had "precipitated a permanent sediment of disillusionment and bitterness," born of hardship, anxiety, and fear for the future. It was difficult to say, they noted, where the balance lay between the two.

The Lynds had first studied Muncie, a typical middle-class city of the time, in 1924 and 1925, when the economy was booming. Upon their return six years into the Depression, they found that petty jealousies over material things had seemed to multiply between neighbors, and that what bonds still existed didn't extend far. "In its relation to outside groups . . . Middletown seems recently to have been building its fences higher. The city is more antagonistic to [outsiders]; individuals in the city are seemingly more wary of one another; need of protection and security is more emphasized."

Trust among strangers and loose acquaintances was eroding, and rising material insecurity had brought with it a "greater insistence upon conformity and a sharpening of latent issues." An intense nationalism had arisen since 1925, the Lynds found, and along with it an increasingly critical attitude toward all things foreign. One op-ed in a local Muncie paper exhorted its readers to "return to the old, sturdy, clean, upstanding America, the America that faced disaster unafraid and that went forward with the Bible and the flag."

Disillusionment among high-school and college graduates, many of them unable to find jobs, became common by the mid-1930s. Suspicions grew that higher education was no longer a sure path to prosperity and that ambition was pointless. Said one college president in a 1936 address, "How are we to teach thrift to those who have lost everything? Why teach youth to rise early when there are no jobs to go to?"

The Lynds interviewed a series of young men and women in their late teens and twenties about their lives and found a "growing apathy." One college graduate who had a job delivering parcels said that many of his peers were "just accepting the fact of a lower station in life and not struggling any longer." A high-school teacher observed of his students, "They're just getting used to the idea of there being no job, and there isn't much explosiveness."

Many young adults who could not find footing in the job market were left permanently scarred. Glen Elder, a sociologist at the University of North Carolina and a pioneer in the field of "life course" studies, has spent much of his career tracking the various generations that lived through the Depression, to see how it shaped their lives. Some three decades after the Depression ended, and even after a long postwar boom, he found a pronounced diffidence in aging men (though not women) who had suffered hardship as twenty- and thirtysomethings during the 1930s. Unlike peers who had been largely spared during those lean years, these men came across, Elder told me, as "beaten and withdrawn—lacking ambition, direction, confidence in themselves."

Yet the period's adolescents were shaped differently. McElvaine observed, "Although the children of the thirties lived through the same economic hardship as their parents did, it meant different things to the new generation. For one thing, children were largely free from the self-blame and shame that were so common among their elders. . . . The Depression's most significant psychological problem was generally absent in the young."

Hardship caused adolescents to take on more responsibility

earlier in life. "There were no working-class 'teenagers' in the 1930s," wrote McElvaine. Boys took jobs after school wherever they could get them. Girls took the place of their mother, who was herself often working, as the custodian of smaller children and keeper of the home. "Ironically," he noted, "the same family hardship that might weaken the self-reliance of a father could strengthen that quality in his child." That's in fact exactly what happened, writes Elder in *Children of the Great Depression*. As adolescents who suffered hardship during the '30s grew into adulthood and middle age, Elder found, they showed no sign of the fatalism and reticence that marked people who were just a few years older. In fact, they became especially adaptable, family-oriented adults.

ON THE ROSTER of history's truly crippling downturns—both inside and outside the United States—the Great Depression as experienced in America stands out for the extent to which society as a whole remained unified and refused reactionary measures. Perhaps the very depth and breadth of the crisis inspired that togetherness. The middle class identified with the poor more than the rich during that time—and generally supported steps to help those brought low in the downturn. And to a large degree, the federal government with one hand protected the rights and interests of the downtrodden, and with the other, the property of the wealthy.

Nonetheless, extremism and rancor did grow stronger throughout the period. Race-based job discrimination became fiercer, and lynchings, as they had in the 1880s and '90s, became more commonplace. A *New Republic* story in 1931 noted that "[d]ust had been blown from the shotgun, the whip, and the noose, and Ku Klux practices were being resumed in the certainty that dead men not only tell no tales but create vacancies."

Father Charles Coughlin, known as "The Radio Priest," regularly spoke to some 30 million or 40 million Americans—the largest radio audience in the world at the time—about the depravity of

Communists, international financiers, and Jews. Coughlin praised Adolf Hitler and other Fascists, seeing in them a strength and moral purity absent from capitalist democrats; as the Depression stretched on, Coughlin became more strident. The Louisiana governor, senator, and presidential hopeful Huey Long, a champion of the poor and the working class, grew in stature. He denounced "imperialistic banking control" and preached a radical populism, rooted in aggressive wealth redistribution, with little respect for democratic principles.

With the onset of World War II and the industrial production that it required, the Depression finally ended (conditions had been improving slowly in the years before the war). But it left the United States ineffably changed. In some respects, the Depression accelerated the evolution of the economy. Innovation was in fact extremely rapid throughout the 1930s, and the period saw an end to the widespread use of domestic servants and the beginnings of an appliance revolution. (John Maynard Keynes wrote at the time that one of the problems of the Depression was "technological unemployment," due to the "discovery of means of economising the use of labour outrunning the pace at which we can find new uses for labour.")

More important were the cultural and political changes that resulted from the social and economic environment of the Depression. Family crowding and the deprivations of city life eventually catalyzed a burst of suburbanization after growth returned. Political reforms—including the Glass-Steagall Act and other banking measures—reshaped the country's business and labor environment, and provided a foundation for decades of growth and social peace. A Democratic political majority, for better or worse, was cemented into place for decades. And the culture was imbued with a spirit of thrift that would last a generation.

THE 1970S

The troubles and turbulence of the 1970s stemmed from many sources. Amidst presidential scandal and military retreat, the United States seemed to have lost its confidence, its moral compass, and much of its luster. But "more than Watergate and Vietnam," wrote the historian Edward Berkowitz in *Something Happened: A Political and Cultural Overview of the Seventies*, "the economy was the factor that gave the seventies its distinctive character."

The seventies saw two major recessions, one beginning in 1973 and the other in 1978. Each involved a sudden spike in the price of oil. Incomes, after rising strongly for decades, were flat, factoring out inflation—even for married couples, and even though married women were entering the workforce in record numbers. Inflation averaged nearly 9 percent a year for the decade as a whole. A third recession, induced by the Fed to arrest inflation as the 1980s began, brought the unemployment rate into the double digits. The economy had mostly recovered by 1983, but prosperity remained elusive for many until the mid-1990s.

The economic challenges that America faced in the 1970s bear some faint resemblance to those the country faces today. Exports failed to keep pace with rising imports (1971 was the first year in the twentieth century in which the United States ran a trade deficit), and American industrial workers felt the sting of international competition. But for the most part, both the origins of the period's economic weakness (oil and agricultural shocks, slowing growth in productivity) and the particular manifestations of weakness ("stagflation") were different from those of today.

Nonetheless, the 1970s are the only other modern period in which the United States experienced long stagnation, punctuated by punishing setbacks. They are instructive primarily for the long-lasting social and political changes that stagnation eventually produced.

In *Something Happened*, Berkowitz describes the burst of civil-rights legislation in the 1960s, following John F. Kennedy's death. But, he notes, that "hopeful legacy began to sour after 1972," as the economy began to sink. The '60s were hardly innocent of white anger over civil rights, but in the '70s, white grievances intensified and spread throughout the country. Conflict grew over busing to achieve racial balance in schools, and protests in Boston turned violent. (One iconic newspaper photo showed young white men trying to impale a black man with an American flag.)

Legal challenges to civil-rights policies began to meet with success. In 1978, the Supreme Court ruled in *Regents of the University of California v. Bakke* that race-based affirmative action was, in some cases, illegal. At the beginning of the '70s, writes the historian Bruce J. Schulman in *The Seventies: The Great Shift in American Culture, Society, and Politics*, most blacks said they wanted to live in integrated neighborhoods and send their children to integrated schools. By the decade's end, more than two-thirds said they felt more kinship with black Africans than with white Americans.

In previous decades, writes Schulman, "American politics and culture had acted like a universal solvent: dissolving ethnic and regional loyalties, diluting sectarian strife and religious enthusiasm." But in the '70s, he says, these same forces acted as a centrifuge, spinning people and communities further apart. Rising individualism, the decline of the WASP social order, and a sexual revolution—themselves inseparable, it might be argued, from the economic transition away from industry and corporate hierarchy and toward a flatter, more creative information age—sowed confusion and concern. Years of economic stagnation, meanwhile, leached away respect for political leaders.

Throughout the '70s, anti-immigrant groups grew stronger. In his 1978 novel, *The Turner Diaries*, William Pierce imagined violent revolution and the extermination of nonwhites. The novel drew a large following across the next decade, as white supremacist movements and antigovernment militias proliferated. The extremism that hard times nourished in society's darker corners left a long legacy. In 1995, as the economy was beginning a remarkable period of growth, Timothy McVeigh bombed a federal office building in Oklahoma, killing 168 people. But the antecedents of McVeigh's ideology can be traced clearly to the anomie and paranoia of the 1970s.

Reactionary violence was by no means limited to whites. In 1992, black residents of South-Central Los Angeles burned, looted, or otherwise damaged some 800 Korean-owned businesses during the riots that broke out after a jury acquitted four white police officers of beating a black motorist. These riots, too, had roots in the '70s, when manufacturing jobs disappeared from inner cities, chronic unemployment rose, neighborhoods began a steep decline that became self-reinforcing, and racial tensions of all sorts grew stronger.

THE 1970s SAW the beginnings of a major shift in economic power, one that irrevocably altered family dynamics, and one that is becoming more pronounced today. Women entered the workforce in great numbers, pushed by economic necessity and pulled by a rising service sector in which physical strength mattered little. In 1970, 43 percent of women in their prime working years held jobs; by 1980, 51 percent did. (Among married women with young children, the increase was sharper still.) In between came the women's-rights revolution—arguably the only major advance of individual rights in that decade. New laws and court decisions put women on more-equal footing in universities and in the workplace, and gave them more-equal access to lending. Many previously all-male colleges went coed.

This revolution, Schulman argued, "was not the product of a conscious feminist ideology so much as it was the result of impersonal economic forces," and it largely accompanied—rather than preceded—the more central role women were finding in family fortunes. As women found the economic means to leave unhappy marriages, divorce rates skyrocketed. Journalists began to write of a crisis of masculinity in blue-collar communities.

The young adults of the 1970s, idle in numbers not seen for a long time, were poorly regarded. (Among sixteen- to twenty-four-year-olds, unemployment for a time surpassed 15 percent, far higher than it had ever been in the 1960s.) Cultural critiques described a "wasted" generation, rootless and uncertain. Still, unemployment never neared 10 percent in the '70s (though it did spike briefly into double digits in the early 1980s, when the Fed raised interest rates to kill inflation). Inflation was the real scourge of the time, eroding people's wages and nest eggs. And it was inflation—not joblessness—that left its deepest mark on the decade's youth.

In *America in Search of Itself*, the historian Theodore White wrote that conversation in the 1970s was

> stained and drenched in money talk, by what it cost to live or what it cost to enjoy life. In the upper classes, one heard cocktail chatter about the cost of a new suit or dress. . . . But the conversation among poor people, among ordinary people, was far more significant. They winced and ached. Some mysterious power was hollowing their hopes and dreams, their plans for a house or their children's college education. . . . Faith in one's own planning was dissolving—all across the nation. The bedrock was heaving.

Families' savings, carefully built over many years and mostly kept in low-interest bank accounts, were destroyed by the inflation of the 1970s, and with them the ideal of thrift that had prevailed since the Depression. At the same time, houses, or at least those secured by fixed-rate mortgages, came to look like great investments; as inflation rose, so too did their prices, for the most part. What's more, fixed-rate mortgage debt became cheap as inflation rose. As Joseph Nocera wrote in *A Piece of the Action: How the Middle Class Joined the Money Class*, "[I]t became nearly impossible to go to a dinner party in a large American city and not wind up spending half the night discussing real estate prices." Middle-class Americans "no longer bought a house so much as they 'invested' in one."

All of these developments were duly noted by young Boomers, who—it seems in retrospect—drew lifelong lessons from these formative years. Nocera quotes a young Paine Webber economist, Christopher Rupkey, who in 1979 offered advice to his generation in an op-ed published by the *New York Times*: " 'Never buy what you can't afford' was the admonition of our parents," he began. "Today, the statement has been changed to, 'You can't afford not to buy it.' . . . Get your money out of the bank and spend it! Inflation gives the most it has to give to those with the largest pile of debts." And so from the fruit of one crisis grew the seeds of the next.

One shouldn't overstate America's economic transformation during the seventies, but by the decade's end, the foundations of the economy we have today had been partly laid. Industry emerged gaunt from the period, and bewildered industrial workers questioned their future and identity. Bill Gates emerged from his garage with a new software company, and rode the wave of the information age. *Newsweek* dubbed 1984 the "Year of the Yuppie," describing a novel type of young worker whose affinities and loyalties lay not with past custom or nation or employer, but with a social network of similarly educated, like-minded professionals. The term was an insult from the start, and soon disappeared from the vernacular, but yuppies would in fact continue to multiply, forming the center of the new economy. Today we call them the meritocratic elite, and their actions and attitudes have shaped the course of the current crisis.

WHAT SHOULD WE take away from these three periods of long economic distress?

For modern readers, accustomed by life experience to the idea that recessions and market downturns are rare and rapidly self-correcting—mere blips between long stretches of growth—each of these periods serves as a bracing caution. All contained growth spurts, false starts, and green shoots. But these upturns proved brief and unsustainable: in each case, for more than a decade, most Americans saw their prospects grow dimmer.

Policy mistakes (or, in the case of the late nineteenth century, the absence of sufficient policy tools) played a part in deepening or extending all of these downturns. And ultimately, the nation's political balance shifted during each of them, with one party losing credibility and the other gaining traction for a number of years or even decades thereafter.

It is perhaps significant that the downturns of the 1890s and 1930s, both precipitated by major financial crises, were preceded by rapidly rising income inequality and the concentration of wealth. (Recent academic research suggests that inequality heightens the risk of financial meltdowns, perhaps by inducing the middle class to take on debt in a futile effort to keep up with the Joneses.) Both crises also led, ultimately, to policy reforms that helped reduce inequality in the following decades—decades we remember for their broadly shared prosperity.

History is messy, and one thing evident from a comparison of these three periods is that culture and politics do not respond uniformly to economic shocks. Both the Gilded Age and the 1970s, for instance, saw great spiritual awakenings, as Americans sought order, meaning, and comfort amidst the disruptions of those eras. Yet nothing comparable occurred during the Depression; indeed, by some accounts, religious intensity and adherence slackened.

Yet in all three periods, one can clearly see a slow buildup of social discord, a rise in racial antipathies and anti-immigrant sentiment, the corrosion of trust, and, in general, the mobilization of efforts geared toward trying to recapture some past idyll rather than those that squarely confronted the future.

Perhaps the most-significant transformations were the ones that occurred in private, inside American bedrooms and kitchens or in backyards. Long slumps change marriages, shrink families, and alter the character of neighborhoods. And they shift the path of whole generations. The longer the current slump lasts, the more pronounced these same sorts of shifts and changes will be. But no matter when the slump ends, we'll be living with the changes for decades to come.

4

GENERATION R: THE CHANGING

FORTUNES OF AMERICA'S YOUTH

'M DEFINITELY SEEING A LOT OF THE OLDER GENERATION SAYING, 'Oh, this [recession] is so awful,' " Robert Sherman, a 2009 graduate of Syracuse University, told the *New York Times* in July 2009. "But my generation isn't getting as depressed and uptight." Sherman had recently turned down a $50,000-a-year job at a consulting firm, after careful deliberation with his parents, because he hadn't connected well with his potential bosses. Instead, he was doing odd jobs and trying to get a couple of tech companies off the ground. "The economy will rebound," he said.

Over the past two generations, particularly among many college grads, the twenties have become a sort of netherworld between adolescence and adulthood. Job-switching is common, and with it, periods of voluntary, transitional unemployment. And as marriage and parenthood have receded farther into the future, the first years after college have become, arguably, more carefree. Early in this recession, the term *funemployment* gained some currency among single twentysomethings, prompting a small raft of youth-culture stories in the *Los Angeles Times* and *San Francisco Weekly*, on Gawker, and in other venues.

Most of the people interviewed in these stories seem merely to be trying to stay positive and make the best of a bad situation. They note that it's a good time to reevaluate career choices; that since joblessness is now so common among their peers, it has lost much of its stigma; and that since they don't have mortgages or kids, they have flexibility, and in this respect, they are lucky. All of this sounds sensible enough—it is intuitive to think that youth will be spared the worst of the recession's scars.

But in fact a whole generation of young adults is likely to see its life chances permanently diminished by this recession. Lisa Kahn, an economist at Yale, has studied the impact of recessions on the lifetime earnings of young workers. In one recent study, she followed the career paths of white men who graduated from college between 1979 and 1989. She found that, all else equal, for every one-percentage-point increase in the national unemployment rate, the starting income of new graduates fell by as much as 7 percent; the unluckiest graduates of the decade, who emerged into the teeth of the 1981–82 recession, made roughly 25 percent less in their first year than graduates who stepped into boom times.

What's truly remarkable is the persistence of the earnings gap. Five, ten, fifteen years after graduation, after untold promotions and career changes spanning booms and busts, the unlucky graduates never closed the gap. Seventeen years after graduation, those who had entered the workforce during inhospitable times were still earning 10 percent less on average than those who had emerged into a more bountiful climate. When you add up all the earnings losses over the years, Kahn says, it's as if the lucky graduates had been given a gift of about $100,000, adjusted for inflation, immediately upon graduation—or, alternatively, as if the unlucky ones had been saddled with a debt of the same size.

When Kahn looked more closely at the unlucky graduates at mid-career, she found some surprising characteristics. They were significantly less likely to work in professional occupations or other prestigious spheres. And they clung more tightly to their jobs: average job tenure was unusually long. People who entered the workforce during the recession "didn't switch jobs as much, and particularly for young workers, that's how you increase wages," Kahn told me. This behavior may have resulted from a lingering risk aversion, born of a tough start. But a lack of opportunities may have played a larger role, she said: when you're forced to start work in a particularly low-level job or unsexy career, it's easy for other employers to dismiss you as having low potential. Moving up, or moving on to something different and better, becomes more difficult.

"Graduates'. first jobs have an inordinate impact on their career path and [lifetime earnings]," wrote Austan Goolsbee, now a member of President Obama's Council of Economic Advisers, in 2006. "People essentially cannot close the wage gap by working their way up the company hierarchy. While they may work their way up, the people who started above them do, too. They don't catch up." Recent research suggests that as much as two-thirds of real lifetime wage growth typically occurs in the first ten years of a career. After that, as people start families and their career paths lengthen and solidify, jumping the tracks becomes harder.

This job environment is not one in which fast-track jobs are plentiful, to say the least. According to the National Association of Colleges and Employers, job offers to graduating seniors declined 21 percent in 2009. They rebounded by 5 percent in 2010 and are expected to rise again in 2011, but not by nearly as much as they've fallen. In the San Francisco Bay Area, an organization called JobNob has been holding networking happy hours since the recession began to try to match college graduates with start-up companies looking primarily for unpaid labor. Julie Greenberg, a cofounder of JobNob, says that at the first event she expected perhaps 30 people, but 300 showed up. New graduates didn't have much of a chance; most of the people there had several years of work experience—quite a lot were thirtysomethings—and some had more than one degree. JobNob has since held events for alumni of Stanford, Berkeley, and Harvard; all have been well attended (at the Harvard event, Greenberg tried to restrict attendance to seventy-five people, but about a hundred managed to get in), and all have been dominated by people with significant work experience.

When experienced workers holding prestigious degrees are taking unpaid internships, not much is left for newly minted B.A.s.

Yet if those same B.A.s don't find purchase in the job market, they'll soon have to compete with a fresh class of graduates—ones without white space on their résumé to explain. This is a tough squeeze to escape, and it only gets tighter over time.

Strong evidence suggests that people who don't find solid roots in the job market within a year or two have a particularly hard time righting themselves. In part, that's because many of them become different—and damaged—people. Krysia Mossakowski, a sociologist at the University of Miami, has found that in young adults, long bouts of unemployment provoke long-lasting changes in behavior and mental health. "Some people say, 'Oh, well, they're young, they're in and out of the workforce, so unemployment shouldn't matter much psychologically,' " Mossakowski told me. "But that isn't true."

Examining national longitudinal data, Mossakowski has found that people who were unemployed for long periods in their teens or early twenties are far more likely to develop a habit of heavy drinking (five or more drinks in one sitting) by the time they approach middle age. They are also more likely to develop depressive symptoms. Prior drinking behavior and psychological history do not explain these problems—they result from unemployment itself. And the problems are not limited to those who never find steady work; they show up quite strongly as well in people who are later working regularly.

As we've seen, young men who suffered hardship during the Depression carried scars for the rest of their lives; even forty years later, unlike peers who had been largely spared in the 1930s, they generally displayed a lack of ambition, direction, and confidence in themselves—a belief that they were powerless before the fates. Today in Japan, according to the Japan Productivity Center for Socio-Economic Development, workers who began their careers during the "lost decade" of the 1990s and are now in their thirties make up six out of every ten cases of depression, stress, and work-related mental disabilities reported by employers.

A large and long-standing body of research shows that physical health tends to deteriorate during unemployment, most likely through a combination of fewer financial resources and a higher stress level. The most-recent research suggests that poor health is prevalent among the young, and endures for a lifetime. Till Von Wachter, an economist at Columbia University, and Daniel Sullivan, of the Federal Reserve Bank of Chicago, recently looked at the mortality rates of men who had lost their jobs in Pennsylvania in the 1970s and '80s. They found that particularly among men in their forties or fifties, mortality rates rose markedly soon after a layoff. But regardless of age, all men were left with an elevated risk of dying in each year following their episode of unemployment, for the rest of their lives. And so, the younger the worker, the more pronounced the effect on his lifespan: the lives of workers who had lost their job at thirty, Von Wachter and Sullivan found, were shorter than those of workers who had lost their job at fifty or fifty-five—and more than a year and a half shorter than the lives of workers who'd never lost their job at all.

JOURNALISTS AND ACADEMICS have thrown various labels at today's young adults, hoping one might stick—Generation Y, Generation Next, the Net Generation, the Millennials, the Echo Boomers. Recently, the *New York Times* reporter Steven Greenhouse has aptly suggested Generation Recession, or simply Generation R. All of these efforts contain an unavoidable element of folly; the diversity of character within a generation is always infinitely larger than the gap between generations. Still, the cultural and economic environment in which each generation is incubated clearly matters. It is no coincidence that the members of Generation X—painted as cynical, apathetic slackers—first emerged into the workforce in the weak job market of the early to mid-1980s. Nor is it a coincidence that the early members of Generation Y—labeled as optimistic, rule-following achievers—came of age during the Internet boom of the late 1990s.

Many of today's young adults seem temperamentally unprepared for the circumstances in which they now find themselves. Jean Twenge, an associate professor of psychology at San Diego State University, has carefully compared the attitudes of today's young adults with those of previous generations when they were the same age. Using national survey data, she's found that to an unprecedented degree, people who graduated from high school in the aughts dislike the idea of work for work's sake, and expect jobs and career to be tailored to their interests and lifestyle. Yet they also have much higher material expectations than previous generations, and believe financial success is extremely important. "There's this idea that, 'Yeah, I don't want to work, but I'm still going to get all the stuff I want,' " Twenge told me. "It's a generation in which every kid has been told, 'You can be anything you want. You're special.' "

In her 2006 book, *Generation Me*, Twenge notes that self-esteem in children began rising sharply around 1980, and hasn't stopped since. By 1999, according to one survey, 91 percent of teens described themselves as responsible, 74 percent as physically attractive, and 79 percent as very intelligent. (More than 40 percent of teens also expected that they would be earning $75,000 a year or more by age thirty; the median salary made by a thirty-year-old was $27,000 that year.) Twenge attributes the shift to broad changes in parenting styles and teaching methods, in response to the growing belief that children should always feel good about themselves, no matter what. As the years have passed, efforts to boost self-esteem—and to decouple it from performance—have become widespread.

These efforts have succeeded in making today's youth more confident and individualistic. But that may not benefit them in adulthood, particularly in this economic environment. Twenge writes that "self-esteem without basis encourages laziness rather than hard work," and that "the ability to persevere and keep going" is "a much better predictor of life outcomes than self-esteem." She worries that many young people might be inclined to simply give up in this job market. "You'd think if people are more individualistic, they'd be more independent," she told me. "But it's not really true. There's an element of entitlement—they expect people to figure things out for them."

Ron Alsop, a former reporter for the *Wall Street Journal* and the author of *The Trophy Kids Grow Up: How the Millennial Generation Is Shaking Up the Workplace*, says a combination of entitlement and highly structured childhood has resulted in a lack of independence and entrepreneurialism in many twentysomethings. They're used to checklists, he says, and "don't excel at leadership or independent problem solving." Alsop interviewed dozens of employers for his book, and concluded that unlike previous generations, Millennials, as a group, "need almost constant direction" in the workplace. "Many flounder without precise guidelines but thrive in structured situations that provide clearly defined rules."

All of these characteristics are troubling, given a harsh economic environment that requires perseverance, adaptability, humility, and entrepreneurialism. Perhaps most worrisome, though, is the fatalism and lack of agency that both Twenge and Alsop discern in today's young adults. Trained throughout childhood to disconnect performance from reward, and told repeatedly that they are destined for great things, many are quick to place blame elsewhere when something goes wrong, and inclined to believe that bad situations will sort themselves out—or will be sorted out by parents or other helpers.

In his 2009 commencement remarks, as the *New York Times* reported, University of Connecticut president Michael Hogan addressed the phenomenon of students' turning down jobs, with no alternatives, because they didn't feel the jobs were good enough. "My first word of advice is this," he told the graduates. "Say yes. In fact, say yes as often as you can. Saying yes begins things. Saying yes is how things grow. Saying yes leads to new experiences, and new experiences will lead to knowledge and wisdom. *Yes* is for young people, and an attitude of yes is how you will be able to go forward in these uncertain times."

Larry Druckenbrod, the university's assistant director of career services, told me, "This is a group that's done résumé building since middle school. They've been told they've been preparing to go out and do great things after college. And now they've been dealt a 180." For many, that's led to "immobilization." Druckenbrod said that about a third of the seniors he talked to were seriously looking for work; another third were planning to go to grad school. The final third, he said, were "not even engaging with the job market—these are the ones whose parents have already said, 'Just come home and live with us.' "

According to a recent Pew survey, 10 percent of adults younger than thirty-five have moved back in with their parents as a result of the recession. But that's merely an acceleration of a trend that has been under way for a generation or more. By the middle of the aughts, for instance, the percentage of twenty-six-year-olds living with their parents reached 20 percent, nearly double what it was in 1970. Well before the recession began, this generation of young adults was less likely to work, or at least work steadily, than other recent generations. Since 2000, the percentage of people ages sixteen to twenty-four participating in the labor force has been declining (from 66 percent to 56 percent across the decade). Increased college attendance explains only part of the shift; the rest is a puzzle. Lingering weakness in the job market since 2001 may be one cause. Twenge believes the propensity of this generation to pursue "dream" careers that are, for most people, unlikely to work out may also be partly responsible. (In 2004, a national survey found that about one out of eighteen college freshmen expected to make a living as an actor, musician, or artist.)

Whatever the reason, the fact that so many young adults weren't firmly rooted in the workforce even before the crash is deeply worrying. It means that a very large number of young adults entered the recession already vulnerable to all the ills that joblessness produces over time. It means that for a sizable proportion of twenty- and thirtysomethings, the next few years will likely be toxic.

· · ·

NO YOUNG PEOPLE were present at a seminar for the unemployed held on November 4, 2009, in Reading, Pennsylvania, a blue-collar city about sixty miles west of Philadelphia. The meeting was organized by a regional nonprofit, Joseph's People, and held in the basement of the St. Catharine's parish center. All thirty or so attendees, sitting around a U-shaped table, looked to be forty or older. But one middle-aged man, one of the first to introduce himself to the group, said he and his wife were there on behalf of their son, Errol. "He's so disgusted that he didn't want to come," the man said. "He doesn't know what to do, and we don't either."

I talked to Errol a few days later. He was twenty-eight and had a gentle, straightforward manner. He graduated from high school in 1999 and had lived with his parents since then. He worked in a machine shop for a couple of years after school, and had also held jobs at a battery factory, a sandpaper manufacturer, and a restaurant, where he was a cook. The restaurant closed in June 2008, and apart from a few days of work through temp agencies, he hadn't had a job since.

He called in to a few temp agencies each week to let them know he was interested in working, and checked the newspaper for job listings every Sunday. Sometimes he went into CareerLink, the local unemployment office, to see if it had any new listings. He did work around the house, or in the small machine shop he'd set up in the garage, just to fill his days, and to try to keep his skills up.

"I was thinking about moving," he said. "I'm just really not sure where. Other places where I traveled, I didn't really see much of a difference with what there was here." He still had a few thousand dollars in the bank, which he'd saved when he was working as a machinist, and was mostly living off that; he'd been trading penny stocks to try to replenish those savings.

I asked him what he foresaw for his working life. "As far as my job position," he said, "I really don't know what I want to do yet. I'm not sure." When he was little, he wanted to be a mechanic, and he did enjoy the machine trade. But now there was hardly any work to be had, and what there was paid about the same as Walmart. "I don't think there's any way that you can have a job that you can think you can retire off of," he said. "I think everyone's going to have to transfer to another job." He said the only future he could really imagine for himself now was just moving from job to job, with no career to speak of. "That's what I think," he said. "I don't want to."

As the recession has ground on, the belief among some young workers that this period is just a speed bump—something that can be easily endured or perhaps even enjoyed—has become harder to sustain. The early posts on the tongue-in-cheek blog Stuff Unemployed People Like, begun by a twenty-six-year-old Internet company worker laid off in December 2008, betray flashes of exuberance ("#7 Buying Game Consoles with Unemployment Checks," "#8 Pretending to Look for a Job," "#15 Taking Friends Out 'On the Government' "). Later entries are less frequent, flatter, and more sallow ("#143 Thrift Stores," "#145 Cramming in Their Health Care," "#146 Staring at Their Useless Diploma(s)," "#150 Wishing They'd Started Job Searching Sooner").

Aubrey Howell, who'd tweeted about funemployment shortly after being laid off as the manager of a Nashville tea shop in 2009, and was featured in a *Los Angeles Times* story soon afterward, told me half a year later that she initially saw the layoff as an opportunity to clear her head, refocus, and "go after what I'm really passionate about"—music and graphic design. "I realize the gravity of my situation," said Howell, twenty-nine. "I was just trying to stay positive." But that was getting harder. "I've had to start selling things off," she said—two guitars, her amps, a violin, a mandolin. To give her days some structure, she volunteered frequently at her church, and also did some free design work there, but she hadn't found paid work, and when we talked, her unemployment benefits were about to run out. "I've definitely broadened the job search," she said. She'd worked in marketing in her early twenties, in a good-paying job, but she'd felt it was a poor fit, and anyway that was some years ago. At this point, she said, "if Starbucks offered me a good job, I'd take it."

Recently, the same career conservatism that Lisa Kahn found in prior generations who'd entered the job market during downturns has begun to appear in this one, too. Asked in 2010 to rate the importance of various career priorities—high pay, intellectual stimulation, creative opportunities, the chance to make a difference in society, and more—Millennials put "job security" above everything else. And when offered a hypothetical choice between the prospect of a long-term job with a single company and the opportunity to change employers throughout their career, only a third chose the latter. Median job tenure rose among workers age twenty to thirty-four between January 2008 and January 2010, more so than among older workers. Overall, job tenure increased to its highest level since the Bureau of Labor Statistics starting tracking tenure in 1996.

These trends are dispiriting when you look at the type of work that young people—even those with college degrees—have been finding. Among college graduates aged twenty-five to thirty-four, according to the economist Michael Mandel, government employment grew the most between August 2009 and August 2010, followed by jobs in professional and technical services. But hotel and restaurant employment was third. Among sectors that are predominantly for-profit, hotel, restaurant, repair, maintenance, and personal-services jobs accounted for 28 percent of all new jobs obtained by four-year college graduates under the age of thirty-five.

Young adults with college and graduate degrees are doing much better than those without; for 2010 as a whole, the unemployment rate among sixteen- to twenty-four-year-olds was 9.4 percent for four-year college graduates, 22.5 percent for those with only a high-school diploma, and 31.5 percent for high-school dropouts. The deepest pain, by far, is concentrated in the latter two groups. But that doesn't mitigate the disappointment and gathering self-doubt of the former, many of whom now have the twin privileges of a bad job and heavy student debt to go along with their degree.

In the fall of 2010, I had coffee with an elfin-featured, blond-haired twenty-seven-year-old law school graduate, whom I'll call

Mark Nickelsen, in Washington, DC. (He asked not to be named because he doesn't want to rock the boat with his current employer.) The only son of an auto-parts machinist and a secretary, Nickelsen grew up in Toledo, Ohio, went to public school, and put himself through the University of Cincinnati, working two jobs and graduating debt-free. But when he was accepted into law school in Boston in 2006, he didn't hesitate to take on a student loan, which would eventually total $145,000. "I figured it was 'good debt,' " he said.

In the fall of 2008, entering his final year in law school, he lined up a job with the Massachusetts Office of the Attorney General, but because of state budget cuts, the offer was rescinded early in 2009, after private law firms had largely finished what little hiring they did that year. He applied for various federal legal internships, and got to the final round of interviews for one of them, but then that position was cut, too. To try to maximize his possibilities, he sat for both the Massachusetts and New York bar exams shortly after graduation in the spring of 2009, passing both. But he couldn't find legal work in either state.

In August, Nickelsen sold most of his furniture and moved to Washington, figuring the legal economy there might be better insulated. He made the rounds of the city's law firms, federal agencies, university law libraries, and professional temp firms—13 of them—showing up in person, in a suit, to deliver his résumé. He also sought out informational interviews through networking contacts. For three months, he spent much of each day in a corner of Rosslyn, in Northern Virginia, where he could access free Wi-Fi, scanning job listings and setting up networking appointments. "I tried to treat it as a job—just go every day and focus," he said.

In October, with his savings depleted and his credit cards nearly maxed out, Nickelsen took a job in the café at Barnes & Noble for about $8 an hour, a little less than he'd made at Arby's in high school. Cass Sunstein, a famous legal scholar he admires, ordered a coffee from him once, but Nickelsen didn't introduce himself. "There was a line, and besides . . ." he said, trailing off with a shrug and a pale smile. His parents took out a home-equity loan to allow him to con-solidate his credit-card and bar-preparation-course debt at a lower interest rate. And they offered to give him his room back if he wanted to return to Toledo. "It just got very dark for me for a time," he said.

In January 2010, things brightened somewhat: Nickelsen got a two-year job at the U.S. Department of Homeland Security through a federal fellowship program. "It's professional work," he said, a re-assurance that may have been meant more for himself than for me. He gathers information from other arms of the government, updates spreadsheets, takes notes in meetings. The job doesn't make use of his law degree, and he doesn't advertise that degree around the office, he said. Whenever a colleague finds out, "they're like, 'You went to law school? What are you doing here?' "

Nickelsen told me he realizes that other people have taken much larger hits than he has. And he's grateful for his salary. Still, it's no-where near what lawyers typically make, and even with the night job he's taken with Kaplan Test Preparation, he doesn't have much left over after making his monthly debt payments. What gnaws at him most is the sense that the things he used to take for granted about his future—not riches, necessarily, but merely the basic pleasures and privileges of a fully adult life—keep receding from him, rather than drawing closer.

"My dad worked in a factory . . . and when he was twenty-two, he had a house and two children," Nickelsen said. "Maybe I bought into it, but you're sort of fed the line that you can't have a normal life unless you get an education. And so you take on this tremendous debt. And so I'm just starting out now at the age of twenty-seven, with prescription glasses and all these payments coming due. And I'm living in an efficiency with a roommate. I had a nicer apartment in law school; I never would have thought that." A house? A family? "There's no *car* in the near future for me. Everything's been pushed back so far, I can't even see it. How did this happen?"

. . .

THE RELATIONSHIP BETWEEN many Millennials and their parents has become complicated since the recession began. In one recent poll, 39 percent of people aged eighteen to twenty-nine said they regularly received money from their parents to help them pay ordinary expenses, and many have moved back home. But these arrangements have worn on both parties. Recent research by the Purdue University psychologist Karen Fingerman indicates that while modern parents do provide more financial support to grown children who are struggling, by and large they prefer to offer their continued guidance and companionship to those who are already succeeding, perhaps because time spent with successful children flatters the parents more.

A May 2010 "Shouts & Murmurs" column in *The New Yorker* captures the ambivalence felt by many "helicopter parents" as their children have returned to the nest. Titled "Your New College Graduate: A Parents' Guide," it begins, "Congratulations! It took four years and hundreds of thousands of dollars, but you're finally the parents of a bona-fide college graduate. After the commencement ceremony is over, your child will be ready to move back into your house for a period of several years. It's a very exciting time." Around the country, family and financial consultants have begun to offer their services to assist with this transition; one consultancy in Los Angeles has created a four-step program that seeks to settle in advance certain questions: What will the child do to earn money if he or she can't find a full-time job? What domestic responsibilities will he or she undertake? What's the target date for moving out?

Near the height of Japan's economic boom in the late 1980s, a relatively small but growing number of teens and twentysomethings began to turn away from well-worn corporate career paths (or at least defer their entry onto them), instead living at home with their parents and taking a string of temporary or part-time jobs. By and large, they valued self-expression and a flexible lifestyle, and many had artistic ambitions. A new term was coined to describe them—*freeters*—and while many criticized them as coddled and lazy, a certain glamour seemed attached to the term.

With the bust of the 1990s, the number of freeters grew rapidly. Aging freeters could not find permanent work; new ones, typically with relatively little education and no designs on an artist's life, found traditional career paths closed off from the start. In 2002, perhaps 2.5 million Japanese between the ages of fifteen and thirty-four were freeters, and year by year their ranks were both increasing and aging. Since the bust, *freeters* has been joined in the Japanese vernacular by a host of other new terms to describe single young people living with parents: *NEETs* (not in education, employment, or training), *hikikomori* (men, mostly, who do not work or socialize, seldom leave their room, and are in some cases physically abusive to aging parents), and several more.

Japan's economy has been troubled for decades, and its culture is in many respects sui generis; one should treat comparisons to the United States with caution. But the evolution of freeters' portrayal in Japan is perhaps telling. By the mid-1990s, most traces of glamour and indulgence were gone. And by the late 1990s, *freeters* had been subsumed into a newly popular term—*parasaito shinguru*, or "parasite singles"—who were blamed for everything from low economic growth to low birthrates. Even as the phenomenon became less a matter of personal choice, the tensions and criticism resulting from it seemed to rise.

Whether the intensive and incessant involvement of today's parents in the daily lives of their children has, in the end, helped the Millennial generation or held it back is a hard question, and one outside the scope of this book. At its worst, one can see in the relationship between helicopter parents and their teenage or twenty-something children a new form of codependency, destructive and debilitating. But it is difficult to criticize parents for offering whatever assistance they can in these times. And it is more difficult still to criticize young adults—particularly those with no degree and few imminent prospects—for taking it.

What often gets lost in the discussion of parents' continuing assistance to their children today is that the children, by and large, have always planned to return the favor. In a 2005 Pew poll, 63 percent of Millennials said they felt a responsibility to allow an elderly parent to live in their home one day if the parent wanted to do so. That's a slightly lower percentage than in Generation X, but much higher than in the generations before that. (Only 55 percent of Boomers and 38 percent of the Silent Generation felt the same way.) By a variety of measures, the bond between this generation of young adults and their parents is stronger than those between past generations of parents and children, and so is the sense of mutual obligation.

But obligations of nearly every sort—current and future—are growing harder for young adults to meet, as high expectations collide with limited means. According to one recent poll, just 16 percent of eighteen- to twenty-nine-year-olds were saving money, and about two-thirds were in debt. In 2009, according to Pew Research, 12 percent of adults younger than thirty-five said they'd acquired a roommate, 15 percent had delayed marriage, and 14 percent had put off having a child. Surely all those numbers are higher now.

In nearly every way, the Great Recession has delayed the ability of young adults to reach the milestones that society has always associated with full adulthood, and to assume the responsibilities that many of them want to accept. With each passing year of economic weakness, more and more of them find themselves swimming in a seemingly endless adolescence, whose taste has long since grown brackish, and from which they cannot fully emerge.

As economic malaise lingers on, the ideas and ideals of twentysomethings—about politics, society, the nature of life—are slowly changing. Millennials entered the Great Recession as the most politically liberal generation in many decades, and as the most socially liberal ever. And between 2008 and 2010, the number who called themselves liberal held steady. Yet cynicism about government's efficacy is growing. By 2010, 37 percent of Millennials said that although they might like to see the government play an active role in the economy in theory, they weren't sure they could trust the government to do that effectively. When asked whom they trusted more to solve the country's economic problems—President Obama or Republicans in Congress—27 percent said "neither." Confidence in elected officials fell between 2009 and 2010.

Economic troubles are sanding away the generation's openness and confidence as well. According to one 2010 survey, just 28 percent of adults younger than thirty believed that most people could be trusted, a lower figure than in prior years. And nearly one in three said they believed their financial well-being primarily depended not on their own actions but on events outside their control. Forty-two percent, a plurality, believed globalization had decreased the opportunities available to them.

The changes now taking place in Millennials' political ideals and social attitudes will shape American politics and culture for decades. A recent paper by the economists Paola Giuliano and Antonio Spilimbergo shows that previous cadres of young adults who endured a recession emerged with different beliefs than they'd held before—and that those new beliefs then stayed with them for the rest of their lives. They became more concerned about inequality, more cognizant of the role luck plays in life, and more likely to support government redistribution of wealth, but also less confident in the efficacy of government institutions—changes, for the most part, that can be seen happening again today.

The optimism of the Millennial generation has not been completely dispelled. A Pew survey early in 2010 found that even among those who were struggling financially, 89 percent were confident that they'd have "enough" income in the future, a characterization that was basically unchanged from 2006. Fewer Millennials were dissatisfied with the country's direction than were other adults. And overall, Millennials were as happy with their lives as other generations, or happier.

This period has not been without silver linings for some young adults. Due to poor job prospects, college attendance has risen since 2007; as a result, some people who would not have gotten a college degree now will; whatever the economic climate today, they'll almost certainly find better long-term prospects than they would have otherwise. Houses are cheaper throughout the country, allowing young adults who have good, secure jobs to buy sooner if they wish to do so. For some twenty- and thirtysomethings on the fast track, aggressive workplace restructuring has meant bigger responsibilities more quickly. And to the extent that young adults embrace thrift the way Depression-era twentysomethings did—still an open question for the generation as a whole—they will leave themselves less vulnerable to shocks that happen later in their lives.

Many factors throughout a lifetime affect generational character. No one can know what technological and scientific breakthroughs await us in the coming years, but it's hard to believe that the nation's material standards in 2030 and 2050 won't be far higher than they are now. Nonetheless, for young adults, perhaps more than anyone else, the key question is: How much longer? How much longer will we remain mired in a weak economy with bad jobs or no jobs for people just beginning their careers? The Great Recession has indelibly changed the lives of many twentysomethings already. The longer this generation marinates in it, the more widely those changes will spread and the deeper they will be. Over the past year, as I've talked with young adults around the country, I've often had the sense of lives in abeyance—particularly among the jobless. Many hopes and many futures can still be realized—or at least nearly so—if the job market soon rebounds. But as the months and years tick by, more of those hopes and futures will become irretrievable. The urgency of recovery is highest for the young.

5

HOUSEBOUND: THE MIDDLE CLASS
AFTER THE BUST

IF YOU DRIVE NORTH FROM TAMPA ALONG I-75 FOR ABOUT TWENTY-
five miles, then take the off-ramp onto Wesley Chapel Boulevard
and drive east a few miles more, you'll eventually come upon Curley
Road, up on the left. And if you take that left, you'll see before you
a clean divide between suburb and country. On the right side of
the road lie vast acres of cow pastures, and beyond them an electrical power station. On the left lie subdivisions, neatly set, one after
another.

The last and largest of them, before you hit the orange groves, is
Bridgewater, a planned community of some 760 houses built mostly
in 2005 and 2006, at the height of the housing boom. It's a nice if
generic-looking community of McMansions and somewhat smaller
homes. Many of the houses back up onto one of the development's
several artificial lakes. All are painted in neutral, inoffensive colors.
Visually, the neighborhood is indistinguishable from innumerable other exurban communities that have promised the trappings
of affluence to millions of middle-class families, and that have become, arguably, the physical representation of the modern American
Dream.

Drive around a bit, though, and you'll quickly notice many of
the dissonant images that now appear in exurban neighborhoods
nationwide. More driveways sit empty than you'd expect, and the
streets are curiously quiet, even by suburban standards. In other
driveways, there are too many cars altogether—jumbles of pickups

and old Camrys; more cars, seemingly, than bedrooms in the house behind them. On some streets, most of the houses are for sale.

Since the recession began, about 80 percent of Bridgewater's houses have been in foreclosure at one time or another. Midway through 2010, nearly half were occupied by renters. Sixty or seventy were vacant.

On a Friday afternoon in August 2010, I chatted with an attractive young couple I saw washing their car in front of their house on one of the subdevelopment's many identical streets. They'd been living there for the past two years, they told me, because the rent couldn't be beat. But that was the only reason. "It's not what you'd expect by just looking at it," said the man, a leanly muscled police trooper with a buzz cut. "The people here are the kind of people I encounter in my line of work," he said, pausing. "People I arrest." Half the houses on the street were vacant—"that one, that one, the one over there"—and he didn't count any friends among those neighbors he had. He kept his police car parked prominently in the driveway of one of those vacant houses, to scare off undesirables.

Mark Spector is one of Bridgewater's original homeowners and now the president of its homeowners association. I sat down with him in the kitchen of his spacious, six-bedroom house that same day, as his seven-year-old daughter, Chloe, played in the living room, and he told me the story of the community. Spector had bought his house for $350,000 in 2005, as the subdevelopment was still being built out. He and his wife—who both have a graduate degree—had moved from California to be closer to her family, and he'd taken a job in business development at a large health-care company. When we talked, he was forty-one, and behind his wire-rimmed glasses, more often than not, he wore an expression of weary bemusement, colored by a deeper bitterness, as he described the past five years.

As their house was being built, Spector said, he tracked other neighborhood house sales with no little excitement—every month the prices seemed to go up by $5,000 or more. At the peak of the market, about a year after he'd moved in, houses with floor plans like his were selling for $550,000. By then he was enjoying the new swimming pool he'd put in, financed by a $50,000 home-equity loan.

Spector knew things were going to go wrong, he told me, when he began to see contractors who'd been working in the neighborhood snapping up houses, planning to flip them. But he wasn't prepared for how far wrong they'd go, or how quickly. In fact, more than half of Bridgewater's home buyers were speculative investors. When the market turned down and they couldn't sell profitably, many went into foreclosure almost immediately. Overcapacity turned out to be so severe—not just in Bridgewater, but everywhere in the region—that even finding steady renters proved difficult. Section 8 voucher recipients became desirable, because their rent payments were assured.

As the neighborhood became more transient, its character began to change. People in the midst of foreclosure stopped keeping their yards carefully; some stripped their houses of appliances and electrical fixtures as they left. Unkempt lawns and visible disrepair became more widespread as new renters and other residents saw that the neighborhood standard of upkeep was not always high. As the months went by, vacant houses, low rental prices, and budding disorder began to attract criminals, Spector told me, and for a time drug sales became a problem; a Miami-based gang briefly established an outpost in the neighborhood and tagged its streets with graffiti. On at least a couple of occasions, he said, gunfire was exchanged. Through it all, people continued to wash in and out of the community, and they still do today; on the first and last day of each month, a "parade of U-Hauls" goes up and down Bridgegate Drive.

"My daughter is always telling me, 'I have a new classmate' " at school, Spector said. But then the classmate will disappear a few months later. No small number of the neighborhood's renters, he said, will pay the deposit and the first month's rent and then just wait to be evicted, which can take several months. More than half the kids at Chloe's elementary school now qualify for the free or reduced-price lunch program, Spector told me, and he worries that the school's quality, which was excellent when he moved in, may be declining. "I understand that people are down on their luck," he said, "but this isn't the neighborhood that I moved into. . . . It's never going to recover to what it was."

The waves of foreclosure buffeting Bridgewater seem unending, Spector said. The investors defaulted first, followed by ordinary homeowners who'd been in over their heads from the day of their closing. The latest wave was washing out people who'd lost their jobs in the recession and seen once-manageable payments become impossible. "Every single time you think you've hit some type of stability, the next round comes."

Spector's house was most recently assessed at $179,000, though he's not sure he could sell it for that much. "We're completely trapped," he said. "There's no way I can move anywhere unless I'm coming to the table with more than $200,000." And besides, he adds, "where would we move? Wherever you look, it's the same, unless you go to one of the really older communities." Spector's house in Bridgewater isn't his first; he and his wife had previously owned a home, and had reinvested part of the proceeds into this one. "To think that we would have to save up just for a deposit now," he says. "It's like starting from scratch."

SINCE THE 1940S, the story of the American middle class has been tightly intertwined with that of America's suburbs. Middle-class life is, to a large extent, measured by housing, and the purchase of a house in the suburbs is, for many families, an emblem of achievement—signifying fully-adult status, economic security, and some measure of prosperity. And of course a home is by far the largest store of wealth for most families as well—a savings account, rainy-day fund, and retirement asset all rolled into one.

As middle-class incomes have faltered over the past two decades or more, housing has become ever more central to the achievement and maintenance of middle-class life. By the middle of the aughts, many Americans had come to view their house not just as a store of wealth, but as an engine of it, one that seemed to promise the upward mobility and increasing material comfort that flat salaries did not. From 2000 through 2006, real home prices rose by almost 90 percent nationally; in particularly effervescent markets such as Las Vegas, Phoenix, Tampa, and Miami, values more than doubled. Home buyers—more than 50 million of them over that same span—chased those returns eagerly, spending 34 percent of their disposable income on housing, on average, by 2006. Relaxed credit standards both expanded the pool of buyers and allowed them to put little money down, enabling bigger and more-leveraged home purchases. In 2005, nearly one in four new mortgages was an interest-only adjustable-rate loan. In 2006, 20 percent of all new mortgages were subprime, up fourfold since 1994.

Clearly, this kind of appreciation couldn't go on forever—as the economist Robert Shiller has shown, once you account for inflation and home improvements, housing has never been a fast-appreciating asset over the long haul. From 1890 through 2004, U.S. house prices rose just 0.4 percent per year on average, with these factors taken into account. This stands to reason: land remains plentiful in the United States, and the cost of construction materials hasn't risen greatly—if anything, houses are cheaper and faster to build now than they've ever been.

But for almost a decade, typical families saw the value of their home go up by $10,000 or $15,000 a year (more still at the peak). Many cashed out at least part of the increase to fund renovations or annual vacations or new cars. According to the Federal Deposit Insurance Corporation, the value of all outstanding home-equity loans more than doubled between 1998 and 2008, to more than $650 billion. As of 2007, according to the Census Bureau, more than 12 million owner-occupied houses (about one in six) had second or third mortgages on them; another 2 million homeowners had refinanced their mortgage primarily to get cash back.

With the crash, many families have seen their house transformed in a blink from a sort of magical ATM to a heavy burden. Nationwide, housing values fell by about 31 percent from their peak in 2006 to the end of 2010. In Las Vegas, Phoenix, and Tampa, they fell by 58 percent, 55 percent, and 45 percent, respectively. And we still may not have reached the bottom; at the beginning of 2011, home values were still more than 20 percent higher than they were in 2000, after adjusting for inflation. According to the Census Bureau, the total housing vacancy rate in 2009—more than 10 percent, including rental properties that had been vacant for a full year—was higher than it had been since 1965, when the bureau first started tracking that data.

At the beginning of 2011, roughly one in four homeowners was underwater—their house was worth less than the principal still outstanding on their mortgage. (In Arizona and Florida, that number was one in two; in Nevada, two in three.) Roughly one in seven was delinquent on a mortgage. A small fraction of homeowners—currently sitting in the long purgatory between foreclosure and eviction—have extra cash to spend or save, albeit temporarily, because they are paying nothing for the roof over their heads. But a larger number have been struggling to make house payments. As Harvard University's Joint Center for Housing Studies reported in June 2010, "Despite falling home prices, loan modifications, and softening rents, the downturn did not reduce the number of households spending half or more of their income on housing—18.6 million in 2008. Instead, the share with such severe housing cost burdens climbed to a new height."

"Disillusionment is the appropriate word for my current condition," wrote a reader of Andrew Sullivan's in Sullivan's recurring blog feature "The View from Your Recession." The man, a software engineer who'd immigrated from Nigeria and was living in the Midwest, said he'd spent years eating ramen noodles and keeping the thermostat down in the winter so that he could save aggressively, and he'd put the lion's share of his savings into his house and other real-estate properties, which he'd bought and held. "If I had been profligate," he wrote, "at least I would have the memories. It's hard to muster the discipline to save again. It was difficult (horrendous even) to work an average of 75 hours a week for over a decade. It stings to realize that it was all for naught."

THE PROBLEM NOW facing many middle-income families—especially young, striving families who bought into new communities in recent years—is not only that their biggest financial asset has become a liability (though that problem is severe). It's that everything they thought they were buying along with their house—good schools, a good neighborhood, the good life—is also now in question. The suburban idyll, in many places, appears to be vanishing.

For many years, the housing bubble papered over the stagnation of middle-class incomes. But it also changed the geography of middle-class living, in ways that look unhealthy today. As the bubble inflated, first-time buyers found it harder to get in on the action—particularly in high-priced city-regions with diverse and thriving economies like San Francisco, Los Angeles, New York, and Boston. But of course, with most people's salaries and wages going nowhere, getting in on the game was also becoming more urgent. Within city-regions, that fueled explosive growth in faraway exurbs. Nationally, it prompted a helter-skelter rush into lower-priced but fast-appreciating metro areas like Orlando, Tampa, Phoenix, and Las Vegas—the same places now suffering the worst effects of the crash.

This pattern of middle-class migration was not new; both sprawl and the Sun Belt had been growing for decades. But the bubble pushed that growth further and faster. Phoenix grew from just under 1 million people in 1990 to more than 1.5 million in 2007. One of its suburbs, Mesa, is now larger than Pittsburgh.

The economic boom in many of these cities, writes Richard Florida, was, to an uncommon degree, "propelled by housing appreciation: as prices rose, more people moved in, seeking inexpensive lifestyles and the opportunity to get in on the real-estate market where it was rising, but still affordable. Local homeowners pumped more and more capital out of their houses as well," and into the local economy. "Cities grew, tax coffers filled, spending continued, more people arrived. Yet the boom itself neither followed nor resulted in the development of sustainable, scalable, highly productive industries or services. It was fueled and funded by housing, and housing was its primary product. Whole cities and metro regions became giant Ponzi schemes."

At the peak of the market, housing construction and related activities accounted for more than a quarter of the economy in Phoenix and Las Vegas, and 30 percent in Orlando. Florida posits that these cities, among others hit especially hard by the housing crash, may never recover. The very nature of their attraction has left them with large populations, but not an especially high level of human capital; the country's economic elite have for the most part clustered elsewhere. So, too, have recent immigrants with high economic potential. According to the Brookings Institution, relatively highly educated immigrants have crowded into places like Seattle, Minneapolis, San Francisco, and New York. By contrast, "immigrants with the lowest levels of English language ability and educational attainment cluster in Texas, inland California, and Sunbelt markets that experienced fast growth during the decade's housing boom." With the mirage of opportunity in these places dispelled, revealing shrunken, low-wage, slow-growth economies, many homeowners have discovered not only that they bought into a Ponzi scheme, but that the local economy cannot provide the sorts of job opportunities that might help them rebuild lost wealth.

In his 2008 *Atlantic* essay, "The Next Slum?" the real-estate developer and land-use strategist Christopher Leinberger argued that even in less frenzied markets, traditional suburbs (and in particular newer exurban communities far from city centers) were headed for a long decline—that today's McMansions might turn into tomorrow's tenements. The suburbs had been massively overbuilt throughout the aughts, Leinberger observed. Meanwhile, inexorable demographic changes (an aging population, fewer and smaller families), rising gas and energy prices, and a tectonic shift in cultural preferences toward urban living all suggested decades of declining demand for oversized houses on the suburban fringe. In 2006, the Virginia Tech housing expert Arthur C. Nelson concluded, after a detailed analysis of housing supply, population growth, and recent consumer research, that by 2025, there would likely be a surplus of some 22 million large-lot homes nationwide, or roughly 40 percent of all large-lot homes then in existence.

It's worth noting the difficult compromises that many middle-class families have made in recent years in their effort to own a piece of the American Dream. Nearly one in four people surveyed by Fannie Mae in 2010 said they were "sacrificing a great deal" to own a home. Even in 2000, roughly 3.5 million Americans were making "extreme commutes" (defined as daily, round-trip travel of three hours or more), and that number had doubled since 1990. Roughly one in eight workers was leaving for work by six o'clock each morning. Whatever it may mean for romantic notions of the human spirit, over the years economists have consistently found that a short commute is one of the more important keys to happiness; few things affect general life satisfaction more than commuting time. Related research shows that people who commute through heavy traffic typically accumulate higher concentrations of stress hormones in their blood, get sick more often, and fight more with office mates at work and with family members at home. Perhaps these compromises were worth making to build equity for the future or provide a better environment for the children. But in many places that equity is now gone and the environment is changing.

Once suburban communities begin to falter, Leinberger wrote, they can tip quickly into irreversible decline. Typically, municipal revenues on the suburban fringe are heavily dependent on property taxes and fees associated with new construction; a smaller tax base means fewer and poorer municipal services, including policing and schools. Widespread vacancies inevitably lead to the eventual conversion of houses into rental units—and not just of the single-family sort. And because most modern houses, even McMansions, are built so cheaply today in comparison to the houses and brownstones of decades past, they are ill-suited to rental, because they show wear quickly.

A 2010 Brookings Institution study, "The State of Metropolitan America," found that in a historic reversal, more poor people have recently come to reside in America's suburbs than in its cities. And the number is climbing rapidly; over the past decade, the suburban population living below the poverty line grew by 25 percent, nearly five times faster than the urban poor population in America's largest metro areas. In the exurbs, just 19 percent of adults had a college degree in 2008, well below the national average. And in places like Memphis and Charlotte, crime, too, has migrated to the suburbs, while in some cases declining in the central city.

In the 1960s and '70s, for the most part, those urban residents who could leave American cities did, and urban decline became self-reinforcing for more than a decade. Today, that same general phenomenon—or rather, its mirror image—may be under way, as those who have the wherewithal leave the exurbs for smaller houses or rental units in closer suburbs or resurgent cities. But the transition of places from middle-class to poor, from populous to vacant, is inevitably messy and contentious. Inner cities took the better part of two decades to empty of the middle class. Astonishingly, as of 2009, Detroit remained America's eleventh-largest city, despite a decline spanning generations and an average home price that fell below $20,000 during the recession.

Today, after years of rapid growth, Las Vegas is now shrinking. In 2005, as Sin City beckoned, U-Haul charged people renting a truck from Los Angeles to Las Vegas almost four times what it charged those going in the opposite direction. In 2010, demand had reversed, and so had U-Haul's prices. That's no surprise: Nevada led the nation in both unemployment and foreclosures as of September

2010, and Las Vegas, noted the *New York Times*, was facing "its deepest slide since the 1940s." What's surprising is that the outflow hasn't been faster. "We're in such bad shape here you'd think a lot more people would be leaving," said John Restrepo, a Nevada economic-development analyst, to the *Las Vegas Sun* in September 2010. "And maybe they would if they could, but they're kind of stuck."

Most people cannot easily uproot themselves from their community, even if they'd rather live elsewhere. Jobs, schools, and family commitments tug at some. Years of savings poured into down payments, mortgage payments, and renovations make others reluctant to cut their losses. Scant savings make it difficult to relocate, and impossible to do so without significant downsizing. Anchored by houses they couldn't afford to sell, more Americans stayed put in 2008, the first year of the recession, than in any year since the Census Bureau began tracking moves in 1948. In 2009, the rate of migration rose minimally—in large part because foreclosures began to force more people to move—but was still historically low.

And so, for the foreseeable future, it looks likely that millions of American families who had imagined themselves to be economically successful and upwardly mobile will be both metaphorically and physically stuck, rooted in places that are changing in ways they did not anticipate and do not welcome. How they react to that circumstance will, to a large degree, shape the contours of American community life for the next several years or more.

IN THE NATIONAL imagination, hard times bring communities together. Neighbors exchange favors, watch out for one another, even cover each other's debts in times of need. And surely this recession has produced untold acts of kindness and generosity; according to one recent Pew survey, for instance, about half of all Americans have lent money to a friend or family member since the downturn began, and roughly a quarter say they've been a recipient of such a loan.

But as many social critics have noted, the suburbs were never really designed for togetherness. As Kenneth T. Jackson writes in his classic history of suburbia, *Crabgrass Frontier*, the initial mid-twentieth-century push into the suburbs was driven by cheap housing, yes, but also by the desire to get away from a more crowded and public way of life—and all too often by racial prejudice. The advent of air-conditioning heralded the abandonment of front porches, the closing of windows, and a further retreat into private lives behind private walls. Indeed, the growth of the suburbs—and with it the privatization of most aspects of daily living—is sometimes given as one reason why Americans became more politically conservative in the latter half of the twentieth century.

I asked Mark Spector if the recession and all its attendant problems had brought Bridgewater's residents any closer together. "It's the exact opposite," he replied. As in many recently built subdivisions, the community didn't have a deep reservoir of local spirit or goodwill to begin with. The homeowners-association meetings, Spector said, have "never had a quorum. . . . Even with all the trials and tribulations, the largest number of people we've ever had—even with proxies—was something like sixty-five. And we need 152." But whatever shallow reservoir once existed now seems utterly depleted by the stresses of community decline—and by the strenuousness of the efforts to reverse it.

Against the backdrop of Florida's epic housing crash, and among subdivisions built near the height of the bubble, Bridgewater is actually something of a success story for its ability to arrest its decline. If you want to see what failure looks like, head south to Carriage Pointe in Gibsonton, where the ubiquitous and exotic real-estate signage—FOR SALE, SHORT SALE, NEIGHBORHOOD STABILIZATION PROGRAM SALE—is frequently obscured by thigh-high weeds; where the detritus of foreclosure and eviction (old couches, broken TVs, cardboard boxes) sits forlornly in driveways and on curbs; and where some of the people who still live among the vacant shells around them will not open their door in the daytime to a fortyish man who says he's a reporter. In Bridgewater, by contrast, the lawns are now neatly trimmed, the yards are once again tidy, and neighborhood crime has decreased from its post-crash highs.

But this order has come at a price. Lacking any organic means of bringing the community together and pulling it back up from its descent, Spector and the other association officers have turned instead to the cudgel available to homeowners associations nationwide, and they have wielded it ruthlessly: hypervigilant rules enforcement—backed by heavy, quick-trigger fines and liens—has become a dominant feature of community life.

To one extent or another, lawyerly yard challenges have always been characteristic of America's planned communities, where one can find occasional acts of exquisite pettiness in even the best of times. And Bridgewater's approach has worked cosmetically, allowing the community to find new home buyers and limit vacancies. But to achieve that goal, the association has levied thousands of dollars in fines on some households. When a lawn isn't kept to code, for instance, the association will issue a warning, and if the violation isn't quickly cured, it will simply put the house on a list of properties for which the association will do lawn care whenever the lawn is in violation, without notice, billed punitively at $100 a cut. The same is true, more or less, for mulching, edging, tree trimming, and exterior house upkeep. Cars parked on the street are quickly towed. Off-duty policemen are paid by the association to patrol the community and keep it safe; they sometimes confront and question people they believe are acting suspiciously.

These tactics have not always gone over well in a community that is already struggling. Some residents told me they believe the association has been especially aggressive toward undesirable renters, burying them or their landlords in fines for small transgressions until they leave. Neighborly relations, meanwhile, have turned hostile, as some families have come to suspect that others do not welcome their presence and are constantly on the watch for minor violations to report. One mixed-race couple who in 2008 bought a foreclosed three-bedroom house— their first—told me that trust within the community is almost completely absent. The neighborhood is more black than it used to be, said the husband, an African American, and some residents didn't seem to like that. He didn't believe the association was targeting blacks—"it has more to do with class than race." But tensions had risen between renters and owners, blacks and whites, higher-income owners who'd initially bought into the neighborhood and lower-income owners who'd bought in more recently.

I asked him whether crime in the neighborhood was ever a problem, and he gave a little laugh. "Maybe it's where I grew up," he said, but since he'd moved in, he'd never felt unsafe or been worried about burglars. What had worn on him instead was the vibe he sensed from a few of his neighbors—and the way he thought some of the community's struggling families were being treated. "It's not the community we thought we were moving into," he said, echoing Spector's words precisely, though for different reasons.

Like Spector, the husband and wife, who asked not to be identified, were now well underwater on their house, though they'd thought they were buying it cheaply. They felt they had no choice but to stay put. But "I don't feel like it's a neighborhood, a community," the wife told me. "It just doesn't feel like a community I should be raising my kids in. I don't really talk to the neighbors much anymore. If we could move, we'd move today."

In his 2008 book, *The Big Sort*, Bill Bishop presented compelling evidence that since about 1980, America's suburbs have become ever more finely segregated—by income, political beliefs, education, and general sensibility. Most, today, are finely attuned to social class. When these delicate ecosystems change suddenly, the results can be jarring for all their residents, new and old, and the reactions are not always graceful.

"People move into neighborhoods because they want to be among their peers," Spector told me. As we talked, it became clear that he resents some of his neighbors, and it isn't so hard to understand why. They are constant reminders that he has stopped moving forward and has instead fallen back—physical embodiments of his disillusionment with the American Dream. "I've done everything right," he said. "I didn't buy a bigger house than I could afford. . . . We have owners here who haven't made a bank payment in four years now; that's what I see on a day-to-day basis. And that makes me scratch my head and think, *What the hell am I doing wrong?* I did everything the way I was taught, everything the way I grew up believing was correct. But at the same time I see all these deadbeats—well, I used to call them deadbeats, now I call them brilliant people, because they're walking away scot-free, not paying any penalty, even getting the difference in a short sale."

By contrast, he said, he can't even get his bank to talk to him about refinancing, because he's made his payments diligently. And in a year and a half, his loan will reset to a variable rate, and he'll be at the mercy of the market. "We love the house; I can't say I love the community. The community is just very different from what we thought we were getting into. I have a Ph.D., my wife has a master's. We were expecting to be among our peers. We're not. Most of the people here will be lifelong renters. That's not the community we moved into."

In 2008, Spector and Bridgewater's other board members had video surveillance cameras mounted outside their front doors. "I've had death threats," Spector told me. "I had someone show up at my front door with a gun because his truck had been towed away. Another guy showed up with a claw hammer." He told me he worked "constantly" to try to keep the neighborhood from slipping—"it's my second full-time job." He'd logged 4,500 cell-phone minutes the prior month on association business, many of them spent talking to an attorney about various motions. "I've lost five years of my life to this," he said. "It's just a battle against everything."

"I do this because my family has to live here," he said, "and I don't want gunfire on the streets. That's what I get out of this—knowing that if I have to travel on business, my house isn't necessarily going to be robbed." But you can see it's more than that. Resignation still seems to vie in him with the unextinguished hope that somehow, if he works hard enough, he can restore the community to something approximating what he imagined when he moved in—and also turn back the clock on neighborhood home values. "What I would love to do is get to a point where I can refinance my house, you know?"

The last time I spoke with Spector on the phone, he had to go abruptly. He'd just received a call on the other line; a neighborhood resident had pulled a gun on a contractor who works for the association. Spector had to go meet the police, who were on their way.

ONE SHOULD NOT overestimate the extent of middle-class status anxiety today. A Pew study released in June 2010 revealed that 71 percent of the self-described middle class felt that their class status was secure, and 70 percent—a higher percentage than in either the lower or upper class—believed that America is still a land of prosperity and economic progress. Asked whether their living standard was higher than that of their parents at the same age, a majority of middle-income Americans (though a relatively small majority, at 58 percent) said yes.

Many of those who've lost their job and are now experiencing downward mobility must feel differently about these questions. But while the Great Recession has accelerated the hollowing of the middle class, the unemployed—along with those who've found new, but much lower-paying, work after a job loss—are still in a distinct minority. Most of Middle America has so far felt the recession primarily through its impact on home values.

The housing bust has of course weighed more heavily on some families and communities than on others; Bridgewater is an extreme case. People who bought long ago in established, upscale suburbs are typically still on high, dry ground, enjoying neighborhoods and schools as good as ever, or nearly so. Likewise, people who took advantage of an inattentive mortgage industry at the height of the bubble—putting no money down on houses they could not afford .

and depending on an ever-rising market to bail them out—have lost little. It's the people in between—younger, moderately educated families in starter homes on the suburban fringe; striving minorities in fragile neighborhoods who took subprime loans at the bubble's height; middle-aged couples who'd come to rely on home equity to spruce up unglamorous lives—who've been knocked flat.

Some of the optimism that can still be found in the suburban middle class today, particularly outside the worst-hit communities, seems justified. Particularly for people with four-year degrees from good colleges living in nice neighborhoods around dynamic cities, the future, in the long view, looks bright. But middle-class optimism also seems to stem from another source: the persistent, widespread belief that housing values will soon start appreciating again, and rapidly. A 2010 Pew survey revealed that 80 percent of Americans believed owning a house was the best long-term investment a person could make. According to Fannie Mae's Fourth Quarter 2010 National Housing Survey, 66 percent believed it was a good time to buy. Asked to name "safe" investments, 64 percent of homeowners checked "buying a house" (for comparison, 77 percent listed putting money into a savings account). More than one in three homeowners, when describing the "major" reasons to buy a house, checked "it gives me something I can borrow against if I need it."

The housing bubble during the aughts was unprecedented in American history; there has never been a run-up that even comes close to it. At a minimum, it is unlikely to be repeated. In their analysis of the economic aftershocks of more than a dozen major post–World War II financial crises worldwide, Carmen Reinhart and Kenneth Rogoff found that housing values typically keep falling for longer than anyone might initially suspect—for six years, on average, and by a total of 35 percent. In Japan—an extreme case—housing never recovered from the crisis that began in 1991; residential urban land prices have declined in every year since then, and in 2009 were 44 percent below their peak value. In recent years, the *New York*

Times has taken to running stories of dispirited Japanese homeowners who've held on throughout, and are now finally selling at half or a third of what they paid long ago.

The optimism and future orientation of the middle class have always been among America's most precious assets, ensuring social peace and underlying the nation's astonishing capacity for reinvention. The connection of that optimism to magical thinking about housing, from as early as the 1980s straight through to the present day, is deeply troubling.

Middle-class culture is changing in the wake of the recession. Evidence of a growing financial and personal conservatism can be found in the nation's personal savings rate, which rose from about 2 percent of disposable income in 2007 to more than 5 percent in 2010. As it relates to housing, however, the gambling spirit of the middle class has not been fully exorcised. In Cleveland, masses of houses sit vacant and boarded, ruined by squatters or mold or the elements. But as Alex Kotlowitz wrote in the *New York Times Magazine*, that hasn't stopped investors and speculators from as far away as California from buying them by the dozen on eBay, at a few thousand dollars each, sight unseen.

In Las Vegas and Phoenix, a few builders are already raising new subdevelopments out beyond the old, half-empty ones—and finding demand for them. "Our customers wouldn't care if there were fifty homes in an established neighborhood of 1980 or 1990 vintage, all foreclosed, empty, and for sale at $10,000 less," said Brent Anderson, a marketing executive with Meritage Homes, to the journalist David Streitfeld. "They want new." In 2010, under a pilot program called Affordable Advantage, several states began offering mortgages for $1,000 down, then selling them to Fannie Mae. "With only $1,000 down, affordable monthly payments and no private mortgage insurance required," read one ad, "the dream is closer than you think."

The Fannie Mae program was quickly halted; the federal agency that oversees Fannie Mae had never approved it. But none of these other, private initiatives appear likely to end well. Houses are not magical assets; basic logic dictates that over the long haul, they simply cannot appreciate faster than the incomes of the people expected to buy them. So what will happen when the nonprofessional middle class finally and fully awakens from its dream of financial security through rising home values? One of the biggest imperatives the nation faces in the years ahead is making sure its middle class retains its sense of optimism and opportunity. Ultimately, housing is too flimsy a foundation upon which to build that ethos. We need to replace it with one that is sound.

6

PLUTONOMY: THE VERY RICH IN
RECESSION AND RECOVERY

IN OCTOBER 2005, THREE CITIGROUP ANALYSTS RELEASED A REPORT describing the pattern of growth in the U.S. economy. If you really wanted to understand the future of the economy and the stock market, they wrote, you first needed to recognize that there was "no such animal as the U.S. consumer," and that concepts such as "average" consumer debt or average consumer spending were highly misleading.

In fact, they said, America was composed of two completely distinct groups: the rich and the rest. And for the purposes of investment decisions, you needed to simply ignore the second group; the masses didn't matter, and tracking their spending habits or worrying over their savings rates was a waste of time. All the action in the American economy was at the top: the top 1 percent of households earned as much each year as the bottom 60 percent put together; they possessed as much wealth as the bottom 90 percent; and with each passing year, a greater share of the nation's treasure was flowing through their hands and into their pockets. It was this segment of the population, almost exclusively, that held the key to future growth and future returns. The analysts, Ajay Kapur, Niall Macleod, and Narendra Singh, had coined a term for this state of affairs: *the plutonomy*.

In a plutonomy, Kapur and his coauthors wrote, "economic growth is powered by and largely consumed by the wealthy few." America had been in this state twice before, they noted—during the Gilded Age and the Roaring Twenties. In each case, it was a result of rapid technological change, global integration, laissez-faire government policy, and "creative financial innovation." In 2005, the rich were nearing the heights they'd reached in those previous eras, and Citigroup saw no good reason to think they wouldn't keep on climbing this time around. "The earth is being held up by the muscular arms of its entrepreneur-plutocrats," the report said. The "great complexity" of a global economy in rapid transformation would be "exploited best by the rich and educated" of our time.

The report was a hit with investors, prompting a series of follow-up papers on how to craft an investment portfolio to take advantage of the plutonomy (the answers generally involved buying shares in the makers of luxury goods). In the fall of 2006, Citigroup held a conference on the topic, which was summarized in a report titled "The Plutonomy Symposium—Rising Tides Lifting Yachts."

Kapur and his coauthors were wrong in some of their specific predictions about the plutonomy's ramifications—they argued, for instance, that since spending was dominated by the rich, and since the rich had very healthy balance sheets, the odds of a stock-market downturn were slight, despite the rising indebtedness of the "average" U.S. consumer. Nonetheless, their overall characterization of the economy remains trenchant. The rich continue to dominate as they seldom have before.

In 2007, on the eve of the recession, the top 10 percent of American families made half of the nation's personal income, according to the analysis of Emmanuel Saez, an economist at the University of California at Berkeley. The top 1 percent—people with a family income of roughly $400,000 or more—earned 23.5 percent. Since 1993, this tiny minority has captured more than half of all income growth in the United States, and its share has been growing. Between 2002 and 2007, out of every three dollars of American income growth, one was divided among the bottom 99 percent of workers. The other two went to the top 1 percent. And even within the top 1 percent, incomes were heavily concentrated among the superstars at the very top of the distribution. The top one-tenth of 1 percent—

mostly business executives and financiers—earned at least $1.7 million in 2008, and their incomes have grown faster than anyone else's.

Income inequality usually shrinks during a recession, but in the Great Recession it hasn't. From 2007 to 2009, the most recent years for which data are available, it widened a little. The top 1 percent of earners did see their incomes drop more than that of other Americans in 2008. But that fall was due almost entirely to the stock-market crash, and with it a 50 percent reduction in realized capital gains. Excluding capital gains, top earners saw their share of national income rise even in 2008. And in any case, the stock market has since rallied. Corporate profits have marched smartly upward, quarter after quarter, since the beginning of 2009, and executive incomes have risen with them. According to *Forbes* magazine, in 2010 the net worth of the 400 wealthiest Americans rose about 8 percent, to $1.37 trillion collectively—still down a bit from its 2007 high of $1.54 trillion, but higher than it had been in 2006.

Even in the financial sector, high earners have come back strong. In 2009, the country's top 25 hedge-fund managers earned $25 billion between them—more than they had made in 2007, before the crash. That same year, Goldman Sachs also made more money than ever before, and paid out more than $16 billion in salaries and bonuses. In 2010, payouts were expected to rise to $17.5 billion. The crisis may have begun with mass layoffs on Wall Street, but the financial industry has remained well shielded compared with other industries; from the first quarter of 2007 to the first quarter of 2010, finance shed 8 percent of its jobs, compared with 27 percent in construction and 17 percent in manufacturing. Throughout the recession, the unemployment rate in finance and insurance has been substantially below that of the nation overall.

"Finance Firms Rev Up Hiring," announced the *Wall Street Journal* in June 2010, when the national unemployment rate stood at 9.5 percent: " 'War for Talent' Intensifies; Staff in Areas Such as Commodities Are Getting Offers Up to 40% Higher Than a Year Ago." By then, Manhattan's whole economy was in the midst of a sharp rebound (while New York City's less affluent outer boroughs remained troubled). The city's most exclusive restaurants were fully booked again by August, and sales at Tiffany & Co. on Fifth Avenue were up 16 percent on the year.

The ease with which the rich have shrugged off the recession shouldn't be entirely surprising; strong winds have been at their backs for many years, and if anything, the recession only intensified them. While technological innovation and global economic integration have been harmful to some Americans, these forces have clearly benefited successful entrepreneurs, financiers, executives, and other highly educated, highly skilled workers. New ideas have never been easier or faster to bring to market, and new products find wider markets than ever before, making it possible for successful innovators and their partners in the financial and creative communities to accumulate more wealth, more quickly, than ever before. Social norms have also changed; mid-twentieth-century taboos against extremely high pay are long since gone. And the outsized political influence of the rich, especially those in the financial industry, has also played a major role in their rise and recovery.

The recession, meanwhile, has put downward pressure on common wages and enabled faster, more brutal restructuring and off-shoring, leaving many corporations with lower production costs and higher profits—and their executives with higher pay. "It looks like every year we move toward greater inequality," Saez told me, "and every year the market forces driving inequality seem stronger. I don't think there's necessarily a limit, short of triggering a policy response. The market itself doesn't impose a limit on inequality, especially for those at the top."

Anthony Atkinson, an economist at Oxford University, has studied the effect of recent financial crises on income distribution—and found that in their wake, the rich have usually strengthened their economic position. Atkinson examined the financial crises that swept Asia in the 1990s as well as those that afflicted several Nordic countries in that same decade. In most cases, he says, the income of the middle class suffered for a long time after the crisis, while the top 1 percent were able to protect themselves—using their cash reserves to buy up assets very cheaply once the market crashed, and emerging from the crisis with a significantly higher share of assets and income than they'd had before. "And I think we've seen the same thing to some extent in the United States" since the 2008 crash, he told me. "Mr. Buffett has been investing." The Boston Consulting Group found that the percentage of America's wealth held by its millionaires increased to 55 percent in 2009—a higher level than it had reached before the recession began.

"The rich seem to be on the road to recovery," says Saez, while those in the middle, especially those who've lost their job, "might be permanently hit." Coming out of the deep recession of the early 1980s, Saez notes, "you saw an increase in inequality . . . as the rich bounced back, and unionized labor never again found jobs that paid as well as the ones they'd had. And now I fear we're going to see the same phenomenon, but more dramatic." Middle-paying positions, in which some American workers have been overpaid relative to the cost of offshore labor or technological substitution, "are being wiped out. And what will be left is a hard and a pure market," with the many paid less than before, and the few paid even better—a plutonomy strengthened and perfected in the crucible of the post-crash years.

ONE OF THE more curious aspects of the times in which we are living is the unmistakable disjuncture between how the American economic elite is faring and how some of its members are behaving. As executives and—especially—financiers have recovered from the hiccup in their fortunes, no small number have adopted a profound sense of aggrievement as they have resumed their ascent.

Since the crash and the bailout that followed, *New York* magazine, the *New York Observer*, and other publications have sent their reporters out prospecting for stories of continuing greed, entitlement, and hubris on Wall Street. And Wall Street's titans have continually obliged them with gem after gem. In a 2009 *New York* article aptly titled "The Wail of the 1%," financiers making seven- and eight-figure incomes complained bitterly to Gabriel Sherman about the prospect of paying somewhat higher taxes. "The government wants me to be a slave!" declared one hedge-fund analyst. Said another, "I'm not giving to charity next year! When people ask me for money, I tell them, 'If you want me to give you money, send a letter to my senator asking for my taxes to be lowered.'" "No offense to Middle America," a Citigroup executive e-mailed a colleague, "but if someone went to Columbia or Wharton, [even if] their company is a fumbling, mismanaged bank, why should they all of a sudden be paid the same as the guy down the block who delivers restaurant supplies?"

In the weeks that followed the fall of Lehman Brothers, Treasury committed some $700 billion to propping up the nation's banking system through the Troubled Asset Relief Program, or TARP, by far the largest bailout program in American history. The Fed, meanwhile, began an intervention without precedent, making almost $7 trillion available for troubled-asset purchases, new lending, and direct company bailouts. To help stabilize financial institutions, the Fed had already dramatically widened access to its discount window, and has since kept interest rates near zero. Without these and other measures—some of which have come at extraordinary expense to taxpayers and savers—Wall Street's survivors would not have survived at all. Because of these actions, along with an implicit guarantee that the government will rescue the large banks should they get into trouble again, they have quickly returned to rude health. (In 2009, Wall Street's five largest banks—Bank of America, Citigroup, Goldman Sachs, JPMorgan Chase, and Morgan Stanley—earned $147 billion before taxes and employee compensation. The banks saved $31 billion for investment and balance-sheet strengthening and distributed $2 billion to their shareholders; the rest, $114 billion, went to their employees.)

In return for this largesse, the federal government has demanded relatively little. Government officials decried some 2009 bonus payments by AIG, placed some limits on compensation during the time that banks were being propped up by government TARP funds, and considered closing a loophole that allows hedge-fund managers to pay income taxes at a rate of just 15 percent. After decades of continual financial deregulation, regulatory authority has been increased, as have capital requirements, but the basic structure of the industry remains intact; no banks have been broken up, and few executives have been sacked (at least at the government's behest). President Obama, despite a few populist jabs against the "fat cats" on Wall Street, has acted with remarkable restraint given the political circumstances, and has gone out of his way to say, for instance, that he didn't begrudge Jamie Dimon and Lloyd Blankfein—the CEOs of JPMorgan and Goldman Sachs, respectively—their wealth and success.

Wall Street's response has been largely graceless. *New York* magazine's John Heilemann wrote that at a dinner he attended with ten financial-industry executives in early 2010, Obama was described as a "vilifier" and a "thug." Another industry insider, Heilemann reported, called him a "Chicago mob guy." Stephen Schwarzman, cofounder of the Blackstone Group, called the proposal to close the 15 percent tax loophole an act of war, comparing it to "when Hitler invaded Poland." Daniel S. Loeb, the founder of the hedge fund Third Point, intimated in his August 2010 investor letter that the pattern of government actions toward high financiers (including a lawsuit against Goldman Sachs) amounted to a violation of the U.S. Constitution's protections against the "persecution of the minority." After the January 2010 announcement of a White House proposal to cap the size of banks in order to limit the fallout from any future failures (with the cap set higher than any bank's current size), the CEO of one of the nation's biggest banks told Heilemann, "For a lot of us Wall Street people, it was like, 'Okay, first you slap us in the face, now you kick us in the balls. Enough is enough. I mean, we're done.'"

The public-relations initiatives of top financiers since the crash and bailout have been tin-eared, to say the least. In November 2009, Blankfein sat for a long interview with the *Times* of London, in which he claimed to be "doing God's work" by making investment capital available to companies. The prior month, in a speech at St. Paul's Cathedral in London, Brian Griffiths, another Goldman executive, also described Wall Street's benevolent purpose in religious terms. Defending the huge bonuses his firm was planning to pay that year, he said, "The injunction of Jesus to love others as ourselves is a recognition of self-interest. . . . We have to tolerate the inequality as a way to achieving greater prosperity and opportunity for all." On April 30, 2010, Blankfein told Charlie Rose, "We're very important, but the public doesn't see that."

In 1895, in the midst of a potentially catastrophic run on gold that had the U.S. government teetering on the brink of default, J. P. Morgan took the train down to Washington and offered to gather and supply some 3.5 million ounces of gold from within and outside the country to staunch the panic, in return for U.S. government bonds (the value of which was uncertain); he did, and the panic ended. Years later, during the panic of 1907, Morgan and a handful of other financiers stopped a potentially catastrophic bank run by pouring loans and deposits into the banks that might be strong enough to survive, again staunching the panic. Morgan also bailed out several trusts, the stock exchange, and the government of New York City during that crisis. (In the midst of the panic of 1929, the next generation of New York bankers also pooled money to try to support the stock market, though their efforts failed.)

Morgan was pompous, vain, and ruthless in search of profit, and the industry titans who were his peers were called robber barons for a reason; shameless avarice and other bad behavior among the powerful are hardly new phenomena. And ultimately, Morgan did make money as a result of the transactions of 1895 and 1907. But as the economic historian Richard Sylla, an expert on the history of the financial industry, told me, "People like Morgan realized that they did have a responsibility for the system." In times of national crisis, Sylla said, Morgan acted with a mixture of public and private motives, "taking risk and exercising public responsibility," even though "things might have gone wrong" for him. Above all, when the stakes were highest, he "wanted to save the system. I think he did feel a higher responsibility."

In this respect, the actions of Wall Street's current titans do not resemble those of their forebears. In the spring of 2008, as economic warning signs began to flash red, Morgan's namesake firm did buy Bear Stearns, which was collapsing, in a deal brokered by the Treasury Department; but as Simon Johnson and James Kwak note in their book, *13 Bankers,* JPMorgan agreed to pay only about as much as Bear Stearns's building was worth, and that was only after the government agreed to assume almost all of the downside risk on $30 billion of Bear Stearns's illiquid securities; to many observers, the deal looked like a gift. A few months later, when Treasury and the Fed tried to convince Wall Street's titans to pitch in and rescue Lehman without substantial federal guarantees, they were given the coldest of shoulders, despite the enormous systemic risk that Lehman's failure would pose.

The most public-spirited action taken by the heads of America's major financial firms during the crisis involved taking money. On the heels of Lehman's collapse, they agreed to take billions in TARP money from the federal government. Without these funds, some financial institutions would have failed almost immediately; others, notably JPMorgan and Goldman Sachs, claimed they didn't need the cash, though there seems little doubt that if the implosion of the financial sector had continued unabated, these firms would have failed, too. In any case, it was essential that all the big banks take TARP money, because if only a few did, investors would have concluded that they were the weakest, prompting runs that might have pulled those firms down, despite the intervention.

In the end, the banks agreed to take injections of federal cash, but with no small drama. "People did what [Treasury Secretary Henry] Paulson asked," Sylla noted, "but almost immediately, there was a sense of resentment." Concerned with the optics of the bailout, the Obama administration put temporary restrictions on the pay of executives of TARP institutions while they were being supported by TARP funds. That, it seems, was simply too much for the financial elite to swallow silently. When the current head of JPMorgan, Jamie Dimon, eventually repaid the TARP funds in 2009, he read aloud from a fake letter he'd written to Timothy Geithner, who'd succeeded Paulson as Treasury secretary: "Dear Timmy," he said, "we are happy to be able to pay back the $25 billion you lent us. We hope you enjoyed the experience as much as we did."

The Federal Reserve did not exist in Morgan's day, so he and his banking peers could not rely on the federal government to stop panics if they didn't themselves. And because the big investment banks are now public companies, their partners and CEOs have to consider their duty to shareholders and creditors, substantially muddying the ethics of public-spirited action; if the government truly expected an entirely private rescue of Lehman, it was expecting too much. Still, the behavior of the financial sector's leaders in this crisis stands out in troubling ways. Faced with overwhelming evidence that their recklessness had nearly destroyed the economy, and following an unprecedented federal bailout, they generally "didn't admit that they made terrible mistakes, and then seemed to resist reforms," Sylla told me. "I have a sense that they were less responsible than in the past."

Bankers make easy targets today, and many of the hedge-fund managers and investment bankers who complain that they are being tarred indiscriminately are right. Many—indeed, most—successful financiers played no role in the crisis, and the idea that Wall Street as a whole is fundamentally parasitic is wrong. Nonetheless, the widespread failure among rich financial professionals to come to grips with the causes of the financial crisis, to empathize publicly with the millions of people who have taken much harder blows than themselves as a result, and to subsume their own interests—even for a moment, even in the worst economic calamity of our lifetimes—is difficult to miss and disheartening to watch.

Well before Wall Street's meltdown, students of the rich and powerful in America had been noticing that elite attitudes seemed different from those in past generations—that the rich and power-ful appeared more inwardly focused and less concerned with public matters. Barbara Kellerman, a professor at Harvard University's Center for Public Leadership, told me that executives today don't have it easy—they face more scrutiny, from a more skeptical public, than leaders in the past. But, she said, at least some of that skepticism may be warranted. When we think of the generations that came of age in the 1930s and '40s and '50s, she said, "what we generally have a sense of . . . is an elite that was at least in the mind's eye more concerned with the public good and the common good than we generally assume now." Kellerman has written that even within the companies they lead, many executives have become too distant to be completely effective: the yawning income gap between executives and rank-and-file employees—and the perception that executives are rewarded even when they or their companies perform poorly—has begun to hurt morale and productivity (in part by engendering a more mercenary attitude throughout the organization, discouraging employees from building company-specific skills that their next employer may not value).

Even David Brooks, in his perceptive and generally positive anthropology of the new rich, *Bobos in Paradise*, voices doubts about the sense of social responsibility felt by today's best and brightest. "By and large they have not devoted their energies to national life," he writes. "When we look back at the postwar ruling class, we see some mistakes and some hubris. But we also see a group of men and women who made genuine commitments to America that sometimes overrode their self-interest." Brooks listed a few of them—George C. Marshall, Dwight Eisenhower, Dean Acheson, John McCloy; people who understood that "to those who are blessed much is expected." Which of us, Brooks wrote, "doesn't long for an updated version . . . of that sober patriotism?"

• • •

LEAVING ASIDE THE question of whether the modern rich have well and truly earned their money (the answer, of course, will vary dramatically from person to person), the defining characteristic of today's elite is its unshakable belief that it deserves every penny (and is perhaps underpaid). The rise of the meritocracy—in which the rich and powerful win their standing through uncommon hard work, intelligence, and chutzpah in a sort of grand economic tournament open to all—is a narrative now deeply ingrained in the U.S. culture. And indeed, society's winners are drawn from more-diverse backgrounds than they used to be, while hereditary advantages have diminished. Ivy League classes look more colorful today than they did in the 1960s, and are populated more consistently with the nation's smartest and most disciplined students. And after college, those who prosper the most do so as a result of their own labor, not a trust fund; the lion's share of income earned by the top 1 percent comes from their career.

In the United States, the rise of the meritocracy has typically been met with celebration, and in most respects it should be. But this recession has underscored the meritocracy's less savory characteristics. In his final book, *The Revolt of the Elites and the Betrayal of Democracy,* published posthumously in 1995, the social critic Christopher Lasch painted a dismal picture of the destination toward which meritocratic progress may lead. Precisely because modern elites believe their status is the exclusive result of their own efforts, Lasch argued, they lack their predecessors' sense of social obligation. "Although hereditary advantages [still] play an important part in the attainment of professional or managerial status," he wrote, "the new [upper] class has to maintain the fiction that its power rests on intelligence alone. Hence it has little sense of ancestral gratitude or of an obligation to live up to responsibilities inherited from the past. It thinks of itself as a self-made elite owing its privileges exclusively to its own efforts."

The rise of the meritocracy has coincided with— and is inseparable from—the disintegration of boundaries between both local communities and nations, and the evolution of a more transient lifestyle for the best-educated and most-successful Americans. Overwhelmingly, today's elites have uprooted themselves from the towns of their birth and congregated in a handful of power centers and creative enclaves both within and outside the United States—New York, San Francisco, Seattle, London, Hong Kong, Shanghai, and so on. They circulate frequently among these cities. Globally connected, many of them associate and identify more with meritocratic winners of foreign nationality than they do with ordinary workers at home. Patriotism, Lasch wrote, "does not rank very high in their hierarchy of virtues." And the far-flung networks that are their primary social and professional communities bear "little resemblance to communities in any traditional sense of the term."

Consequently, Lasch argued, modern elites tend to "exercise power irresponsibly, precisely because they recognize so few obligations to their predecessors or to the communities they profess to lead. Their lack of gratitude disqualifies meritocratic elites from the burden of leadership, and in any case, they are less interested in leadership than in escaping from the common lot—the very definition of meritocratic success."

IF YOU WANT to see the plutonomy up close, you can do worse than to spend some time in Aspen, Colorado. I traveled there in July 2010 for the Aspen Ideas Festival, a weeklong colloquy of the rich and powerful, loosely in the model of the World Economic Forum at Davos or the TED conference in Long Beach, California (anyone can buy a ticket to the Aspen festival—unlike Davos—but it will set you back about $5,000 for the week). Each year, hundreds of well-heeled people arrive in Aspen for the festival, many on their own jet (I counted forty or fifty private jets on the tarmac of the town's airport, parked neatly in four long rows). Once there, they spend long days discussing pressing social issues, policy problems, and technological developments, and hobnobbing with the likes of Bill Gates, Alan Greenspan, Thomas Friedman, Sebastian Junger, and Kurt Russell.

The crowd at Aspen is not a bad cross section of today's meritocratic elite—hardworking, cosmopolitan, earnest if a little self-involved—and most of the people there seemed seriously engaged by the big global problems and potentially novel solutions being discussed. During breaks, fit men and attractive women milled about in casual, understated clothing, drinking pomegranate juice and snacking on oversized cookies or fresh fruit. A few were a touch too eager to chat about the World Cup games they had attended in South Africa the week before (in the company of Jacob Zuma, South Africa's president), or to proffer what they'd gleaned from their most recent conversation with President Obama. A larger number used the breaks to focus on their BlackBerrys, iPhones, or iPads, transacting ad hoc business. (One fortysomething man sitting next to me at a panel discussion was, by turns, listening to the discussion, checking a feed on his iPad, and, in short bursts, working two different BlackBerrys.)

Bill Gates was one of the featured attractions of the conference. With the recession still biting deeply in the United States, Walter Isaacson, the president of the Aspen Institute, kicked off an onstage interview with him by asking what he was optimistic about. Gates replied easily, "I'm optimistic about most things." He went on to list some of them: global health and education were improving markedly; literacy was way up in Africa, and childhood deaths were down; technological and scientific progress were continuing worldwide. Gates didn't mention America or its prospects; his frame of reference encompassed the whole globe. And why shouldn't it? This expansive view of how we should think about economic and social fortune is both logically unimpeachable and morally laudable.

It is also deeply liberating for American business elites today. In a recent essay, the journalist Chrystia Freeland recounted a conversation she'd had with the CEO of a U.S.-based investment fund, one of the world's largest. The firm's investment committee often discusses the likely winners and losers from continuing globalization, the CEO told her. Recently, he said, one of his colleagues had been arguing that the travails of American workers shouldn't be a source of angst. "His point," the CEO continued, "was that if the transformation of the world economy lifts four people in China and India out of poverty and into the middle class, and meanwhile means one American drops out of the middle class, that's not such a bad trade."

Not that long ago, the interests of American capitalists and American workers—while never the same—were in some important respects aligned. Firms were dependent on domestic labor, domestic financing, and the domestic consumer market; the strength and competitiveness of America's economy and workforce were essential to the fortunes of large American companies—and those of their executives. What was good for General Motors was good for America, and vice versa.

But in Aspen, one could see how much these ties have weakened—and how little the entrepreneurs and executives at the conference seemed to depend on the health of other classes of Americans. In a public interview at the conference, Michael Splinter, the founder of Applied Materials, a large, California-based supplier of chip-making equipment that has pushed heavily into green technology, and that recently decided to move its largest R&D operations to China, said, "This year, almost ninety percent of our sales will be outside the United States. The pull to be close to our customers, and most of them are in Asia, . . . is enormous." At a panel discussion on the future of the middle class, Tom Wilson, the CEO of Allstate, said, "I can get [workers] anywhere in the world. . . . I have 1,500 people in Belfast, 1,000 people in India, people in the Philippines." The employment difficulties of citizens with limited education "is a problem for America, but it is not necessarily a problem for American business," Wilson said. Business "will adapt."

David Hale, the founder of David Hale Global Economics, a consulting firm that counsels large corporations and investment firms, celebrated that adaptation: Since the fourth quarter of 2009, he said at a panel discussion, U.S. firms had "enjoyed very large gains in productivity, very large gains in profits. . . . No other country in the world could do what America did to its workforce twelve and eighteen months ago. In this recession, the American economy had an output decline of 3.8 percent—we reduced private sector employment by 7.5 percent." Because of its uniquely aggressive actions, "American business today is 10 to 15 percent more competitive than it was a year ago compared to Europe and Japan."

The particular sense of community at the Aspen Ideas Festival is difficult to put your finger on. Freeland has described the international conference circuit as the natural habitat of the new, global meritocratic elite—a replacement for the balls and fox-hunting parties that filled the social calendar of hereditary elites generations ago, with an updated focus on networking; continual learning; and sober discussion of the economic, political, and technological changes that might lead to business opportunity. At Aspen, while the participants were overwhelmingly American, the ambitions and affinities were global.

And yet these sentiments of global citizenship and global ambition were matched by a near-total insularity from non-elites, and a personal detachment from the struggles of other Americans. Several people I spoke with said that from their enclaves and offices in Boulder or the Bay Area, the recession appeared mild or invisible—though of course they knew it wasn't, really. That same sentiment could be observed in the popularity (or lack thereof) of different events at the conference: the talks on emerging technologies were generally well attended, and a panel discussion about the federal deficit and the future of taxes was standing room only; the panel on reigniting job growth, on the other hand, was less than half full when it started, though more people eventually trickled in. There was no shortage of gloomy speechifying at Aspen, but many attendees seemed to sort of float through that, intellectually aware and suitably concerned in an abstract way, yet personally untouched.

Onstage, Bill Gates sat talking about global progress, and then, as the interview continued, about a host of other issues, from green energy to fixing U.S. schools. At this point in his career, Gates is as benign an icon of the meritocratic elite as one could imagine, the physical embodiment of the meritocracy's promise. Whatever one may think of the latest version of Windows, he made his vast fortune by creating something that has improved the work and lives of countless people. And now, in his fifties, he is in the midst of giving most of that fortune away. The Bill & Melinda Gates Foundation was endowed with some $36 billion as of September 2010, and Gates was in the midst of a nationwide effort to convince America's richest people to join him in a pledge to give away half their wealth within their lifetime or upon their death. (More than fifty billionaires have agreed.)

"There's a lot to be optimistic about if you look at it the *right way*," Gates emphasized. His charitable endeavors reflect that optimism; they're designed around the idea that by trying new approaches to solving old problems, we can not only alleviate suffering but achieve permanent progress in areas ranging from health to education. About 84 percent of the Gates Foundation's distributions in 2009 were international, reflecting the belief that the return on giving is generally highest outside the United States, in places where, for example, so many children are being stunted by malnutrition or killed by preventable disease. But roughly 16 percent—$489 million in total—was focused inside the United States, the lion's share of it on fixing American schools and providing college scholarships.

Gates talked about that issue in his interview. As to both equality of opportunity and international competitiveness, he said, nothing was more important than education: a country that doesn't offer good educational opportunities to all its people is simply wasting much of its IQ. Maximizing national IQ was high on Gates's list for curing what ails America; he mentioned it again when the discussion turned to immigration, calling IQ "the most important import into the United States" and noting the benefits of a larger inflow of accomplished and highly educated immigrants to the country's tech companies. And, of course, Gates was right. Gathering up the best and brightest undoubtedly serves the national interest, and bringing more of them into closer proximity with one another is likely to speed technological progress.

When I listen to Gates and to other meritocratic winners reflecting on good works or good policy or their legacy, I can't help but think that Christopher Lasch was perhaps too harsh, or at least too sweeping, in his characterization of the new rich. Breaking into the elite requires neither virtue nor vile character, and the elite as a whole contains both elements in ample supply. Yet I also can't shake the sense that, among the elites who are publicly minded at all, what many care most about, in the end, is perfecting the meritocracy—ensuring that every boy and girl has the same educational and entrepreneurial chances that they did so that the cream might always rise to the top. This is an admirable and, indeed, an essential goal. Yet it seems incomplete. It isn't so much that today's elites think poorly of Americans who lack the genetic endowment of IQ required to climb the modern economy's ladder; by and large, many elites just don't think about them much at all.

DOWNTOWN ASPEN SITS perhaps half a mile from Aspen Meadows, the campus on which the Aspen Ideas Festival takes place. It is lovely in July; cafés and upscale shops line leafy streets and boulevards, arranged in miniature blocks that march out primly from the feet of stately green mountains. But the town has not escaped the recession. Many of Aspen's wealthy homeowners were swindled by Bernie Madoff, and foreclosures have multiplied. The depth of distress is difficult to gauge; as a *New York Times* article published during my stay in Aspen noted (albeit using data that are merely suggestive), high-income Americans appear more likely than other classes to treat a home like any other investment, and simply walk away when it slips underwater.

Whatever their depth, from these troubles one can trace quite clearly the trickle-down effect of the plutonomy, and better appreciate the livelihoods that elites' spending sustains. COMPLETE STORE CLOSING LIQUIDATION read the large banner outside Ingrid Antoni Designs, one of several tony stores in town bearing out-of-place signs advertising store closures or deep discounts. On the other hand, business was "way up," a cashier told me, at the Thrift Store of Aspen, a nonprofit that's been in operation since 1947. Most of the new demand was coming from the small army of contractors and construction workers and maids and waitresses who live in the area (though rarely in Aspen itself) to serve wealthy residents and vacationers.

I spoke with Diane Turner, an agent for the Aspen Real Estate Company, at her street-front office in town. She is a gregarious, middle-aged brunette, quick to smile. As we talked, her husband, an erstwhile builder, came in from a mountain-bike ride—"that's what you do here when there's no work," he said, not altogether unhappily. Turner told me how fully "the town's working class depends on the rich and the skiing industry," and described how tough things had been. She showed me the front page of the *Aspen Daily News,* which announced a bank's plan to foreclose on a big resort at nearby Snowmass. Turner asked me about my job and my current reporting, and I gestured vaguely toward her and said I was trying to see how the recession was affecting middle-class people around the country. "We're working-class," she said, interrupting me. And indeed, they are. In Aspen, you are one or the other, rich or the rest. There is nothing to bridge the gap in between.

7

UNDERCLASS: MEN AND FAMILY

IN A JOBLESS AGE

IN HIS 1996 BOOK, *WHEN WORK DISAPPEARS*, THE HARVARD SOCI-ologist William Julius Wilson connected the loss of jobs from inner cities in the 1970s to the social ills that overwhelmed many inner-city neighborhoods after that. "The consequences of high neighborhood joblessness," he wrote, "are more devastating than those of high neighborhood poverty. A neighborhood in which people are poor but employed is different from a neighborhood in which many people are poor and jobless. Many of today's problems in the inner-city ghetto neighborhoods—crime, family dissolution, welfare, low levels of social organization, and so on—are fundamentally a consequence of the disappearance of work."

In the mid-twentieth century, most urban black men were employed, many of them in manufacturing. But beginning in the 1970s, as factories moved out of the cities or closed altogether, unemployment began rising sharply. Between 1973 and 1987, the percentage of black men in their twenties working in manufacturing fell from roughly 37.5 percent to 20 percent. As inner cities shed manufacturing jobs, men who lived there, particularly those with limited education, had a hard time making the switch to service jobs. Service jobs and office work of course require different interpersonal skills and different standards of self-presentation from those that blue-collar work demands, and movement from one sector to the other can be jarring. What's more, Wilson's research shows, downwardly mobile black men often resented the new work they could find, and displayed less flexibility on the job than, for instance, women or first-generation immigrant workers. As a result, employers began to prefer hiring women and immigrants, and a vicious cycle of resentment, discrimination, and joblessness set in.

The community breakdown that followed—drinking and drug sales and addiction; an accelerating decline in the prevalence of nuclear families; the sclerosis of church groups and other social institutions—has been well documented. But it is nonetheless troubling, as an outsider, to witness everyday life in a nongentrified inner-city neighborhood today. In October 2010, I visited Kensington, a large, multiethnic neighborhood in Philadelphia, where the death rate of young black men during the early aughts was comparable to that of U.S. soldiers in Iraq, and where it was plain to see how the neighborhood's character and economy combined to stifle the life chances of its residents.

Storefront businesses are not altogether absent from Kensington; on and around the main strip is a collection of pawnshops, takeout restaurants, strip clubs, bail-bond offices, hair salons, and furniture-rental stores. But even at noon on a Monday, some of the more obvious signs of economic activity involved streetwalking prostitutes and "corner boys" just beginning to emerge from dilapidated row houses to sell drugs.

Many of those row houses once had screen doors and metal sashes, but metal can be sold for scrap, and the doors and sashes have mostly been taken. On one street, two women, working separately, pushed shopping carts filled with metal piping and other scavenged junk down the sidewalk. Other neighborhood women get work as babysitters or day-care providers or hairstylists; relatively few young men work regularly, at least in the formal economy. According to the sociologist Maria Kefalas, the high-school dropout rate in Kensington is above 50 percent for boys, and heavy daily absences from school are common.

These sorts of problems are not exclusive to inner cities. In *The*

Big Sort, Bill Bishop describes the economic decline of the Coal Belt in rural Appalachia and the social dysfunction that followed. Although Appalachia has long been associated with poverty, in fact much of the area has made great material progress over the past fifty years. But the region's "coal counties" suffered greatly during the 1980s and 1990s, shedding tens of thousands of mining jobs (between 1980 and 1995, coal-mining employment in West Virginia fell by more than half). In the early '90s, unemployment topped 20 percent in parts of the region. It has since come down, partly because so many people have left the area—"rational people leave, if they can," the president of Concord University in Athens, West Virginia, told Bishop—and partly because so many who've stayed behind have instead left the workforce, in many cases for a place on the disability rolls. Today, jobs remain scarce and poverty high.

In McDowell County, West Virginia, about 6 percent of the adult population has a bachelor's degree; 40 percent didn't finish high school. The term *shotgun wedding* has sometimes been associated with Appalachia, perhaps unfairly, but whatever the circumstances, in the past people did marry. That's less often the case today; more than one in three children in McDowell County were born out of wedlock in 2010. According to Bishop, "civic dysfunction" and political corruption are rife throughout the region.

Abuse of drugs like OxyContin has ravaged coal country, and is especially prevalent among former miners. In 2005, FedEx stopped delivering prescription drugs to several counties in eastern Kentucky. Its trucks were being surrounded by staggering addicts eager for their delivery; drivers feared being robbed or mobbed. "Everybody here has a close personal friend or a relative who is on OxyContin," the director of a drug-treatment clinic director in Evarts, Kentucky, a town of just 1,000 people, told Bishop. In Harlan County, one young woman talked about what it's like to live in the area: "The quality of life is so low. . . . When you deal with what people have to deal with here. I don't know how to say it. . . . Me and my son were on our own and everywhere I went I began to feel like a failure. I never dreamed I would turn to drugs but it seemed to be the easy way out." She'd been selling her furniture to pay for her habit.

Pockets of chronic joblessness, poverty, and social dysfunction have of course been a part of the nation's geography for a long time. Every now and then, a book or television show will come along that brings some national focus to these areas—*The Other America, The Wire*—but because such places are so cut off from mainstream American life, they generally have been easy to ignore.

The Great Recession has deepened the misery in many of these places. Year by year, it is also creating more of them. It's a long way, both economically and culturally, from most blue-collar neighborhoods or less affluent suburbs to Kensington or Harlan County. But the distance is slowly growing shorter. The steady disappearance of nonprofessional middle-class jobs is creating the possibility that a larger underclass could form in the United States, one that becomes self-perpetuating and extends across generations. The elements that ultimately produce a true underclass are varied, and they interact in complicated ways. But the ingredients for such a soup are present today, and the recession has stirred them. One of the most important—the one that typically sets everything else in motion—is the failure and frustration of working-class men.

THE WEIGHT OF this recession has fallen most heavily upon men, who suffered roughly three-quarters of the 8 million job losses in 2008 and 2009. Male-dominated industries (construction, manufacturing) have been particularly hard-hit, while sectors that disproportionately employ women (education, health care) have held up relatively well. In January 2011, 18.8 percent of all men in their prime working years, twenty-five to fifty-four, did not have jobs; since the recession began, fewer prime-age men have been employed than at any time since the Bureau of Labor Statistics began tracking the statistic in 1948. During the recession, for the first time in U.S. history, women came to hold a majority of the country's jobs.

In this respect, the recession has merely intensified a long-standing trend. Broadly speaking, the service sector, which employs more women, is growing, while manufacturing, which employs more men, is shrinking. The net result is that men have been contributing a smaller and smaller share of family income—and working less and less over time.

One of the great puzzles of the past thirty years has been the way that men, as a group, have responded to a declining market for blue-collar jobs. Opportunities have expanded for college graduates over that span, and for nongraduates, jobs have proliferated within the service sector (at wages ranging from rock-bottom to middling). Yet in the main, men have availed themselves of neither of these opportunities. The proportion of young men with a bachelor's degree today is about the same as it was in 1980. And as the sociologists Maria Charles and David Grusky noted in their 2004 book, *Occupational Ghettos,* while men and women now mix more easily on different rungs of the career ladder, many individual industries and occupations have remained astonishingly segregated, with men continuing to seek work in a dwindling number of manual jobs and women "crowding into nonmanual occupations that, on average, confer more pay and prestige." Between 2000 and 2009, for instance, the ratio of women to men in education and health services remained unchanged at about three to one.

As recently as 2001, U.S. manufacturing still employed about as many people as did health and educational services (roughly 16 million each). But since then, those latter, female-dominated sectors have added about 4 million jobs, while manufacturing has lost about the same number. And while men made no inroads into these growing sectors over that time, they did consolidate their hold on manufacturing jobs—those dwindling jobs, along with jobs in construction, transportation, and utilities, were more heavily dominated by men in 2009 than they'd been at the beginning of the decade.

"Forty years ago, thirty years ago, if you were one of the fairly constant fraction of boys who wasn't ready to learn in high school, there were ways for you to enter the mainstream economy," says Henry Farber, an economist at Princeton. "When you woke up, there were jobs. There were good industrial jobs, so you could have a good industrial, blue-collar career. Now those jobs are gone." And men have yet to adjust. In 1967, 97 percent of thirty- to fifty-year-old American men with only a high-school diploma were working; in 2010, just 76 percent were. Declining male employment is not unique to the United States. It's been happening in almost all rich nations as they've put the industrial age behind them.

In her 2010 *Atlantic* essay "The End of Men," the journalist Hanna Rosin posed the question "What if the modern, postindustrial economy is simply more congenial to women than to men?" What if the exodus of men from the workforce that began in the malaise of the 1970s, and has continued at a more measured pace since then, is once again gaining speed—especially in the bottom half of the economy?

"I'm deeply concerned" about the prospects of less-skilled men, says Bruce Weinberg, an economist at Ohio State. "Looking over the past forty years, deindustrialization has been bad for men." Weinberg's research has shown that in occupations in which "people skills" are becoming more important, employment is skewing more and more toward women. And that category of occupations is large indeed. In his National Bureau of Economic Research working paper, "People People," Weinberg and his two coauthors found that interpersonal skills typically become more important and more highly valued in occupations in which computer use is prevalent and growing, and in which teamwork is important. They also become more important in "firms which have recently gone through organizational changes," as so many have in this recession. Even for jobs in traditionally masculine fields like home improvement, people skills and customer service have arguably become more important than they used to be.

In surveys, women are more likely than men to say they are effective at "people tasks." They're also more cooperative in Prisoner's Dilemma games (in which teamwork is necessary to the achievement of the best result for both players). Needless to say, a great many men have excellent people skills, just as a great many men do well in school. And many of the differences we observe between the genders may be the result of culture rather than genetics. All that notwithstanding, a meaningful minority of men have struggled badly as the economy has evolved, and have shown few signs of successful adaptation.

Many women are also struggling because of the recession. After the crash, in 2009, the unemployment rate among single mothers was 13.6 percent. And indeed, while employment among women with only a high-school degree rose sharply from the mid-1960s through 2000, it has declined somewhat since then (albeit less dramatically than it has for men). The disappearance of middle-skill jobs has hurt members of both sexes, and has increased the number of men and women who drift in and out of the labor force, weakly attached to low-wage, low-status, generally unpleasant jobs at the bottom of the economy.

Nonetheless, the structural changes in the economy, accelerated by the recession, have been hardest on men. And male unemployment, historically, has been hardest on society. Three years after the crash, its social consequences are becoming visible once again.

"I LIKE IT outside, you know?" said Frank Massoli (a pseudonym), a former construction foreman who lives outside Reading, Pennsylvania, in December 2010. "You see all these office buildings—you stick me in one of them, I'd be completely clueless. . . . I don't like being penned up with the same people each day."

Massoli, a stocky, balding forty-seven-year-old with fat brown sideburns and a thick, hoop-shaped silver earring, has worked much of his life outside; at different times, he's been a well-digger and a construction worker. Long ago, he worked in a factory, but he lost that job in his twenties. Before the recession, he was a foreman with a small construction outfit. "Things were pretty good," he said. "I was working six days a week, we went to Outback Steakhouse once a month. We were doing pretty good."

In July 2008, he lost that job, and couldn't find another one for more than two years. By 2010, his wife had left and they'd split custody of their eight adopted children. Four initially lived with him, although a fifteen-year-old daughter went to live with her mother after she became pregnant and stole money from Massoli.

Over those two years, Massoli went to some meetings for the unemployed sponsored by his church—"I was feeling pretty down," he said, and he thought he could use some guidance and support. But he says he wasn't qualified for the jobs that were posted by the group—most of them were in customer service or required more than a high-school degree—and he didn't feel like he fit in. He stopped going after he had a run-in with a human-resources consultant the group had brought in. She told him that he would have a hard time getting hired outside of construction, given the way he was describing himself and one of his past employers, for whom he had little respect. "And I was like, 'Kiss my ass.'" He'd never been the sort to sugarcoat things, he told me. He was a good worker, he said, and that's what should count.

Massoli said he'd looked for a job daily since he'd gotten laid off—in construction, delivery, machine operation, kitchen work. He was occasionally able to get some part-time work with his cousin, laying carpet. He knew there were government-sponsored retraining programs available, but he felt he was too old for that, and besides, he'd never been much of a classroom guy.

As time went by, with his savings exhausted and bills going unpaid, he began rooting through neighbors' garbage at night, looking for scrap he might be able to sell. "I'm a hustler," he said. "And I had no health insurance. I was divorced." He'd go out in his pickup with his kids at about six in the evening and cruise around until nine or nine thirty, looking through people's trash. Then he'd get up at about three in the morning and cruise around again for three or four hours on his own. He quickly learned the trash-pickup schedule for neighborhoods as far as thirty miles from his house. "I only took what people left out," he told me, although he wouldn't talk about his scavenging until I agreed not to use his real name. "There was competition," he said. "I remember one night driving around a corner, and I missed a washing machine, which is worth like twenty bucks, by like ten seconds, because someone got there before me."

His kids would help him tear apart the appliances they found, separating out the coated wire, brass fittings, and other components that could be resold. He would fix old lawn mowers he'd picked up, and resell them. Usually, he could make $75 or more a day, though fuel for his truck ate pretty heavily into that. He feared getting sick, because he had no health insurance—but also because he was living hand-to-mouth and couldn't afford days off.

To his great relief, in August 2010 Massoli found steady work again, digging geothermal wells with a company he used to work for long ago. "It's hard," he said, "and I'm not young." It didn't pay nearly what his job as a construction foreman did, but it had health benefits and was steady—though he didn't know if it would remain that way. The company was not doing well, he said, but the checks were still clearing. He'd bought a good steak and cooked it up for his kids recently. "I got bills to pay," he said. "But you got to do something once in a while." I asked him what would happen if the company were to fail. "I'll be back to scrappin'. What else am I gonna do?" •

NUCLEAR FAMILIES, WITH both parents present in the home, are of course less the norm today than they used to be. And "traditional" marriages, in which men engage in paid work and women in home-making, have long been in eclipse. Particularly in blue-collar families, where many husbands and wives work staggered shifts, men routinely handle a lot of the child care. Still, the ease with which gender bends in modern marriages should not be overestimated. When men stop doing paid work—and even when they work less than their wives—marital conflict usually follows.

Between 2007 and 2010, calls to the National Domestic Violence Hotline rose continually, by almost 20 percent in total; as was the case during the Depression, unemployed men are vastly more likely to beat their wives or children. More common than violence, though, is a sort of passive-aggressiveness. In *Identity Economics,* the economists George Akerloff and Rachel Kranton find that among married couples, men who aren't working at all, despite their free time, do only 37 percent of the housework, on average. And some men, apparently in an effort to guard their masculinity, actually do less housework after becoming unemployed.

Many working women struggle with the idea of partners who aren't breadwinners. "We've got this image of Archie Bunker sitting at home, grumbling and acting out," says Kathryn Edin, a professor of public policy at Harvard, and an expert on family life. "And that does happen. But you also have women in whole communities thinking, *This guy's nothing.*" Edin's research in low-income communities shows, for instance, that most working women whose partner stayed home to watch the kids—while very happy with the quality of child care their children's father provided—were dissatisfied with their relationship overall. "These relationships were often filled with conflict," Edin told me. Even today, she says, men's identities are far more defined by their work than women's, and both men and women become extremely uncomfortable when men's work goes away.

The national divorce rate fell slightly in 2008, and again in 2009, and that's not unusual in a recession: divorce is expensive, and many couples delay it in hard times. But joblessness corrodes marriages, and makes divorce much more likely down the road. According to

W. Bradford Wilcox, the director of the National Marriage Project at the University of Virginia, the gender imbalance of the job losses in this recession is particularly noteworthy, and—when combined with the depth and duration of the jobs crisis— poses "a profound challenge to marriage," especially in lower-income communities. It may sound harsh, but in general, he says, "if men can't make a contribution financially, they don't have much to offer." Two-thirds of all divorces are legally initiated by women, and women who earn substantially more than their husband are vastly more likely to initiate them. Wilcox believes that over the next few years, we may see a long wave of divorces, washing no small number of discarded and dispirited men back into single adulthood.

Among couples without college degrees, says Edin, marriage has become an "increasingly fragile" institution. In many low-income communities, she fears it is being supplanted as a social norm by single motherhood and revolving-door relationships. As a rule, fewer people marry during a recession, and this one has been no exception. But "the timing of this recession coincides with a pretty significant cultural change," Edin says: a fast-rising material threshold for marrying, but not for having children, in less affluent communities.

Edin explains that poor and working-class couples, after seeing the ravages of divorce on their parents or within their communities, have become more hesitant to marry; they believe deeply in marriage's sanctity, and try to guard against the possibility that theirs will end in divorce. Studies have shown that even small changes in income have significant effects on marriage rates among the poor and the lower middle class. "It's simply not respectable to get married if you don't have a job—some way of illustrating to your neighbors that you have at least some grasp on some piece of the American pie," Edin says. Increasingly, people in these communities see marriage not as a way to build savings and stability, but as "a symbol that you've arrived."

Childbearing is the opposite story. The stigma against out-of-wedlock children has by now largely dissolved in working-class communities—more than half of all new mothers without a college degree are unmarried. For both men and women in these communities, children are commonly seen as a highly desirable, relatively low-cost way to achieve meaning and bolster identity—especially when other opportunities are closed off. Christina Gibson-Davis, a public-policy professor at Duke University, recently found that among adults with no college degree, changes in income have no bearing at all on rates of childbirth.

"We already have low marriage rates in low-income communities," Edin told me, "including white communities. And where it's really hitting now is in working-class urban and rural communities, where you're just seeing astonishing growth in the rates of nonmarital childbearing. And that would all be fine and good, except these parents don't stay together. This may be one of the most devastating impacts of the recession."

Many children are already suffering in this economic climate, for a variety of reasons. Among poor families, nutrition can be inadequate in hard times, hampering children's mental and physical development. And regardless of social class, the stresses and distractions that afflict unemployed parents also afflict their kids, who are more likely to repeat a grade in school, and who on average earn less as adults. Children with unemployed fathers seem particularly vulnerable to psychological problems.

But a large body of research shows that one of the worst things for children, in the long run, is an unstable family. By the time the average out-of-wedlock child has reached the age of five, his or her mother will have had two or three significant relationships with men other than the father, and the child will typically have at least one half sibling. This kind of churning is terrible for children—heightening the risks of mental-health problems, troubles at school, teenage delinquency, and so on—and we're likely to see more and more of it, the longer this malaise stretches on.

"We could be headed in a direction where, among elites, marriage and family are conventional, but for substantial portions of society, life is more matriarchal," says Wilcox. The marginalization of working-class men in family life has far-reaching consequences. "Marriage plays an important role in civilizing men. They work harder, longer, more strategically. They spend less time in bars and more time in church, less with friends and more with kin. And they're happier and healthier."

One 2005 study shows that after marriage, men begin to work more hours than they used to, and eventually earn higher wages than their single counterparts; all in all, marriage adds nearly 20 percent to their income over time. Higher incomes, meanwhile, encourage men to stay married. And so, where the economy is healthy and marriage is the norm, a virtuous circle sets in, one that has benefited most American communities for most of America's history.

By contrast, communities with large numbers of unmarried, jobless men take on an unsavory character over time. Edin's research team spent part of the summer of 2009 in Northeast and South Philadelphia, conducting in-depth interviews with residents. She says she was struck by what she saw: "These white working-class communities—once strong, vibrant, proud communities, often organized around big industries—they're just in terrible straits. The social fabric of these places is just shredding. There's little engagement in religious life, and the old civic organizations that people used to belong to are fading. Drugs have ravaged these communities, along with divorce, alcoholism, violence. I hang around these neighborhoods in South Philadelphia, and I think, *This is beginning to look like the black inner-city neighborhoods we've been studying for the past 20 years.* When young men can't transition into formal-sector jobs, they sell drugs and drink and do drugs. And it wreaks havoc on family life. They think, *Hey, if I'm 23 and I don't have a baby, there's something wrong with me.* They're following the pattern of their fathers in terms of the timing of childbearing, but they don't have the jobs to support it. So their families are falling apart—and often spectacularly."

• • •

EVEN AS WEAK job prospects have spread family and community problems more widely, they have also deepened them in many of the same neighborhoods that were plagued by joblessness in the 1970s and '80s, and that have been struggling unsteadily to make their way back ever since. Urban minorities tend to be among the first fired in a recession, and the last rehired in a recovery. Overall, black unemployment stood at 15.7 percent in January 2011; among Hispanics, that figure was 11.9 percent. Even in New York City, where the financial sector, which employs relatively few blacks, initially shed tens of thousands of jobs, unemployment increased much faster among blacks than it did among whites.

In June 1999, the journalist Ellis Cose wrote in *Newsweek* that it was then "the best time ever" to be black in America. He ticked through the reasons: employment was up, murders and out-of-wedlock births down; educational attainment was rising, and poverty less common than at any time since 1967. Middle-class black couples were slowly returning to gentrifying inner-city neighborhoods. "Even for some of the most persistently unfortunate—uneducated black men between 16 and 24—jobs are opening up," Cose wrote.

But many of those gains are now imperiled. "It's like someone bombed my city," A. C. Wharton told the journalist Michael Powell in 2010, describing how foreclosure and unemployment have hollowed out neighborhoods in Memphis. Memphis was poised to become one of the country's first black-majority metro regions that year, and Wharton was the city's mayor. The median income of Memphis's black homeowners, which had been growing through the middle of the aughts, is now as low as it was in 1990, and black middle-class neighborhoods like Orange Mound, Whitehaven, and Cordova have been decimated by foreclosures and vacancies. "It's done more to set us back than anything since the beginning of the civil rights movement," Wharton said.

At the start of 2011, unemployment among black teens ages sixteen to nineteen was more than 45 percent, and the unemployment rate for black men age twenty or older was almost 17 percent. With so few jobs available, the sociologist William Julius Wilson told me, "many black males will give up and drop out of the labor market, and turn more to the underground economy. And it will be very difficult for these people"—especially those who acquire criminal records—"to reenter the labor market in any significant way." The sociologist Glen Elder, who's done fieldwork in Baltimore, said, "At a lower level of skill, if you lose a job and don't have fathers or brothers with jobs—if you don't have a good social network—you get drawn back into the street. There's a sense in the kids I've studied that they lost everything they had, and can't get it back."

In New York City, 21 percent of low-income blacks and Hispanics reported having lost their job in 2010 as a result of the bad economy, according to a survey by the Community Service Society. More still had had their hours or wages reduced. About one in four low-income New Yorkers often skipped meals in 2010 to save money, and one in five had had the gas, electricity, or telephone turned off. Wilson argues that once neighborhoods become socially dysfunctional, it takes a long period of unbroken good times to undo the damage—and they can backslide very quickly and steeply. "One problem that has plagued the black community over the years is resignation," Wilson said—a self-defeating "set of beliefs about what to expect from life and how to respond," passed from parent to child. "And I think there was sort of a feeling that norms of resignation would weaken somewhat with the Obama election. But these hard economic times could reinforce some of these norms."

Wilson, age seventy-five, is a careful scholar, who chooses his words precisely and does not seem given to overstatement. But he sounded forlorn when describing the "very bleak" future he sees for the neighborhoods that he's spent a lifetime studying. There is "no way," he told me, "that the extremely high jobless rates we're seeing won't have profound consequences for the social organization of inner-city neighborhoods." As economic weakness persists, Wilson believes that "we're going to see some horror stories"—and in many cases a relapse into the depths of decades past. "The point I want to emphasize," he said, "is that we should brace ourselves."

BAD SOCIAL NORMS spread like colds through communities. When their neighbors are idle, people are less likely to find and keep work, whatever the level of local job availability. When a couple divorces, the odds of divorce increase among their friends, coworkers, and other acquaintances.

One of the larger long-term risks to U.S. society is that the norms of a very large class of people, in a very large number of places, are now changing in unhealthy ways. Many of the social and, especially, family changes described throughout this chapter are steadily creeping into the heart of the middle class. The recession did not cause these changes—although they are inextricably linked to economic changes over the past thirty years. Nor has the recession suddenly turned the middle class into an underclass—although the forces that are winnowing the nonprofessional middle class will remain strong even once recovery is complete. The long-run economic troubles that haunt the nation are not limited to a few disadvantaged places. Left unaddressed, they could produce an unwelcome sea change in American culture.

"The newest and perhaps most consequential marriage trend of our time," wrote Brad Wilcox in a 2010 national study of the American family, "concerns the broad center of our society." Among what Wilcox describes as "Middle Americans"—people with a high-school but not a college degree, who make up 58 percent of the adult population—an array of measures of family dysfunction have begun to blink red. Overall, "the family lives of today's moderately edu-cated Americans"—which in the 1970s closely resembled those of college graduates—now "increasingly resemble those of high-school dropouts, too often burdened by financial stress, partner conflict, single parenting, and troubled children."

"The speed of change," writes Wilcox, "is astonishing." By the late 1990s, 37 percent of moderately educated couples were divorcing or separating within ten years of their first marriage, roughly the same rate as among couples who didn't finish high school and more than three times that of college graduates. By the aughts, the percentage in "very happy" marriages—identical to that of college graduates in the 1970s—was also nearing that of high-school dropouts. In 2006–8, 44 percent of all births among moderately educated women occurred outside of marriage, not far off the rate (54 percent) among high-school dropouts; among college-educated women, that number was just 6 percent.

The same pattern emerges—the actions and attitudes of non-professional middle-class families diverging from those of the college-educated and converging with those of high school dropouts—with norm after norm: the percentage of fourteen-year-old girls living with both their mother and father; the percentage of adolescents who say they'd be embarrassed if they got (or got someone) pregnant; the rate of infidelity and number of sexual partners; the percentage of adolescents wanting to attend college "very much"; the percentage of never-married young adults using birth control all the time.

One stubborn stereotype in the United States is that religious roots are deepest in blue-collar communities and small towns, and more generally among Americans who have high-school diplomas but not college ones. That was true in the 1970s. Yet in fact, attendance at religious services has plummeted among moderately educated Americans, and is now much more common among college grads. So, too, is participation in civic groups. High-school seniors from affluent households are more likely to volunteer, join groups, go to church, and have strong academic ambitions than they used to be, and are as trusting of other people as they were a generation ago; high-school seniors from less affluent households have become less engaged on each of those fronts. A cultural chasm—which did not exist forty years ago and which was still relatively small twenty years ago—has developed between the traditional middle class and the top 30 percent of society.

The interplay of economic and cultural forces is complex, and changes in cultural norms cannot be ascribed exclusively to the economy. Wilcox has tried to statistically parse the causes of these changes, finding that about a third of the class-based changes in marriage patterns, for instance, are directly attributable to wage stagnation, increased job insecurity, or bouts of unemployment; the rest he attributes to a decline in civic and religious participation and broader changes in the attitudes and outlook of the middle class.

In fact, all of these variables seem to influence and reinforce one another. Nonetheless, some of the most significant cultural changes within the middle class have accelerated in the past decade, as the prospects of the nonprofessional middle class have dimmed. The number of couples who live together but are not married, for instance, has been rising briskly since the 1970s, but it really took off in the aughts—nearly doubling from 3.8 million to 6.7 million from 2000 to 2009. From 2009 to 2010, that number jumped even more sharply (by 868,000, or 13 percent). In six out of ten of the newly cohabitating couples, at least one person was not working, a much higher fraction than in the past.

The increasing segregation of American communities by affluence and educational attainment has doubtless reinforced the divergence in the personal habits and lifestyle of Americans who lack a college degree and those who have one. In highly educated communities, families are largely intact, educational ideals strong, connections between effort and reward clear, and good role models abundant. None of those things is a given anymore in communities where college-degree attainment is low. The natural leaders and role models of such communities—the meritocratic winners who do well in school, go off to selective colleges, and get their degrees—generally leave them for good in their early twenties.

In their 2009 book, *Creating an Opportunity Society*, Ron Haskins and Isabel Sawhill wrote that most Americans believe strongly that opportunity is widespread in the United States, and success primarily a matter of individual intelligence and skill. But the reality is more complicated. Mobility—up and down—from the middle class has traditionally been high. Among people who were about forty years old near the turn of the millennium, those born to middle-class parents had widely varied incomes. But class was more sticky among those born to parents who were either rich or poor. Thirty-nine percent of children born to parents in the top 20 percent of earners stayed in that same bracket as adults. Likewise, 42 percent of those whose parents were in the bottom income quintile remained there as adults, and only 6 percent reached the top quintile; rags-to-riches stories were extremely rare. A large, healthy, vibrant middle class is essential to the goal of mobility and opportunity. But one must speculate that if the economic and cultural trends under way continue unabated, class mobility will decrease in the future. How could it not?

The prospect of two nations—one wealthy and well educated, one poor and of limited hope—living apart and divided by largely impermeable cultural barriers, seems distant. And in most respects it probably is. Yet one indication of the degree to which American society has already cleaved into two can be seen in the geographic pattern of U.S. military recruitment. Bill Bishop and the statistician Robert Cushing have tracked recent U.S. military casualties by hometown, finding that generally, "the bigger the city, the smaller the percentage of its young people were likely to die" in the wars of the aughts. By early 2007, the casualty rate among military-age residents of Bismarck, North Dakota, was almost ten times that of San Francisco. The Department of Defense, in a 2001 study, found that the "propensity to enlist is lower for high-quality youth, youth with better-educated parents, and youth planning to attend college." In its recruiting, it has zeroed in on places with limited prospects for good jobs or higher education. In Iraq and Afghanistan, "the death rate among military-age residents living in America's high-tech cities has been half that of military-age people from rural America," writes Bishop. "There has been a form of economic conscription at work."

Is a large underclass in America's future? It need not be. The cultural changes now at work on America's middle and working classes are slow-acting, though the recession has sped them for a time. Frank Massoli is not the only blue-collar worker who has found work again; manufacturing jobs have rebounded, albeit very weakly, since the depths of the recession. Some opportunities in construction will come back, and many other nonprofessional middle-class jobs will rebound, too, though the long-term trend for these jobs may remain downward sloping. Indeed, one small service the recession may have done us is to underline men's struggles, the struggles of high-school graduates more generally, and the deterioration of family life in many communities—providing a warning of what may be to come. Yet warnings matter only if we heed them. Should we fail to do so, the very idea of America could change profoundly in the years to come. And American politics—as contentious as they seem already—may take on a new and unwelcome cast.

8

THE POLITICS OF THE
NEXT TEN YEARS

O N THE EVE OF THE GREAT RECESSION, AMERICAN SOCIETY WAS,
by many measures, as open, culturally vibrant, and socially tol-
erant as it had ever been. Economic connections to the rest of the
world were growing stronger year by year. Racial and ethnic tensions
were by many measures diminishing. Volunteerism and political participation had begun to rise, particularly among the young, after a
long period of decline. Just weeks after the crash, the election of
Barack Obama to the presidency seemed—to many independents
who supported him, at least—to promise a political renewal that
would transcend the divisive issues of the past and bring the country
together, into a more hopeful future.

Since then, America's social and civic health have so far held
up better than the economy. Crime rates have stayed low, and hate
crimes have actually fallen somewhat. A variety of polls on social
conflict since 2007 have shown mixed results, but for the most part
they point to continuing, if slowly thinning, amity. Signs of looming
class warfare or racial conflagration, as of this writing, are not much
in evidence. This general pattern fits that of previous downturns,
even steep ones. The worst effects of pervasive joblessness and economic weakness take time to incubate, and they show themselves
only slowly. Brief downturns seldom change politics or culture dramatically—only over the course of many disappointing years does
the national character change.

Still, it has been three years since the crash, and many more since incomes were growing strongly for most Americans; those pre-recession days of increasing openness seem far off now. Economic hardship clearly has weakened the social fabric, and has prompted a retreat into private concerns. The National Conference on Citizenship, a nonpartisan organization that has tracked civic engagement for more than fifty years, reported that in 2009, 72 percent of Americans said they'd cut back on time spent volunteering, participating in groups, and engaging in other civic activities. The organization last observed such a widespread "turning inward," it noted, in the deep recession of the early 1980s.

The seeds of a deeper discontent may slowly be germinating, and with them a more reactionary set of ideas. Public views toward society's more marginal members have hardened since the crash; the percentage of Americans who support government aid to the needy fell from 54 percent in 2007 to 48 percent in 2009, even though poverty and unemployment rose sharply over that span. Mistrust of all things foreign has risen, and support for free trade has declined. A 2010 poll by the *Wall Street Journal* and NBC News found that 53 percent of Americans believed free trade was harmful to the United States, versus 46 percent in 2007 and 32 percent in 1999.

In the spring of 2010, the state of Arizona passed into law the strictest and most far-reaching immigration measure that any state has enacted in decades. Among its more controversial measures, the law requires immigrants to carry registration papers with them at all times or face criminal penalties. It also requires police to ascertain the immigration status of anyone they stop, detain, or arrest if they have a "reasonable suspicion" that the person may be an illegal alien. According to a poll conducted by NBC and the *Wall Street Journal* in May 2010, 66 percent of Americans believed the Arizona law would lead to discrimination against legal Latino immigrants—and yet 64 percent supported it.

Deportations have risen dramatically since the recession began, and prominent senators, including John McCain and Lindsey Graham, have supported hearings to consider amending the Fourteenth

Amendment, which grants citizenship as a birthright, regardless of the immigration status of one's parents. The percentage of Hispanics saying that whites and Hispanics get along "not too well" or "not at all well," according to Pew Research, rose from 24 percent in 2007 to 41 percent in 2009.

Anti-Muslim sentiment has seemed quick to surface since the downturn began (though violence against Muslims has not risen). The number of Americans with a favorable impression of Islam declined from 41 percent to 30 percent between 2005 and 2010. In the summer of 2010, anger erupted over the plan by a moderate Islamic cleric to build an unobtrusive mosque two blocks away from the site of the World Trade Center. Several mosques around the country were defaced or defiled, and a pastor in Florida threatened to burn the Koran. Martin Peretz, then the editor in chief of the *New Republic*, publicly questioned whether American Muslims were "worthy of the privileges of the First Amendment." So quickly did the flames of bigotry seem to rise in some quarters that an "emergency summit" was convened in the nation's capital by prominent Christian, Jewish, and Muslim leaders to try to quell them. A joint statement expressed alarm over the "anti-Muslim frenzy" and pled for tolerance. "This is not America," said Cardinal Theodore McCarrick. "America was not built on hate." •

THESE PROLIFERATING SIGNS of a turning inward and a narrowing of American minds should not be surprising: as hard times linger, they reliably produce resentment toward outsiders, suspicion of unfair treatment, and zero-sum thinking. And as is clear from history, frustration is typically strongest not among the *most* marginalized groups, but among the *newly* marginalized—that is to say, those whose status and self-image have collapsed most abruptly, or are in the greatest danger of doing so. In the United States today, that describes a large part of the nonprofessional middle class.

Middle-class discontent with the federal government has grown markedly since 2007, finding its clearest expression in the Tea Party movement. Candidates affiliated with the Tea Party won forty seats in the House of Representatives in the 2010 midterm elections, and 41 percent of voters polled on Election Day said their attitude toward the movement was generally supportive; 73 percent said they were angry or dissatisfied with the federal government.

The Tea Party's active supporters are overwhelmingly white and about 60 percent male; in a 2010 *New York Times* poll, half described themselves as middle-class and another quarter as working-class (the rest were split among upper-middle-class, lower-class, and upper-class, in descending order of prevalence). A plurality had some college education but not a college degree.

At the core of the Tea Party, it is often asserted, stand older residents of rural regions. And indeed, 75 percent of Tea Party supporters are older than forty-five, and the movement is popular in many rural areas. Yet this characterization is overly narrow and ultimately misleading. An analysis of Tea Party events in the run-up to the 2010 midterms, performed by the political scientist James Gimpel, showed the highest level of activity in former real-estate boomtowns and in newer exurbs around the country—the places where the housing market crashed the hardest.

It appears likely, then, that many of the Tea Party's supporters are people who used to feel prosperous, but whose stars are now falling and whose lifestyles have become insecure. Unemployment itself isn't an overwhelming problem within the Tea Party; just 6 percent of its supporters responding to the *Times* poll said they were temporarily out of work, and 14 percent, less than the nationwide average, said the recession had caused them true "hardship." (The relatively advanced age of many Tea Party members may be one reason why comparatively few are unemployed. Some are retired, and for older workers, the unemployment rate in this recession has been relatively low.) But more than half said the recession had in one way or another made life "difficult" for them and their family—whether due to falling home values, pay cuts, anxiety, or other problems.

At Rand Paul's May 2010 Senate primary celebration in Kentucky, his father, Ron, an elder statesman of the Tea Party who was mobbed by supporters in the crowd, said his son's insurgent victory sent a strong message: "Get rid of the power people, the people who run the show, the people who think they're above everybody else." At the Tea Party's national convention earlier that year, Sarah Palin denounced "elitists" and said America was "ready for another revolution." At a Utah GOP convention, conservative senator Robert Bennett was jeered before his primary ouster for supporting the bank bailout—"TARP! TARP! TARP!" went the chant.

The Tea Party is powered partly by anger toward a financial elite that, abetted by government, seems to be prospering at the expense of regular people. But the movement seems equally suspicious that less favored groups are also unfairly getting a leg up. According to a survey by the Public Religion Research Institute, 61 percent of people who identified with the Tea Party believed that discrimination against whites was as big a problem as discrimination against minorities, and 58 percent said discrimination against women was no longer a problem. Tea Party supporters generally favor lower taxes and the slashing of government programs that do not benefit them directly, with exemption for those, like Medicare and Social Security, that do. The ideal of market freedom is not deeply held within the movement: in October 2010, 63 percent of Tea Party supporters said free trade was "bad for the U.S.," and just 24 percent believed it was good for the country.

If you squint hard enough, you can begin to see some resemblance between the Tea Party and the Populist movement of the late nineteenth century, a movement of downwardly mobile farmers who felt deeply exploited by the financiers of their time. The Populists formed the only grassroots political cause in American history that achieved widespread support and didn't fade quickly away; the movement grew for two decades before reaching its apotheosis in 1896, and for a time, it looked possible that it might upend and remake the traditional two-party system in the United States. Like the Tea

Party, it was born in an environment of rapid economic change, rising inequality, and increasingly burdensome debt—an environment, in the words of the historian Lawrence Goodwyn, in which "a large number of people in the United States discovered that the economic premises of their society were working against them." Like the Tea Party, the Populist movement attracted earnest and well-meaning people, previously uninvolved in politics, who felt that neither Democrats nor Republicans were serving "plain people" like themselves. And like the Tea Party, it developed worrisome characteristics: nationalism side by side with an aggressive provincialism; reflexive anti-elitism; a strong sense of moral superiority; little reverence for the present, and too much for a partly imagined past.

At its core, however, Populism was a class-based movement, with class-based goals. By contrast, as the conservative political analyst David Frum has noted, American populist ire in recent generations has nearly always been focused on the best-educated rather than the wealthy. A key difference between the Populist movement and the Tea Party is that the latter, so far, has not taken on an anti-business or anti-rich cast. Despite its flirtations with protectionism and its loathing of the bank bailouts, the Tea Party still fits relatively easily within the GOP—favoring small government, light regulation, and low taxes at every income level.

Yet if class distinctions continue to grow sharper in the United States, and if educational differences keep looming larger as a filter between the classes, one wonders whether the populist distinction between wealth and education will last very far into the twenty-first century. One of many reasons that Sarah Palin is the natural leader of the Tea Party is that she has achieved power and material success outside of the usual meritocratic channels. But her path to wealth—celebrity—is of course not widely available, even in the age of reality TV.

In his 1951 book, *The True Believer: Thoughts on the Nature of Mass Movements,* the social writer Eric Hoffer argued that all mass movements, whether religious, social, or nationalist, share certain essential characteristics, and are rooted in the failing self-esteem of large groups of people. Ruined middle classes, Hoffer noted, are highly susceptible to movements; they "throb with the ferment of frustration. The memory of better things is as fire in their veins." Over time, feelings of helplessness and worthlessness foster paranoia, which shifts guilt and blame onto others. Boredom with a stagnant life inspires identification with radical causes. To one extent or another, wrote Hoffer, mass movements always breed "enthusiasm, fervent hope, hatred and intolerance." Their stated goals are less important than the psychological and emotional void they fill, and in fact are easily mutable.

The American middle class, while under increasing pressure, is hardly ruined. And aggressive populism—whether embodied in the Tea Party movement or any other—does not look likely to gain dominance over U.S. politics anytime soon. Even the Populist movement, which developed deep institutional roots and had deeper grievances than those of the middle class today, was ultimately crushed by business and financial interests in 1896, once it had become a true threat to them. (The Populists had cast their lot with the Democrats by then, and the Republican Party, fueled by unprecedented campaign contributions, developed a new and more sophisticated campaign machine that would dominate politics for years thereafter.) It is very difficult for any outsider movement to succeed in American politics. That difficulty is all the greater today—and the odds that any genuinely anti-elite movement could succeed are all the longer—because of the nature of our meritocracy, which lifts natural leaders from the communities of their birth and absorbs them.

Yet that very fact also makes modern grassroots movements less apt to develop responsible and coherent positions, and more vulnerable to demagoguery. When discredited ideas and irresponsible proposals gain a wide following, they do eventually exert an influence on policy and on the culture, even if their main proponents never gain power. And of course, the "tail risk" of an inchoate populism should not be overlooked; however unlikely a populist government might seem in any particular year, should economic pressures increase, the dam could someday break. The frustration felt today by many Tea Party supporters is not without basis. It is likely to increase as the cities of the "coastal elite" and other elite enclaves shrug off the recession.

In July 2010, a Penn Schoen Berland poll of Washington, DC, elites—defined as college graduates involved in politics or policy who make more than $75,000 a year—revealed their views about the economy to be much more positive than those of most Americans; nationwide, about two out of three survey respondents said the U.S. economy was on the wrong track, but less than half of the Washington elites surveyed felt the same way. (Elites were also less concerned about immigration than most Americans, and more apt to think the Tea Party was a fad that would "go away soon.") A large majority acknowledged that the current downturn had affected them less than it had most Americans.

A salary of $75,000 is hardly a ticket to high living, especially in Washington, where costs are steep. But it's no mystery why Washington's political elites have a rosier view of the economy than most Americans. The city's professional suburbs are among the very richest in America. And while a relatively large number of poor people do live in Washington itself, many of them are sequestered in corners of the city where the professional class seldom sets foot. The city and its environs are a primary habitat for America's meritocratic winners, and most of the area's professional inhabitants have felt the recession only lightly.

The federal government, of course, did not stand idly by as the recession unfolded. Aggressive action by the Fed and Treasury immediately after the crash almost certainly prevented a true depression. The stimulus package of 2009 helped stabilize the economy, and more modest measures at the end of 2010 were passed explicitly to speed growth in 2011. Hesitancy to do more is understandable;

by 2010, most Americans believed the government had done too much, rather than too little, and worries about the national debt were widespread.

All that notwithstanding, the political will to action undeniably diminished—and the government, to some extent, became unfocused—soon after the stock market began to rally and business profits began to grow again. Over the past two years, I've spoken with many political leaders and officials about the economy, and every one of them seems to genuinely regret the pain that the recession has inflicted on so many Americans. But as early as the fall of 2009, many of them simultaneously seemed to believe that the healing was well advanced. The acceptance of that idea is doubtless made easy by the tenor of their daily interactions with associates, friends, and acquaintances. Within the Washington professional community's social circles, nearly everyone you meet seems to be doing just fine.

In his 2005 paper, "Inequality and Democratic Responsiveness," Martin Gilens, a political scientist at Princeton University, examined the influence that different classes of Americans exert on federal government action. Sifting through detailed survey data on public support for thousands of proposed policy changes from 1981 through 2002, he found that, in essence, the government is responsive *only* to the wishes of the rich. Gilens compared popular support for different initiatives at the tenth, fiftieth, and ninetieth income percentiles. On many issues, poor, middle-class, and rich Americans held similar views. When they didn't, however, it was crystal clear whose interests legislators and other policy makers served. When the rich and poor disagreed about an issue, policy hewed closely to the preferences of the rich, and was "wholly unrelated" to the preferences of the poor. The same was true, more or less, when the opinions of the rich differed from those of median-income Americans. When middle-class preference for any given policy flipped from strong opposition to strong support, the probability of government action rose by only 6 percent, on average, if the rich remained opposed. By contrast, when the rich got behind an issue that the middle class opposed, the chances of government action rose by 30 percent. "Whether or not elected officials and other decision makers 'care' about middle-class Americans," Gilens concluded, "influence over actual policy outcomes appears to be reserved almost exclusively for those at the top of the income distribution."○

The sequestration of the rich and affluent from other Americans—in tandem with the flow of money toward positions that the rich hold dear—may in large part explain the intensity with which certain ideals are held in Washington (unrestrained finance; free trade as an end in itself). A whole ideology of governing has grown over the past thirty years, extending across party lines, that is defensible intellectually, but congenial to the rich and well educated above all. This ideology, for the most part, does not directly *conflict* with the ideal of a broadly shared prosperity. Yet increasingly, it appears to be insufficient for the achievement of that goal—and perhaps indifferent to it.

Some three years after the crash, America's banking institutions are generally larger and more powerful than they were before, and they carry an even stronger implicit government guarantee against failure. The plan to close the loophole that allows hedge-fund managers to pay just 15 percent of their income in taxes died a quiet death in the Senate in 2010. A new free-trade agreement with South Korea, the biggest since NAFTA, was negotiated by the White House near the end of that year. The temporary income-tax cuts passed by the Bush administration, and tilted toward high earners, were extended. Not all of these measures were bad policy, and some of them carry substantial benefits for the middle class. Nonetheless, it is undeniable that throughout the Great Recession, and particularly with regard to long-term policies involving the financial industry, one of the more prominent national political developments has been the furtherance of positions, however unpopular, that benefit and are supported by the elite.

. . .

POLITICAL FORECASTING IS a murky business, but the state of the economy will likely determine the presidential election of 2012. The malaise of the 1970s, to one extent or another, cost both Gerald Ford and Jimmy Carter reelection. Ronald Reagan, whose approval ratings suffered along with the economy through much of his first term, won a landslide reelection in no small part because incomes and the economy were improving extremely quickly by 1984. George H. W. Bush, whose midterm approval ratings were so high that some of the most prominent Democrats decided not to run against him, was not so lucky; recession returned in the latter half of his first and only term (the recession ended a few months before the 1992 election, but that had not yet translated into bigger paychecks when voters cast their ballots). In 1996, the economy was booming when Bill Clinton won his second term, easily dispatching Bob Dole; job growth was strong, and wages were rising.

Other factors besides the economy can of course swing elections. "Incumbent fatigue" tends to hurt the prospects of candidates who follow a two-term president from the same party; that's one reason George W. Bush beat Al Gore by a whisker in 2000, despite a strong economy. Wars and other traumas can override economic concerns; the war on terror almost certainly boosted Bush's reelection prospects in 2004 (economic conditions in that year were middling, on balance).

But economic conditions are usually the dominant factor in modern presidential elections. In particular, voters respond strongly to the *direction* of the economy *during the election year*. As the journalist John Judis has observed, the unemployment rate in November 1984, when Reagan won reelection, was 7.2 percent, the same as it was in July 1981, soon after he'd assumed the presidency. But in between it had been much higher. Voters didn't punish Reagan for the high unemployment and economic contraction that encompassed much of his first term; they rewarded him for strong income growth and a falling rate of unemployment in 1984 itself. Similarly, in 1936, Franklin Delano Roosevelt was easily reelected despite an unemployment rate of about 14 percent; unemployment had been much higher in the years before.

As the election of 2012 nears, the answers to two key questions will likely determine which party will hold the White House in 2013. The first concerns the pace and rhythm of recovery. The second is *which* recovery voters ultimately care about. Although the unemployment rate is usually a fairly good proxy for the health of the economy, since the Great Recession ended, jobs have stayed scarce while economic growth, business profits, and some personal-income growth have returned. Historically, political scientists have found that once you account for income growth, unemployment doesn't matter much at the ballot box; the unemployed, even in times like these, are a small fraction of the electorate, and many don't vote. And Larry Bartels, a political scientist at Princeton, has found that one of the best predictors of incumbent support in presidential elections is income growth at the 95th percentile. (He suggests that the outsized importance of the affluent as potential campaign contributors, as well as their high voting rates and their propensity to occupy positions that lend them large megaphones, may account for that.)

The divergent finances of different classes of Americans make any assessment of the recovery exceedingly difficult, and nearly impossible to capture in a single metric—particularly when one considers the prominent role of housing wealth in the recession. Housing values kept rising throughout the two recessions prior to this one, and typically change slowly enough that they don't seem to have a big impact on elections. We are in uncharted territory this time around.

If the recovery broadens meaningfully in 2012, Barack Obama will likely win a second term, even if improvement is still small compared with the accumulated pain of the past three years, and even though the long-term prospects of most Americans are likely to remain uncertain. On the other hand, if the economy is flat or ebbing—whether due to the tapering off of stimulus measures, a falling housing market, a worsening of Europe's debt crisis, turmoil in the Middle East, or some other shock—the GOP will hold an enormous advantage. The 2012 Republican presidential field appears weak to many political observers. Yet polling in early 2011 showed that nearly every major Republican hopeful was running close to Obama in hypothetical head-to-head match-ups. If the economy dips down again, any GOP nominee would have a good shot at winning the White House.

And if the economy is somewhere in between—shambling slowly forward, with strong gains at the top slowly petering out as one moves down into the broad center of society? In the end, all of these questions and "horse race" analyses may obscure a larger point: no matter who wins the White House in 2012, history suggests that if economic weakness lingers, politics will become smaller, reforms more muted, and experimentation with new ideas less likely.

After the 2010 midterms, the historian David Kennedy wrote that the recent pattern of U.S. elections bore no small resemblance to that of the Gilded Age. The 2010 election, he noted, was America's third consecutive "wave" election—in 2006, control of both houses of Congress changed from one party to the other; in 2008, the presidency did; in 2010, the House of Representatives flipped again. In 2008, some political observers speculated that the GOP was a spent force that would need years in the wilderness before it could once again garner widespread support; the Democrats seemed poised for many years of control. Yet only two years later, political momentum had entirely reversed. Such political volatility recalls that of 1870 through 1900, when control of the House shifted six times in fifteen elections, and when divided government was the norm.

"Generations of American scholars have struggled to find a coherent narrative or to identify heroic leaders in that era's messy and inconclusive political scene," Kennedy wrote. "It is not as if the Gilded Age did not have plenty of urgent and potentially galvanizing issues"—from healing the wounds of the Civil War to navigating the disorienting switch from agriculture to industry. "Yet the era's political system proved unable to grapple effectively with any of those matters."

Kennedy relates the "abject political paralysis" of that period—defined by a political system "both volatile and gridlocked"—to the enormous social and economic dynamism of the times, and the near constant dislocations and disorientation that resulted. And indeed, periods of profound economic transformation, in which both ordinary people and the government are unsure of how to adapt, are likely to be politically unstable, even when the economy is lifting most people up from year to year.

But the failure of most people to benefit strongly from economic dynamism in the 1880s and 1890s—just as they failed to benefit throughout the early 2000s—surely also contributed to political instability. Japan's economy since the early 1990s has hardly been a dynamo, yet its politics have also grown exceedingly volatile as stagnation has deepened. As John Judis has noted, from 1950 to 1970, Japan had six prime ministers; since 2005, it has had just as many. (Since 1990, it has had fourteen.) Several recent leaders initially "stirred hopes of renewal and reform," as Obama did during his campaign, only to be undone by rapid "disillusionment and despair."

In the end, if we remain stuck in an economic climate in which stagnation and disappointment are the norms for large numbers of Americans, the most-likely risks to our politics are not rogue leaders or an insurgent populist party. They are endless vacillation, low levels of public trust, and political options that are stunted by a poisonous atmosphere and heavy discontent. Of course, the bad times could end naturally and relatively quickly; new technological breakthroughs or world events could lift the economy, easing, at least for a time, the economic problems we face. That, by and large, is what happened at the beginning of the twentieth century and at the end of the 1930s.

But the country had advantages then that it no longer possesses—most notably a population that, from top to bottom, was much better educated than that of any other country, and that was rapidly becoming better educated still. National problems are not always self-correcting, and we must be wary of the assumption that because the United States has extricated itself from bad situations in the past, it is predestined to do so in the future. Over many years, a persistently bad economy can create a sort of political trap that is difficult to escape. That is yet one more reason to focus our national energies today on putting a definitive end to this period of malaise, and putting the nation on better footing in the decades to come.

9

A WAY FORWARD

THE SOCIAL LEGACIES OF THE GREAT RECESSION ARE STILL BEING written, but their breadth and depth are immense. They are enormously complex problems, and their solutions will be equally difficult. There is no magic bullet for what ails the United States today.

To be effective, any potential remedies must alleviate the worst symptoms of the current weakness and also confront the problems that lie beneath them. They must bolster the economy now and clear the way for faster long-term growth, help the jobless get back to work and ensure that we are creating the kinds of jobs that allow for a more broadly shared prosperity in the future. I wish I could say I have a proven twelve-step plan to achieve these goals—quickly and without risks or side effects. But these are difficult and contentious issues, and many reasonable people will doubtless disagree with the solutions I propose.

Before proceeding to those remedies, let me make a few brief observations about the *nature* of the problems that the recession has caused or revealed, and how we've perceived—or in some cases misperceived—them. I believe these general principles must undergird any serious effort to improve the nation's footing. If we can agree on them, at least, we will be on our way to better, smarter action.

1. The problems created by the most-severe recessions are typically bigger and longer-lasting than they first appear. Indeed, the damage

that periods like this one do to people, families, and communities is in many cases permanent. The greatest treasure of any modern economy is its human capital, but long, deep slumps slowly drain that away. As we've seen, the life prospects, openness, and energy of young adults are diminishing with each year that economic weakness lingers. The ranks of middle-aged and older workers who've become unemployable by being sidelined too long are swelling. Families are fracturing, and the futures of the children within them dimming. Middle- and working-class communities are tipping into decline.

All of these developments are, above all, personal and local tragedies. But they also leave a national legacy, robbing the economy of human potential for decades. Every year that goes by while masses of people are trapped and idled due to housing woes and high unemployment is not merely one lost year—it's a loss that's paid forward into future years as well, an accumulating deficit of skill, character, and regenerative ability. It's a loss that will restrain America's growth potential and cause social problems for many years to come.

2. Again and again, our tendency in periods like this one has been to hunker down, retreat from one another, and wait for the bad times to pass. When bubbles pop and times grow hard, the animal spirits within all of us turn bearish, money-conscious, sometimes ungenerous, and deeply averse to risk. Some of these changes may be healthy in moderation. But they are of course emotional responses, and unchecked, they can bias our thinking and actions in ways that are just as dangerous and counterproductive as bubble thinking itself.

3. Historically, as a result of these first two factors, we have tended to underestimate the true cost of remaining in periods like this one, and to overestimate the risks of aggressive action to try to hasten recovery. The bias in periods like this one has usually been toward doing too little; if anything, it should be toward doing too much.

4. This was not a vanilla recession, and vanilla responses will not fully end it. Recovery from financial crisis is usually slow and painful. Today, government action is hampered by interest rates near zero, which hamstrings the Fed; and by a high and rising national

debt, which makes fiscal expansion more risky and contentious. Many American workers, meanwhile, are in the wrong places and in possession of skills that are no longer useful. Innovation, a critical engine of jobs, has been disappointing for a decade. Boilerplate responses—cut taxes, raise spending—are insufficient given the nature and variety of these problems, and potentially dangerous if only bluntly applied. We need a combination of actions—some time-honored, some novel—to restore our health.

5. True recovery is not simply a matter of jolting the economy back onto its former path; it's about changing the path. We are in the midst of a major, global economic transformation, one that is steadily thinning the American middle class. The Great Recession has brought this into sharp relief, and in some ways has given us a preview of where America's economy is heading. And while this preview is troubling, it is also clarifying. Many of the deepest economic trends that the recession has highlighted and temporarily sped up will take decades to fully play out. We can adapt successfully to them, if we start now.

6. Culture matters. Everything about this period underlines the connections between the economy and the culture—and the profound way that each influences the other. A cultural separation is accompanying and reinforcing the economic sorting of Americans. It is happening in Middle America and it is happening in Aspen. Much of the nonprofessional middle class is slowly coming to resemble the poor in its habits and values; the rich are simply floating away from everyone else, not just financially but emotionally too. Both developments are profoundly unhealthy. Solutions to the problems of this era cannot be only economic. They must be cultural as well.

These six principles shape and inform the recommendations that follow. I am not a policy analyst by trade, and while I have spent many hours reading, thinking, and talking with experts about the nation's problems, I offer this plan with humility. Collectively, these ideas make sense to me as a way of restoring America's social and economic health. They begin in response to the nation's most-immediate problems and then move to longer-term concerns.

HELPING TO HEAL A SICK ECONOMY

In 1937, as Franklin Roosevelt began his second term, the U.S. economy seemed to be on the mend. Unemployment was still very high, but it had come down greatly, from nearly 25 percent at its peak in 1933 (and nearly 20 percent in 1935) to about 14 percent. The economy was clearly improving, and the private sector seemed to be returning to health. And although worries about jobs and incomes remained intense, they jostled, increasingly, with concerns over government debt. In 1936, after years of deficits, about 65 percent of the American population had said the budget absolutely needed to be balanced, many even supporting higher taxes to do it. And so, in 1937, the federal government raised taxes and slashed spending. Demand plummeted, and in August 1937, the stock market collapsed again; the unemployment rate rose to 19 percent in 1938, and didn't fall below its 1937 level until 1941. World War II and the spending it generated ultimately restored the economy to health.

Deficit spending intuitively feels irresponsible today. It nearly always does during a downturn: in the recession of the early 1980s, for instance, three out of four Americans were somewhat or very worried that government debt would choke off the recovery, although as a share of the economy, the debt was less than half what it is today. (Debt kept rising as a share of the economy through 1995, and remained far above its early-'80s level throughout the boom years of the 1990s.)

The size of the debt really is a cause for serious concern today. The ratio of government debt held by the public to U.S. GDP, about 62 percent in 2010, is still substantially lower than it was during the World War II era (the debt ratio peaked at about 109 percent in 1946, and was above 70 percent from 1943 through 1950; average debt for the 1950s as a whole was about 58 percent). But it's higher now than it has ever been since that time, and it has been growing very quickly since the crash. There are no signs that investors fear an imminent fiscal crisis; they continue to buy U.S. Treasury notes that pay extremely low interest rates. And other countries have more recently carried larger debts than ours for many years without any crisis, although international comparisons are complicated and of limited value. No one knows exactly how large the federal government's debt could grow before it would prompt a crisis—or at least a crippling loss of confidence. Many observers believe that stabilizing the debt at no more than 60 percent of GDP, in the long run, is critical to maintaining confidence in the government.

Yet concerns over the national debt need to be put in their proper context. One reason the debt has grown so much as a share of the economy since 2007 is that the economy shrank and has bounced back only weakly. And lower-than-normal tax receipts, not extra spending, accounted for much of the deficit from 2008 to 2010; actual government revenues in 2010 were roughly $800 billion less than they had been projected to be back in 2007—that's more than half of the 2010 deficit—and a sizable portion of the reduction resulted directly from the economic slump. Revenues will rise automatically, of course, as the economy returns to health.

In the short run, austerity, not deficit spending, would be irresponsible. One clear lesson from the aftermath of other major crashes is that incipient recoveries remain uncertain for a long time, and are vulnerable even to small shocks. When the economy is fragile, measures to cut the deficit can be highly counterproductive, setting off a chain reaction of reduced demand, lower growth, job cuts, and further reductions in the tax base—all yielding a more deeply troubled economy and another large deficit the next year.

Jobs are scarce and out-of-work applicants are plentiful across nearly every sector of the economy today; unemployment in 2010 was roughly double its 2007 rate, or more, in every major sector save for leisure and lodging. The unemployment rate even for young college grads—who have not yet yoked themselves to any particular industry and who have strong, generalizable skills—was 9.4 percent in 2010, nearly double its level in 2007. All of this suggests quite strongly that depressed demand is the biggest problem facing the economy in the near term. As much as Americans were overspending before the crash, they are underspending today as they rebuild their finances; once that process is complete, they'll be able to spend more again. In the meantime, though, the long dip in demand is causing all manner of problems. To avoid economic backsliding and enable a faster, more broadly shared recovery, we will probably need to run large deficits for the next two or three years.

Few would deny that the U.S. government was reckless with its finances during the aughts. And it would be just as reckless to keep running big deficits without highly credible reassurances that the government will begin to balance its books the moment the economy is healthy again. Ultimately, it is not this year's deficit, or next year's, that poses a significant risk to the economy. It is the prospect of endless large deficits—and fears that the government lacks the political will to close them. Those fears have little to do with recession-fighting. The problem has not been deficits during times of economic weakness, but rather their continuation during times of good health. Even more so, fears are driven by the continuing, runaway growth in spending on Medicare—the overwhelming reason why our budgetary future looks grim.

To restore confidence in the federal government without undermining the recovery, we must tie current deficits to binding measures that will close the budget gap and stabilize the national debt in the near future. By early 2011, several bipartisan plans had been developed to do just that, including the Bowles-Simpson plan, developed at the behest of the White House, and the Bipartisan Policy Center's Debt Reduction Task Force's plan. We should immediately pass legislation that requires aggressive deficit cutting, beginning in two or three years and containing automatic triggers that will impose across-the-board spending cuts and tax increases if Congress cannot come to agreement on a budget that conforms to the law. Better still, we should pass a binding commitment to a budgetary balance or surplus whenever the economy is objectively healthy (for instance, whenever unemployment is below, say, 6 percent, and economic growth exceeds a certain threshold). Every category of spending must be on the table for cuts, including defense and entitlements. We should also embark on tax reform to broaden the tax base and close distortionary loopholes.

As painful and contentious as it will be, we should also focus immediately on the real source of our long-term budgetary problems: Medicare. The health-care-reform bill of 2010 contained measures designed to reduce the growth in health-care costs over time, and they may, but it's difficult to take that to the bank today. We should either provide more authority to the new Independent Payment Advisory Board tasked with reducing growth in Medicare spending, or consider converting Medicare into a system of vouchers with which seniors can buy health insurance, with the growth in annual voucher payments strictly limited to a rate below that at which medical costs have historically grown.

Fiscal policy as a means of raising or sustaining demand is inherently leaky—some of the money injected into the economy just flows right out as people use it to buy imported goods, and some people don't spend the extra money in their pockets at all, saving it instead. The initial stimulus, of necessity, was something of a shotgun blast, showering cash into the economy in any way possible at a time when the economy was in free fall. Today, we need rifle shots—targeted efforts that can deliver maximum impact for each dollar spent.

Aid to the states is one good example. Bound by balanced-budget requirements and facing huge tax shortfalls, many state and local governments have begun firing teachers, police, and other employees by the thousands. Initial stimulus funds helped these governments cover shortfalls, keeping people employed. But those funds have largely run out. In early 2011, the city of Camden, New Jersey, laid off 168 police officers—46 percent of its police force—along with 67 firefighters and more than 100 other municipal employees. A resumption of federal aid to states would preserve some of these jobs until tax revenues rise again, and keep more money circulating in local economies throughout the nation. Further measures to support the unemployed would likewise bolster demand efficiently and immediately; the unemployed typically spend their benefits quickly and entirely—they can seldom afford to save.

One of the best targets for spending today—with both jobs and competitiveness in mind—is infrastructure. For years, the United States has let its infrastructure age and deteriorate; in 2009, the average age of public infrastructure was at a forty-year high. The American Society of Civil Engineers gave U.S. infrastructure a D grade overall in its 2009 Report Card for America's Infrastructure, down from a C about twenty years ago; public transit, roads, airports, dams, levees, schools, and energy infrastructure all received D grades. Over the past decade, the United States has slipped considerably in the World Economic Forum's global ranking of physical infrastructure, and it's not hard to see why. China spends about 9 percent of its GDP on infrastructure each year, and Europe 5 percent. The United States, by contrast, spends about 2.5 percent; we've been underinvesting for years.

The 2009 stimulus included heavy funding for infrastructure, but that money is now largely spent. With much of the construction industry idled, materials costs low, and useful projects abundant, what better time to make further investments? Infrastructure is of course the backbone of any economy, and arguably, the free and rapid flow of people and goods becomes more important to sustaining growth as economies become more advanced. We need to renew our commitment not only to maintaining the infrastructure we have, but to building new infrastructure—a good investment regardless of the state of the economy.

Not all of this investment need come at taxpayer expense. Around the country, governments at every level are experimenting with innovative approaches to financing infrastructure investment—

for instance, by using public dollars to subsidize private investment, thus leveraging government funds. By pulling spending forward and partnering with private investors, the government can help create productive jobs now; and by raising our long-term commitment to infrastructure investment, we can sustain many of those jobs in the long run. Those jobs would be of exactly the sort that are attractive and attainable for many men without four-year college degrees, a group whose struggles the Great Recession has intensified.

Tax cuts and government spending won't fix the various *structural* problems that afflict the economy. Simply juicing demand won't magically turn factory workers into nurses any faster, nor will it turn laid-off high-school graduates into more-skilled college grads. These are real problems (more on this in a moment). But demand is the bigger problem in the short run. At an absolute minimum, we should not risk recovery by premature fiscal tightening. And targeted expansion in some areas of the budget could hasten recovery and speed job growth. The Congressional Budget Office estimates that the initial stimulus saved perhaps 3 million full-time equivalent jobs and boosted output by perhaps 2 percent in the fourth quarter of 2010, though its impact was by then diminishing. Stimulus is expensive, no doubt, but, as the economist Adam Posen has written, it is effective when it's tried.

GETTING PEOPLE MOVING AGAIN

The suppleness of the U.S. economy has long been a point of pride for Americans, and rightly so. Historically, few other countries have adapted as quickly or as well to the continual rise and fall of companies, industries, cities, and regions. The government has generally kept red tape to a minimum, allowing companies to hire and fire freely. And American workers have responded quickly to market incentives, moving readily from place to place and from industry to industry. Americans' nomadic tendencies—as to both place and career—have been a boon.

Reviving that nomadic spirit is essential to restoring economic health today. The housing bubble and everything that went along with it has left the economy badly distorted—-with too many workers in construction and too many families in former real-estate boomtowns that can no longer sustain them. Yet rarely have so many Americans been stuck in place.

Economic woes are not distributed evenly across the country today; although unemployment is higher than usual just about everywhere, job opportunities vary widely from city to city and state to state. At the end of 2010, the unemployment rate was 14.9 percent in Las Vegas and 6.5 percent in Minneapolis. In February 2011, the ratio of unemployed people to job vacancies was almost nine to one in Las Vegas and Miami; more than six to one in Detroit; and less than two to one in Baltimore, Hartford, Washington, DC, New York, and San Jose. Some of these disparities are likely to increase as general demand returns; places like Nevada, Florida, and Michigan are all suffering from the collapse of locally dominant industries that may not bounce all the way back. Yet since the recession began, the rate of migration has fallen to its lowest level on record. In a 2010 Rutgers University survey of the unemployed, two-thirds of respondents said they were unable to move to another city or town for a job. Immobility is likely to prolong the jobs recession and prevent a full recovery.

In fact, mobility has been declining for many years, and for many reasons (for one thing, the population is aging, and older people have deeper roots than young ones). But housing is surely one particularly important reason today. The rate of homeownership rose markedly in the aughts, and while widespread homeownership has some social benefits, it also makes moving more difficult and expensive. With the housing market now paralyzed by foreclosures and uncertainty, that problem has become severe. The rising prevalence of two-earner families, perversely, has also left many people stuck in place. An employed spouse or partner has been a godsend to many people who've lost their job. But it has also made moving more risky, particularly in a tough economic climate. As a result, many families are staying put and scraping by in the most depressed places, keeping the unemployment rate elevated and the economy below its potential.

In the short run, the government should do everything it can to get the housing market running smoothly again, so that houses can change hands faster and their real value within each community can be more confidently established. That means policies that will help foreclosures clear more quickly, rather than delay them, and an end to policies that seek to keep people in houses they cannot afford. For the long run, we should reconsider whether the promotion and massive subsidization of homeownership—through mortgage-interest tax deductions and other measures—is doing the nation more harm than good. An end to policies that encourage homeownership over renting would restore some of the workforce flexibility that's been lost, while also eliminating the incentive to overinvest in houses. And the gradual elimination of the mortgage-interest tax deduction would improve the budget outlook.

The Internet has made it much easier for people to identify potential job opportunities from afar. By and large, motivated people can see potential opportunities; they just can't always reach them. A temporary relocation-assistance program could diminish the financial risk of moving and help cover the expense of getting set up in a new city or region, encouraging migration. Under the Trade Adjustment Assistance Program, established in 1974, workers who've been displaced by the movement of jobs overseas are already eligible for reimbursement of some of the costs they incur while looking for work in other regions of the country; moving expenses are also covered. We should offer similar assistance to unemployed workers in badly depressed states or city-regions, to enable faster migration to more dynamic places. As a lower-cost alternative to grants, the economists Jens Ludwig and Steven Raphael have suggested a program of low-interest loans for relocation, payable only once work is found, in the same basic model as college loans.

Many unemployed people today aren't just stuck in the wrong city or region; they're stuck in shrinking industries or with obsolescent skills. Construction, for instance, is unlikely to return to its previous share of the economy, and many of the construction jobs that have been lost will never come back as a result. And across industries, many companies, having restructured operations during the recession, are looking for workers with different skills than the ones they laid off had. In a 2010 survey by the National Association of Manufacturers, about one in three industrial companies reported moderate or serious skills shortages in the local workforce.

Since the crash, the government has provided expanded financial assistance for retraining. Retraining programs have a mixed history, but they can be effective when closely coordinated with the needs of local employers. In some places, what employers need is a higher level of literacy and mathematical ability than is prevalent in the wage-earning population. (For instance, Ben Venue Laboratories, a drug maker located outside Cleveland, posted a hundred new job openings in 2010, at $13 to $15 an hour, but many of the 3,600 applicants could not read and do math at a ninth-grade level, as the jobs required; after several months, the company had hired only 47 people.) Basic training in generalizable skills should always be on offer.

Where jobs simply aren't open, the immediate payoff of retraining will be limited. Nonetheless, by providing people with a new or broader set of skills, these programs enable faster absorption back into the workforce as demand rises. We should support that strongly.

Unavoidably, many people who lost their job in the Great Recession will ultimately end up in jobs that don't make full use of the particular skills they developed in their last job, and that pay much less, too (pay cuts of 20 or 30 percent are typical). That sort of reduction in pay and status can be extremely difficult, both financially and psychologically—so much so that some people hold out as long as they possibly can in the hope, often vain, that they'll find something closely equivalent to their old job. Beyond a certain point, that typically ends up being a bad decision; they would be better off jumping more quickly to a new job or new industry and starting the climb back up. The economy would be better off, too.

That's one reason why time limits on unemployment benefits are important when jobs are widely available. Incentives matter, and a large literature shows that lengthy unemployment benefits (and other welfare spending that is not tied to work) tend to lead to longer bouts of unemployment and lower levels of employment overall. Historically, the comparatively short duration of unemployment benefits in the United States (the duration varies by state, but roughly six months has been typical in normal times), along with efforts to tie other forms of assistance to work, have advantaged the United States over many countries in Europe, for instance—keeping more people in the workforce, speeding economic adjustment, and diminishing the prevalence of chronic unemployment and its associated ills.

That said, these are not normal times, and while some unemployed Americans today are undoubtedly being too picky or simply trying to wait the recession out, as a practical matter it is impossible to distinguish them from the many others who simply cannot get full-time work of any sort, or of a kind that makes at least *some* use of truly valuable skills, knowledge, or abilities that they have developed. The temporary extension of unemployment benefits to up to ninety-nine weeks has been entirely warranted by economic conditions, and we should strongly consider a longer duration still, until unemployment rates come down meaningfully. For people who've been unemployed for more than, say, six months, we might add a requirement that they need to be engaged in either part-time work or some form of retraining, in an effort to keep them attached to the workforce.

So how can we nudge people toward making a jump to a different job or career, even when that means a substantial loss in pay? One measure that deserves serious attention is a "wage insurance" program for middle- and working-class Americans—something that's also already available to workers who've lost their jobs due to trade liberalization. Wage insurance kicks in when unemployed people find a new job that pays less than their old one, making up a part of the difference—say, half—for a couple of years. It makes downward mobility a little less jarring, and might be justified solely on those grounds. But it also provides a positive incentive for unemployed people to accept lower-paying jobs more quickly—allowing them to jump more easily to new careers or growing industries where they might ultimately have a brighter future, and moving the economy more quickly back toward full employment. (To further encourage timely jumps to new jobs, beyond a certain duration of unemployment, the portion of any wage difference that's covered by wage insurance could be gradually reduced.) Wage insurance wouldn't be cheap—one 2007 estimate placed its costs at around $3.5 billion in a typical year—but it would help some people take new jobs more quickly, reducing unemployment benefits paid out and increasing income-tax revenues. And in a tumultuous economy where careers are less secure than they used to be—and where flexibility is more important than ever—it's the sort of measure we should support both inside and outside of recession.

Finally, there is the special matter of the long-term unemployed. Many people who lost their job in the recession have already been unemployed for two years or more, and that number will swell further before recovery is complete. Especially for those with limited skills, finding work again will likely be very difficult. We should consider offering aggressive wage subsidies to employers who hire the long-term unemployed, making that hire extremely cheap for, say, a year before the subsidy is withdrawn. By providing a targeted and temporary incentive, we can help long-displaced workers shed the stigma that they have developed, rebuild skills and work habits, and reenter mainstream society. Even workers who are not retained after the subsidy is removed will emerge with recent work history, reacquainted with the rhythms of the workplace.

It takes time for mid-career workers to acquire new skills, find new industries, and resettle in new places. But the measures outlined above would speed the structural changes that need to happen—helping workers, and helping the economy to recover its dynamism and resiliency. Along with an accommodating fiscal policy, they can help bring to an end the most-urgent problems that the recession has caused.

Still, in the longer term, we need to do more than merely pull ourselves out of the hole that the recession created. As technology and global integration continue to remake the U.S. economy, many of the best characteristics of American society—widespread opportunity, a broad middle class, exuberant growth that borders on the chaotic—are being threatened. The old foundations of our economy and culture are being eroded by powerful, global changes. We need new ones.

DOING WHAT WE DO BEST—BUT BETTER

In 2010, the McKinsey Global Institute released a report detailing just how mighty America's multinational companies are—and how essential they have become to the U.S. economy. Multinationals employed 19 percent of the private-sector workforce in 2007, earned 25 percent of gross private-sector profits, and paid out 25 percent of all private-sector wages. They accounted for nearly three-quarters of the nation's private-sector R&D spending. Since 1990, they've been responsible for 31 percent of the growth in real GDP.

Yet for all their outsized presence, they have been puny as engines of job creation. Over the past twenty years, multinationals have accounted for 41 percent of all gains in U.S. labor productivity—but just 11 percent of the gains in private-sector employment. And in the past decade, that picture has grown uglier: according to the economist Martin Sullivan, from 1999 through 2008, U.S. multinationals shrank their domestic workforce by about 1.9 million, while increasing foreign employment by about 2.4 million.

The heavy footprint of multinational companies is merely one sign of how inseparable the U.S. economy has become from the larger global economy. Still, these figures neatly illustrate two larger points. First, we can't wish away globalization or turn our backs on trade; to try to do so would be crippling and impoverishing. And second, something has nonetheless gone wrong with the way America's economy has evolved in response to increasingly dense global connections, especially in the past decade.

Particularly since the 1970s, the United States has placed its bets on continuous innovation, accepting the rapid transfer of production to other countries as soon as products mature and their manufacture becomes routine, all with the idea that the creation of new products and services will more than make up for that outflow. The nation has nearly always benefited from its orientation toward the future, rather than the past, and from its entrepreneurialism and readiness to adapt. This strategy is very much in keeping with those core precepts, and at times it has paid off big. Rapid innovation in the 1990s allowed the economy to grow quickly and create good, new jobs up and down the ladder to replace those that were obsolescing or moving overseas. Yet in recent years, that process has broken down.

One reason, writes the economist Michael Mandel, is that America no longer enjoys the economic fruits of new innovation for as long as it used to. Knowledge, R&D, and business know-how depreciate more quickly now than they did even fifteen years ago, because global communication is faster, connections more seamless, and human capital more broadly diffused than in the past. Mandel writes:

The value of knowledge capital depends, in part, on how rare it is. The more companies or countries that possess the same knowledge (say, about how to make a commercial airliner), the less valuable that knowledge is. . . . Over the past 10–15 years, the strengthening of information flows into developing countries meant that knowledge capital was being distributed much more quickly around the world. As a result, the normal process of knowledge capital depreciation greatly accelerated in the U.S. and Europe—beneath the radar screen, because no statistical agency constructs a set of knowledge capital accounts.

The product cycle—with initial production in the richest and most innovative places, then moving eventually to lower-labor-cost countries—has sped up in recent decades, and domestic production booms have ended sooner. (IT-hardware production, for instance, which in 1999 the Bureau of Labor Statistics projected would create about 155,000 new jobs over the following decade, actually shrank by nearly 500,000 jobs. Jobs in data processing also fell, presumably as a result of both offshoring and technological advance.) Because innovations depreciate faster, we need more of them than we used to in order to sustain the same rate of economic growth.

Yet in the aughts, as an array of prominent economists and entrepreneurs have recently pointed out, the rate of big innovations actually slowed considerably; with the housing bubble fueling easy growth for much of that time, we just didn't notice. This slowdown may have merely been the result of bad luck—big breakthroughs of the sort that create whole categories of products or services are difficult to predict, and long droughts are not unknown. Overregulation in certain areas may also have played a role. The Columbia University professors Edmund Phelps and Leo Tilman point to a patent system that's become stifling; an increasingly myopic focus among public companies on quarterly results, rather than long-term value creation; and, not least, a financial industry that for a generation has focused its talent and resources not on funding business innovation but on proprietary trading, regulatory arbitrage, and arcane financial engineering. The economist Tyler Cowen, in his 2011 book, *The*

Great Stagnation, argues that the scientific frontier itself—or at least that portion of it that leads to commercial innovation—has been moving outward more slowly, and requiring ever-more resources to do so, for many decades, and that we've now plucked most of the low-hanging fruit from major advances deep in the past.

Process innovation has been quite rapid in recent years. U.S. multinationals and other companies are very good at continually improving their operational efficiency by investing in IT, restructuring operations, and shifting work around the globe. Some of these activities benefit some U.S. workers, by making the jobs that stay in the country more productive. But absent big breakthroughs that lead to new products or services—and given the vast reserves of low-wage but increasingly educated labor in China, India, and elsewhere—rising operational efficiency hasn't been a recipe for strong growth in either jobs or common wages in the United States. New products and services are extremely important to the future of the economy.

America has huge advantages as an innovator. Innovative clusters like Silicon Valley, North Carolina's Research Triangle, and the Massachusetts high-tech corridor are difficult to replicate, and the United States has many of them. Foreign students still flock here, and foreign engineers and scientists who get their doctorates here have been staying on for longer and longer over the past fifteen years. When you compare apples to apples, the United States still leads the world, handily, in the number of skilled engineers, scientists, and business professionals in residence.

But we need to better harness those advantages to speed the pace of innovation, in part by putting a much higher national priority on investment—rather than consumption—in the coming years. Among other things, that means substantially raising and broadening both national and private investment in basic scientific progress and in later-stage R&D—through a combination of more federal investment in scientific research, perhaps bigger tax breaks for private R&D spending, and a much lower corporate tax rate (and a simpler corporate tax code) overall. Phelps and Tilman have proposed the creation of a National Innovation Bank that would invest in, or lend to, innovative start-ups—bringing more money to bear than venture-capital funds could, and at a lower cost of capital, which would promote more investment and enable the funding of somewhat riskier ventures. (The broader idea behind such a bank is that because innovation carries so many ambient benefits—from job creation to the experience gained by even failed entrepreneurs and the people around them—we should be willing to fund it more liberally as a society than private actors would individually.)

Putting more public money into research and innovation of course means putting less of it elsewhere—one more reason why institutionalizing greater budget discipline and continuing the reform of entitlements like Medicare is so critical. And even as we invest more in scientific progress and new business breakthroughs, we need to recognize that because the benefits of innovation diffuse more quickly now, the return on such national investment may be lower than it was in previous decades. Despite these drawbacks and trade-offs, the alternative to heavier investment is dismal to contemplate.

Removing bureaucratic obstacles to innovation is at least as important as pushing more public funds toward it. As Wall Street has amply demonstrated, not every industry was overregulated in the aughts. Nonetheless, the decade did see the accretion of a number of well-intentioned regulatory measures that may have chilled the investment climate (the Sarbanes-Oxley accounting reforms and a proliferation of costly security regulations following the creation of the Department of Homeland Security are two prominent examples).

Regulatory balance is always difficult in practice, but Mandel has suggested a couple of useful rules of thumb. One is that where new and emerging industries are concerned—industries at the forefront of the economy that could provide big bursts of growth—our bias should be toward light regulation where possible, allowing creative experimentation and encouraging rapid growth. (A corollary is that we should be careful not to overburden young, small companies in particular. The Sarbanes-Oxley reforms, for instance, are especially punishing to newer firms, which do not have the same resources to put toward documentation of compliance that larger, more established ones do.) The growth of the Internet in the 1990s is a good example of the benefit that can come from a light regulatory hand early on in an industry's growth; green technology, wireless platforms, and social-networking technologies are perhaps worthy of similar treatment today.

A second rule of thumb is that our regulatory bias should be countercyclical. In times like these, when growth is depressed and companies are hesitant to invest anyway, we should, on the margins, lean toward lighter regulation. In periods of strong growth—when exuberance and the easy availability of investment capital, along with the inattentiveness that typically accompanies both, can inspire mischief—the government should tend toward a more aggressive approach.

One of the cheapest, fastest, and most leveraged actions we can take to increase the country's innovative capacity is to simply let in a larger number of creative, highly educated, highly skilled immigrants each year The United States remains tremendously attractive to entrepreneurial and technically skilled foreigners around the globe, but not many are allowed to work here. Only about 65,000 H-1B visas for highly skilled foreign workers are available each year, along with another 20,000 for those who have an advanced degree from a U.S. university. The supply of willing workers is of course far larger, and so is the demand from U.S. companies. We should vastly increase the number of these visas, ease the path to permanent residency, and create new avenues for foreign entrepreneurs and scientists to relocate here. One group of venture capitalists has suggested a new sort of visa, a "start-up visa," open to any foreigner who has a business idea that a U.S. venture-capital firm is willing to fund; a bill based on this idea, the StartUp Visa Act, is before Congress at the time of this writing. We should pass it.

Most important, of course, an innovation economy depends on an excellent education system and a highly educated workforce—

both historic advantages of the United States that are now diminishing relative to other countries. Improving educational attainment in the United States is essential to keeping America at the forefront of the global economy, and ensuring that high-quality educational opportunities are available to everyone is an imperative social goal.

Over the past decade, the country has taken some good steps toward fixing the problems with its educational system, though more are needed. Commitments to excellence and access beginning even in preschool; to meeting clear standards, school by school; to school choice and experimentation with different educational models; and to subjecting teachers to the same consequences for poor performance that nearly every other American worker faces—all of these measures are crucial to improving the nation's human capital and enabling strong growth in the long run. A special focus on improving the educational opportunities of disadvantaged children is essential: more than half of the children from high-income families graduate from college in the United States; just 11 percent of those from low-income families do the same.

Finally, as we strive toward faster innovation, we also need to prevent the production of new, high-value goods from leaving American shores too quickly. Protectionist measures are generally self-defeating, and can prompt larger trade wars. And while vigilance against the theft of intellectual property and strong sanctions when such theft is discovered are sensible, they are unlikely to alter the basic trends of technological and knowledge diffusion. (Much of that diffusion is entirely legal, and the long history of industrialization and globalization suggests that attempts to halt it will fail.) What *can* really matter economically is a fair exchange rate. Throughout much of the aughts and continuing to the present day, China, in particular, has taken extraordinary measures to keep its currency undervalued relative to the dollar, and this has harmed U.S. industry. We must press China on currency realignment, putting sanctions on the table if necessary.

Given some of the workforce trends of the past decade, doubling down on technology, innovation, and globalization may seem counterintuitive. And indeed, this strategy is no cure-all. Too often, it has been viewed as the beginning and end of what we need to do as a nation to ensure a broadly shared prosperity. We are right to view it as the beginning; without a vibrant, innovative economy, all other prospects dim. But even in boom times, many more people than we would care to acknowledge won't have the education, skills, or abilities to prosper in a pure and globalized market, shaped by enormous labor reserves in China, India, and other developing countries. Over the next couple of decades or more, even if national economic growth is strong, what we do to help and support moderately educated Americans may well determine whether the United States remains a middle-class country.

FILLING THE HOLE IN THE MIDDLE CLASS

In *The Race Between Education and Technology*, the economists Claudia Goldin and Lawrence Katz make a compelling argument that throughout roughly the first three-quarters of the twentieth century, most Americans prospered and inequality fell because while technological advance was rapid—and mostly biased toward people with relatively advanced skills—educational advance was faster still; the pool of people who could take advantage of new technologies kept growing larger, while the pool who could not stayed relatively small. Elementary education had become free and accessible to most citizens in the nineteenth century, and high-school participation and graduation rose meteorically in the first half of the twentieth; a rise, initially rapid, in college completion followed in short order.

Since the 1970s, however, growth in educational attainment has slowed to a crawl; college-completion rates have grown exceedingly slowly since the early 1970s, and even high-school graduation rates have been flat. Meanwhile, with remarkable speed, younger people in many other countries have caught up to or surpassed their

American peers in the classroom. Relatively fewer Americans are in the educational vanguard today, and vastly more foreign workers possess the moderate skills learned in high school (and beyond). These factors have put pressure on the middle and lower classes and increased the income premium that's gone to those Americans who are in the educational vanguard—a vanguard now filled largely by those with graduate degrees, not merely bachelor's degrees.

The call to redouble our national commitment to educational opportunity and advancement is loud for a reason: educational progress has long been at the heart of the nation's success, not only helping the economy grow faster, but also helping to ensure widespread benefits from that growth. There would be no better tonic for the country's recent ills than a resumption of the rapid advance of skills and abilities throughout the population. Clearly there is room for improvement. About 30 percent of young adults finish college today, yet as noted above, that figure is 50 percent among those with affluent parents. It follows that with improvements in the K–12 school system, better home environments, and widespread financial access to college, we eventually could move to a 50 percent college graduation rate. And because IQ worldwide has been increasing slowly from generation to generation—a somewhat mysterious development known as the "Flynn effect"—higher rates still may eventually come within reach.

Yet the past three decades of experience suggest that this upward migration, even to, say, 40 percent, will likely be slow and difficult. (Over the past thirty years of data, from 1979 to 2009, the percentage of people aged twenty-five to twenty-nine with a four-year college degree rose from 23.1 percent to 30.6 percent—or roughly one percentage point every four years.) And ultimately, of course, the college graduation rate is likely to hit a substantially lower ceiling than that for high school or elementary school. For a time, elementary school was the answer to the question of how to build a broad middle class in America. And for a time after that, the answer was high school. College may never provide as comprehensive an answer

in the coming decades. Over the next decade or two, college education simply cannot be the whole answer to the woes of the middle
class, since even under the rosiest of assumptions, most of the middle
of society will not have a four-year college degree.

Among the more pernicious aspects of the meritocracy as we now
understand it in the United States is the equation of merit with test-
taking success, and the corresponding belief that those who struggle
in the classroom should expect little out of life. Progress along the
meritocratic path has become measurable from a very early age. This
is a narrow way of looking at human potential, and it badly under-
serves a large portion of the population. We have beat the drum so
loudly and for so long about the centrality of a college education
that we should not be surprised when people who do not attend
college—or those who start but do not finish—go adrift at age eighteen or twenty. Grants, loans, and tax credits to undergraduate and
graduate students total roughly $160 billion each year; by contrast,
in 2004, federal, state, and local spending on employment and training programs (which commonly assist people without a college education) totaled $7 billion—an inflation-adjusted decline of about 75
percent since 1978.

As we continue to push for better K–12 schooling and wider college access, we also need to build more paths into the middle class
that do not depend on a four-year college degree. One promising
approach, as noted by Ron Haskins and Isabel Sawhill in *Creating
an Opportunity Society*, is the development of "career academies"—
schools of 100 to 150 students, within larger high schools, with a
curriculum that mixes academic coursework with hands-on technical courses designed to build work skills. Some 2,500 career academies are already in operation nationwide. Students attend classes
together and have the same guidance counselors; local employers
partner with the academies and provide work experience while the
students are still in school.

"Vocational training" programs have a bad name in the United
States, in part because many people assume they close off the

possibility of higher education. But in fact, career academy students go on to earn a postsecondary credential at the same rate as other high-school students. What's more, they develop firmer roots in the job market whether or not they go on to college or community college. One recent major study shows that on average, men who attended career academies were earning significantly more than those who attended regular high schools, both four and eight years after graduation. They were also 33 percent more likely to be married and 36 percent less likely to be an absentee father.

Career-academy programs should be expanded, as should apprenticeship programs (often affiliated with community colleges) and other, similar programs designed to build an ethic of hard work; to allow young people to develop skills and make achievements outside the traditional classroom as well as inside it; and ultimately to provide more, clearer pathways into real careers. By giving young people more information about career possibilities and a tangible sense of where they can go in life and what it takes to get there, these types of programs are likely to lead to more-motivated learning, better career starts, and a more highly skilled workforce. Their impact on boys in particular is highly encouraging. And to the extent that they can also expose boys to opportunities within growing fields like health care (and also expose them to male role models within those fields), these programs might even help erode the various stereotypes that seem to be keeping some boys locked into declining parts of the economy.

"Middle-skill" jobs are not about to vanish altogether. Many construction jobs and some manufacturing jobs will return. And there are many, many occupations—from EMTs, lower-level nurses, and X-ray technicians to plumbers and home remodelers—that trade and technology cannot readily replace, and these fields are likely to grow. A more highly skilled workforce will allow faster, more efficient growth; produce better quality; and earn higher pay.

All that said, the overall pattern of change in the U.S. labor market suggests that in the next decade or more, a larger proportion of

Americans may need to take work in occupations that have traditionally required little skill and that have historically paid low wages.
Analysis by David Autor indicates that from 1999 to 2007, low-skill
jobs grew substantially as a share of all jobs in the United States.
And while the lion's share of jobs lost during the recession were middle-skill jobs, job growth since then has been tilted steeply toward
the bottom of the economy; according to a survey by the National
Employment Law Project, three-quarters of American job growth in
2010 came within industries paying less than $15 an hour on aver-
age. One of the largest challenges that the United States will face in
the coming years will be adjusting to this reality and doing what we
can to make the jobs that have traditionally been near the bottom
of the economy better, more secure, and more fulfilling—more like
middle-class jobs, in other words.

As Richard Florida writes in *The Great Reset*, part of that process
may be under way already, due to the actions of individual companies. A growing number of companies have been rethinking retail
workforce development, to improve productivity and enhance the
customer experience, leading to more-enjoyable jobs and, in some
cases, higher pay. Whole Foods Markets, for instance, one of *Fortune*
magazine's best companies to work for, organizes its workers into
teams and gives them substantial freedom as to how they go about
their work; after a new worker has been on the job for thirty days,
the team members vote on whether the new employee has embraced
the job and the culture, and hence whether he or she should be
kept on. Best Buy actively encourages all of its employees to suggest improvements to the company's work processes, much as Toyota
does, and favors promotion from within. Trader Joe's requires that
full-time employees earn at least a median income within their community; store captains, most of them promoted from within, can
earn six figures.

The natural evolution of the economy will surely make some service jobs—even in retail—more productive, independent, and en-
joyable over time. Yet even in the best case imaginable, productivity

improvements at the bottom of the economy seem unlikely to be an adequate answer to the economic problems of the lower and middle classes, at least for the foreseeable future. Indeed, the relative decline of middle-skill jobs combined with slow increases in college completion suggests a larger pool of workers chasing jobs in retail, food preparation, security, and the like—and hence downward pressure on wages.

Whatever the unemployment rate over the next several years, the long-term problem facing American society is not that employers will literally run out of work for people to do—it's that the market value of much low-skill and some middle-skill work, and hence the wages employers can offer, may be so low that many American workers will not strongly commit to that work. Bad jobs at rock-bottom wages are a primary reason why so many people at the lower end of the economy drift in and out of work, which in turn creates highly toxic social and family problems. With little economic security and low prospects for advancement, ambivalence toward low-wage work is common, and resentments can come easily to the surface, leading to serial job loss and financial instability.

American economists on both the right and the left have long advocated the subsidization of low-wage work as a means of social inclusion—offering an economic compact with everyone who embraces work, no matter their level of skill. The Earned Income Tax Credit, begun in 1975 and expanded several times since then, does just that, and has been the country's best anti-poverty program. Yet by and large, the EITC helps only families with children. In 2008, it provided a maximum credit of nearly $5,000 to families with two children, with the credit slowly phasing out for incomes above around $16,000 and disappearing altogether at roughly $39,000. The maximum credit for workers without children (or without custody of children) was only $438. We should at least moderately increase both the level of support offered to families by the EITC and the maximum income to which it applies. Perhaps more important, we should offer much fuller support for workers without custody of children. That's a matter of basic fairness. But it's also a measure that would directly target some of the biggest budding social problems in the United States today. A stronger reward for work would encourage young, less skilled workers—men in particular—to develop solid, early connections to the workforce, improving their life prospects. And better financial footing for young, less skilled workers would increase their marriageability.

Finally, we should take steps to open the country's most dynamic cities and affluent communities to more middle- and working-class Americans. The geographic segregation of society by income and education is unhealthy in any number of ways. Within dynamic major cities, we should loosen zoning requirements, allow taller buildings, and take other measures to promote greater density and more housing supply—a strategy that would promote growth as well as reduce the price premium on housing in these areas. Around them, we should improve public transit, to make faster, cheaper commutes available. And in affluent communities that are still being built out, we should seriously consider requiring the construction of some number of low-cost housing options, as contentious as that may be, to promote more class mixing, better economic opportunities, and better access to good schools.

A continued push for better schooling, the creation of clearer paths into careers for people who don't immediately go to college, better access to affluent communities and dynamic cities, and stronger support for low-wage workers—together, these measures can help mitigate the economic cleavage of U.S. society, strengthening the middle. Combined with wage insurance and the recently passed health-care bill, which sought to make portable, continuous coverage available to everyone, these measures would help bring greater stability to most Americans in an otherwise unstable era. They would hardly solve all of society's problems, but they would create the conditions for more predictable and comfortable lives—all harnessed to continuing rewards for work and education. These, ultimately, are the most critical preconditions for middle-class life and a healthy society.

THE LIMITS OF MERITOCRACY

The panic of 1893, the crash of 1929, and the meltdown of 2008 all share a common antecedent: inequality, in the run-up to each of those disasters, was exceedingly high. Recent research has shown that this is a common pattern; highly unequal societies seem more vulnerable to financial crisis. The reasons are murky. Perhaps the middle class extends itself too much as it chases the status objects of the rich; perhaps spending by the rich on some goods, like housing, forces overspending by middle-class families who wish to live in dynamic city-regions or good school districts. Or perhaps too much money sloshing into elite investment accounts itself creates bubbles and busts (the rich save more of their money than the middle class, and invest more of those savings in high-risk instruments; when too much money is chasing limited investment opportunities, investing standards decline).

Up to a point, inequality creates incentives for education, hard work, and entrepreneurialism, and speeds economic growth. And at a more basic level, the ideal of "social justice" cuts both ways; people should of course be allowed to enjoy the fruits of their honest labor. As a society, we should be far more concerned about whether most Americans are getting ahead than about the size of the gains at the top.

Yet extreme income inequality causes a cultural separation in society that is unhealthy on its face and corrosive over time. Ultimately, it is prone to reaction, particularly when much of society is struggling.

The rich have not become that way while living in a vacuum. Technological advances, freer trade, and wider markets—along

with the policies that promote them—always benefit some people
and harm others. Economic theory is quite clear that the winners
gain more than the losers lose—the people who suffer as a result
of these forces, it is often said, can be fully compensated for their
losses; society as a whole still gains. This precept has guided U.S.
government policy for thirty years. Yet in practice, the losers are
seldom compensated, not fully and not for long. And while many
of the gains from trade and technological progress are widely spread
among consumers, the pressures on wages that result from these
same forces have been felt very differently by different classes of
Americans. Income statistics don't fully capture the improvement
in living standards brought about by technological advance (the Internet, of course, did not exist in 1970). At a minimum, however,
the income gains powered by these forces have been extraordinarily
lopsided for several decades. In the aughts, incomes grew *only* at the
top of the pyramid.

What's more, some of the policies that have most benefited the
rich have little to do with greater competition or economic efficiency.
Fortunes on Wall Street have grown so large in part because of implicit government protection against catastrophic losses, combined
with the steady elimination of government measures to limit excessive risk taking, from the 1980s right on through the crash of 2008.

Over time, the United States has expected less and less of its elite,
even as society has oriented itself in a way that is most likely to maximize their income. The top income-tax rate was 91 percent in 1960,
70 percent in 1980, 50 percent in 1986, 39.6 percent in 2000, and is
now 35 percent. Income from investments is taxed at a rate as low as
15 percent. The mortgage-interest tax deduction is most generous,
of course, to the affluent, and while it's small potatoes to anyone who
makes a good income, so, too, is the savings incentive provided by
401(k) plans. The estate tax, meanwhile, has been gutted.

As the winners have been separated more cleanly from the losers, the idea of compensating the latter out of the pockets of the
former has run into stiff resistance: that would run afoul of a dif-

ferent economic theory, dulling the winners' incentives, dispelling their entrepreneurial spirit, and punishing them for their success; some might even leave the country. And so, in a neat and perhaps unconscious two-step, some elites have pushed policies that benefit them by touting theoretical gains to society, then ruled out measures that would distribute those gains widely.

What will become of American society if these trends keep up? Even as we continue to strive to perfect the meritocracy—for of course family background still matters greatly today—signs that things may be moving in the other direction are proliferating. The increasing segregation of Americans by education and income, and the widening cultural divide between families with college-educated parents and those without them, suggests that built-in advantages and disadvantages may be growing. And the concentration of wealth in relatively few hands opens the possibility that much of the next generation's elite might achieve their status through inheritance, not hard work.

Soaking the rich is not the answer to America's problems. Holding all else equal, we would need to raise the top two tax rates to roughly 90 percent, then unrealistically assume no change in the work habits of the people in those brackets, merely to bring the deficit down to 2 percent of GDP in a typical year. Even with strong budget discipline and a reduction in the growth of Medicare costs, somewhat higher taxes for most Americans—in one form or another—seem inevitable. While we can and should cut spending in many areas, we also need to increase our national investment in infrastructure and innovation, and to provide some assistance to an increasing number of people who are falling out of the middle class. The professional middle class in particular should not expect exemption from tax increases.

But high earners should pay considerably more than they do now. Top tax rates of 50 percent for incomes in the seven-figure range would be considerably lower than their level throughout much of the postwar era, and should not be out of the question—nor should an estate-tax rate, for large estates, of similar size. Investment income should be taxed at ordinary income-tax rates (especially as the corporate tax is reduced).

We should not nourish the mercenary tendencies within today's elite. America remains a magnet for talent, for reasons that go beyond the tax code, and by international standards, none of the tax changes recommended here would create an excessive tax burden on high earners. And while we should continue to celebrate people who make great accomplishments in their work, we should also seek to inculcate a sense of social and civic responsibility among today's meritocratic winners—one that's been lost, to some extent, in recent generations. If certain financiers choose to decamp for some small island-state in search of the smallest possible tax bill, we should wish them good luck.

We need to diminish the extraordinary power held by the rich over American government. Most Americans have little problem with high earnings won on a level playing field. But wealth always brings influence, and the self-reinforcing relationship between the two can lead to policies that are unfair, anticompetitive, and bad for the economy. Nowhere is this clearer than in the financial industry, which concentrates gains in the hands of a few and—because of its relationship to the government—distributes losses among the broader public. Lax regulation of finance combined with an implicit government guarantee against failure has inspired much mischief, made many fortunes, and left the country poorer. The specifics of financial reform to limit moral hazard and rent-seeking are beyond the scope of this book (I recommend *13 Bankers,* by Simon Johnson and James Kwak, as a starting place for interested readers). But these problems remain enormous; the financial reforms undertaken since the crash have not solved them.

To the extent possible, we should keep money out of politics. Strict restrictions on campaign contributions and issue advertising, along with lobbying reform, would make our democracy healthier. The Supreme Court has struck down some measures that were designed to achieve these goals, saying they unconstitutionally violate free speech. Those decisions should be reconsidered. The former labor secretary Robert Reich has argued that all campaign contributions should go through "blind trusts" so that political candidates and office-holders cannot know who contributed to their campaigns, or how much they contributed. "The quid," he writes, "would be severed from the quo."

ONE CULTURE

Economic tumult has frayed the social fabric; if we remain in a period of slow growth and high unemployment, many aspects of public life and social relations could become more bilious than they are today. And even once employment rises back to more-normal levels again, the most-powerful economic forces of our times will remain fundamentally divisive, concentrating wealth at the top of society and putting more pressure on the middle. The great challenge of our times is adapting to and ameliorating these forces.

Politics will not be easy in the coming years, in part because the problems we face have no easy, painless political solutions. As Tyler Cowen wrote in *The Great Stagnation,* we should not pretend that they do—and we should resist the tendency to reflexively demonize those who disagree with us, rather than trying, where possible, to find common ground.

Many of the ideas presented in this chapter would help decrease the social distance that has grown between different American cliques and classes, a crucial charge if the United States is to retain a common culture. A society in which the different classes jostle more frequently alongside one another—living in the same communities and cities, harboring the same hopes and expectations for their children—is inherently healthier than one in which they are segregated physically and split by cultural norms. Broader exposure to one another would foster the ideals of civic equality and equal opportunity that are our cultural bedrock.

The information age—individualistic, experimental, boundary-breaking—has eroded other once-common virtues, ones that we do not associate as strongly with a distinctly American character, but that are nonetheless essential to a cohesive, successful society: from family commitment rooted in marriage, to civic responsibility. The Great Recession has merely cast light on the extent of that erosion. The past is not a hallowed place, and we would not want to return to it even if we could. But we do need to sow those virtues again as we move forward—through education and through our own private actions and expectations.

As with the end of the nineteenth century, the Great Depression, and the 1970s, when we look back on this period, we will see it as a time when much that was familiar came to an end. But we will also see many new beginnings. After years of profligacy, the crash and its aftermath may mark a generational turning toward thrift and personal responsibility, changes that would serve the country well for decades. We will likely remember the Great Recession not only as a time when women first became a majority of the workforce, but also more broadly as a transition from a male-centered economy to one built more around women. The end of the housing-construction boom—and the financial sector's preoccupation with housing—will surely clear the way for growth in other industries, and for the rise of new ones.

The most-important legacies of this period are, of course, unknowable today. Will education take another leap forward, as it has during the major economic transitions of the past? Will the long trend toward the concentration of income be altered—and in what manner? Will the middle class retain its optimism and its sense of unbounded opportunity?

We should not underestimate the size of the challenge the United States faces in the coming decades. But nor should we underestimate the resourcefulness of the American people in meeting it—through private invention and decisive government action, through continuing competition tempered by mutual support. The journalist James Fallows has observed that worrying over national decline is a time-honored American pastime frequently in vogue since the very foundation of the republic. Cycles of crisis and renewal appear throughout our history; at critical moments, we have always found the courage to fix what was broken in our politics, our economy, and our society.

Can we find the national courage to do that again today, though it surely means sacrifice? Can we still discern a national interest above our personal ones? Amid the strains and fissiparous forces of a new, global era, can we still find ways to mix and balance liberty with justice, self-interest with cooperation? If we are to remain one nation, in any meaningful sense of the word, we must.

NOTES

1: NOT YOUR FATHER'S RECESSION

13 *The Great Recession ended*   National Bureau of Economic Research, "Report by the Business Cycle Dating Committee," September 20, 2010, http://www.nber.org/cycles/sept2010.html5.

13 *It was the decade's second*   Bureau of Economic Analysis, "Table 1.1.6 Real Gross Domestic Product, Chained Dollars," U.S. Department of Commerce, April 28, 2011.

13 *The average house*   S&P/Case-Shiller Home Price Indices, U.S. National Index Levels, Standard & Poor's; Social & Demographic Trends Project, "How the Great Recession Has Changed Life in America," Pew Research Center (June 30, 2010), 31; Jesse Bricker, Brian Bucks, et al., "Surveying the Aftermath of the Storm: Changes in Family Finances from 2007 to 2009," Board of Governors of the Federal Reserve System, March 2011.

13 *The Dow, from peak to trough*   Gerald P. Dwyer, "Stock Prices and the Financial Crisis," Federal Reserve Bank of Atlanta, September 2009.

13 *One hundred and sixty-five commercial banks*   Federal Deposit Insurance Corporation, "Failures and Assistance Transactions: 2007–2009," http://www2.fdic.gov/hsob/HSOBSummaryRpt.asp?BegYear=2009&EndYear=2007&State=1.

13 *"I think the unemployment rate"*   Tom Raum, "Higher Jobless Rates Could Be Here to Stay," Associated Press, October, 19, 2009.

14 *What few jobs*   National Employment Law Project, "A Year of Unbalanced Growth: Industries, Wages, and the First 12 Months of Job Growth After the Recession," February 2011.

14 *Inevitably, the rhythm of life*   Joe Rojas-Burke, "Does Our Health Actually Get Better in Some Ways During a Down Economy?" *Oregonian* (Portland), April 22, 2009; National Highway Traffic Safety Administration, "National Statistics," www.fars.nhtsa.dot.gov/main/index.aspx; Pierre Brochu et al., "The 'Trendiness' of Sleep: An Empirical Investigation into the Cyclical Nature of Sleep Time" (working paper 0909E, Department of Economics, University of Ottawa, 2009); Benjamin Schwarz, "Life in (and After) Our Great Recession," *Atlantic*, October 2009.

14   *Pop songs become*   Terry F. Pettijohn and Donald F. Sacco, "The Language of Lyrics: An Analysis of Popular Billboard Songs Across Conditions of Social and Economic Threat," *Journal of Language and Social Psychology* 28, no. 3 (September 2009): 297–311.

14   *Fewer weddings have been celebrated*   "Births, Marriages, Divorces, and Deaths: Provisional Data for 2009," *National Vital Statistics Reports* 58, no. 25 (August 2010), http://www.cdc.gov/nchs/data/nvsr/nvsr58/nvsr58_25.pdf; National Center for Children in Poverty, http://www.nccp.org/.

14   *Bewilderment . . . has filled*   Peter S. Goodman, "Despite Signs of Recovery, Chronic Joblessness Rises," *New York Times*, February 20, 2010; Emily Yoffe, "The Visit That Never Ends," *Slate,* December 21, 2010, http://www.slate.com/id/2277569/.

15   *"There's no end to this"*   Peter S. Goodman, "Real Estate in Cape Coral, Florida, Is Far from a Recovery," *New York Times*, January 2, 2010.

15   *Part of the answer stems*   Carmen M. Reinhart and Kenneth S. Rogoff, "The Aftermath of Financial Crises," *American Economic Review* 99, no. 2 (May 2009): 466–72, http://www.nber.org/papers/w14656.pdf.

16   *the housing bubble distorted*   Michael Mandel, "Why We Struggle: Too Much Housing, Too Little Information Technology," *Mandel on Innovation and Growth* (blog), August 29, 2010, http://innovationandgrowth.wordpress.com/2010/08/29/why-we-struggle-too-much-housing-too-little-information-technology/.

17   *The construction, real-estate*   Bureau of Economic Analysis, "Value Added by Industry as a Percentage of Gross Domestic Product," U.S. Department of Commerce, 2010.

17   *the ten years prior*   David Leonhardt, "A Decade with No Income Gains," *New York Times*, September 10, 2009.

17   *Housing is . . . the largest asset*   Edward N. Wolff, "Recent Trends in Household Wealth in the United States: Rising Debt and the Middle-Class Squeeze—An Update to 2007" (working paper 589, Levy Economics Institute of Bard College, March 2010), http://www.levyinstitute.org/pubs/wp_589.pdf.

17   *more families have lost*   Justin Lahart, "The Great Recession: A Downturn Sized Up," *Wall Street Journal*, July 28, 2009.

17   *Nationwide, nearly one in four houses*   Zillow.com, "Real Estate Market Report," February 9, 2011, http://zillow.mediaroom.com/index.php?s=159&item=221.

17   *one in seven mortgages*   Mortgage Bankers Association, "National Delinquency Survey," 2007 and 2010.

17   *And it is by no means clear*   Gary Shilling, "Here's Why House Prices Will Now Drop Another 20%," *Business Insider*, October 5, 2010, http://www.businessinsider.com/gary-shilling-house-prices#.

18   *The ratio of household debt to disposable income*   Reuven Glick and Kevin J. Lansing, "Consumers and the Economy, Part I: Household Credit and Personal

Saving" (economic letter, Federal Reserve Bank of San Francisco, January 10, 2011), http://www.frbsf.org/publications/economics/letter/2011/el2011-01.html.

18 *as Raghuram Rajan* Raghuram Rajan, *Fault Lines: How Hidden Fractures Still Threaten the World Economy* (Princeton, NJ: Princeton University Press, 2010).

18 *exports make up only* Bureau of Economic Analysis, "Table 1.1.5. Gross Domestic Product," U.S. Department of Commerce, March 18, 2011.

18 *One big reason* The CBO estimates full-time equivalent job savings of between 1.8 and 5 million, and a boost to real GDP of between 1.1 and 3.5 percent. See Congressional Budget Office, "Estimated Impact of ARRA on Employment and Economic Output from October 2010 Through December 2010," *Director's Blog*, February 2011, http://cboblog.cbo.gov/?p=1852.

19 *with federal government debt* Martin Crutsinger, "Obama Sends Congress $3.73 Trillion Budget," Associated Press, February 14, 2011.

19 *55 percent of American workers* Social & Demographic Trends Project, "How the Great Recession Has Changed Life in America," i.

19 *In January 2011* U.S. Bureau of Labor Statistics, "Employment Situation Summary," January 2010; U.S. Bureau of Labor Statistics, "Labor Force Statistics From the Current Population Survey: Average Weeks Unemployed," January 2010.

19 *Unemployment benefits have been* Arthur Delany, "3.9 Million Americans Ran Out of Unemployment Benefits in 2010: Report," *Huffington Post,* February 10, 2011, http://www.huffingtonpost.com/2011/02/10/2010-unemployment -benefits-exhausted_n_820957.html.

19 *In February 2011* Heidi Shierholz, "February Rebounds, but Road to Jobs Recovery Remains Years Long," Economic Policy Institute, March 4, 2011.

19 *According to Andrew Oswald* Andrew Oswald, conversation with author, 2009.

20 *one attendee, Gus Poulos* Gus Poulos, conversation with author, 2009.

21 *A 2010 study* Debbie Borie-Holtz, Carl Van Horn, and Cliff Zukin, "No End in Sight: The Agony of Prolonged Unemployment" (paper, Rutgers University, May 2010), available at http://www.scribd.com/doc/32165839/Work-Trends -May-2010-No-End-in-Sight-The-Agony-of-Prolonged-Unemployment.

22 *a White House study* Peter Baker, "The White House Looks for Work," *New York Times Magazine,* January 19, 2011.

22 *As the end of 2010 approached* in e-mail message to author, "Economic Projections of Federal Reserve Governors and Reserve Bank Presidents," Board of Governors of the Federal Reserve, November 2010; Neil Irwin, "Fed Lowers Economic Expectations for 2011," *Washington Post,* November 23, 2010.

22 *If the labor recovery* Heidi Shierholz (Economic Policy Institute), conversation with author, 2009; David Leonhardt, "In the Rearview, a Year That Fizzled," *New York Times,* December 28, 2010.

22 *Jobs came back more slowly* Josh Bivens and Heidi Shierholz, "For Job Seekers, No Recovery in Sight," EPI Briefing Paper 259, Economic Policy Institute, March 31, 2010.

22 *American workers never* U.S. Bureau of Labor Statistics, "Labor Force Statistics," Current Population Survey.

22 *the economy sits* Heidi Shierholz, "February Rebounds."

23 *More than half of all the jobs* Social & Demographic Trends Project, "How the Great Recession Has Changed Life in America," 20.

23 *"In a sense"* Gary Burtless (Brookings Institution), conversation with author, 2009.

23 *the phone maker Sony Ericsson* Laura Bassett, "Disturbing Job Ads: 'The Unemployed Will Not Be Considered,' " *Huffington Post,* June 4, 2010, http://www.huffingtonpost.com/2010/06/04/disturbing-job-ads-the-un_n_600665.html; Chris Isidore, "Looking for Work? Unemployed Need Not Apply," CNNMoney.com, June 16, 2010, http://money.cnn.com/2010/06/16/news/economy/unemployed_need_not_apply/index.htm.

24 *The blight of high unemployment* Laurence Ball, "Hysteresis in Unemployment: Old and New Evidence" (working paper 14818, National Bureau of Economic Research, March 2009).

25 *The number of active militias* Southern Poverty Law Center, "Active Patriot Groups in the United States in 2010," *Intelligence Report* (Spring 2011); Southern Poverty Law Center, "Active Patriot Groups in the United States in 2007," *Intelligence Report* (Spring 2008).

25 *Business profits approached* Catherine Rampell, "Corporate Profits Were the Highest on Record Last Quarter," *New York Times,* November 23, 2010, http://www.nytimes.com/2010/11/24/business/economy/24econ.html.

2: THE TWO-SPEED SOCIETY

26 *But some of the entries* Andrew Sullivan, "The View from Your Recession," *Daily Dish* (blog), *Atlantic,* May 13, 2009, http://andrewsullivan.theatlantic.com/the_daily_dish/2009/05/the-vi.html.

26 *Another writer noted* March 17, 2009, http://andrewsullivan.theatlantic.com/the_daily_dish/2009/03/the-view-fro-45.html; January 18, 2010, http://andrewsullivan.theatlantic.com/the_daily_dish/2010/01/the-vi.html, supplemented by conversation with author.

27 *Among others writing in* March 4, 2009, http://andrewsullivan.theatlantic.com/the_daily_dish/2009/03/the-view-fro-11.html; February 28, 2009, http://andrewsullivan.theatlantic.com/the_daily_dish/2009/02/the-view-fro-38.html; March 3, 2009, http://andrewsullivan.theatlantic.com/the_daily_dish/2009/03/the-view-from-4.html.

27 *One unmistakable pattern* April 6, 2009, http://andrewsullivan.theatlantic.com/the_daily_dish/2009/04/the-view-from-your-recession-2.html.

27 *In March 2011, the unemployment rate* U.S. Bureau of Labor Statistics, e-mail message to author, April 2011. Findings are based on the Current Population Survey.

27   *job postings in February 2011*   Juju.com, "Job Search Difficulty Index," February   2011,   http://www.job-search-engine.com/press/Juju-Releases-Job -Search-Difficulty-Index-for-Major-Cities-February-2011.

27   *wages were essentially flat*   Edward Glaeser, "The Information Economy Powers Wage Increases," *Economix* (blog), *New York Times*, October 26, 2010, http://economix.blogs.nytimes.com/2010/10/26/the-information-economy -powers-wage-increases/.

28   *A 2010 Pew Research Center study*   Social & Demographic Trends Project, "How the Great Recession Has Changed Life in America," Pew Research Center (June 30, 2010), 34.

28   *The recession has even proved*   Anna Turner, "Jobs Crisis Fact Sheet," Economic Policy Institute, 2010; Hanna Rosin, "The End of Men," *Atlantic*, July/August 2010, http://www.theatlantic.com/magazine/archive/2010/07/the -end-of-men/8135/.

28   *men have reported*   Social & Demographic Trends Project, "How the Great Recession Has Changed Life in America," 59.

29   *"The Great Recession has quantitatively"*   David Autor, "The Polarization of Job Opportunities in the U.S. Labor Market: Implications for Employment and Earnings," Center for American Progress and Hamilton Project, April 2010, 2–9.

30   *"Technology has changed the game"*   Jack Welch quoted in Fareed Zakaria, "How to Restore the American Dream," *Time*, October 21, 2010, http://www .time.com/time/nation/article/0,8599,2026776,00.html#ixzz161WI283S.

30   *the total number of people*   U.S. Bureau of Labor Statistics, "Employment, Hours, and Earnings From the Current Employment Statistics Survey (National)," 2011.

31   *the United States was the second-largest*   CIA World Factbook staff, e-mail message to author, January 5, 2011.

31   *Alan Blinder estimated*   Alan Blinder, "How Many U.S. Jobs Might Be Offshorable?" (working paper 142, Center for Economic Policy Studies, Princeton University, March 2007).

32   *job losses hit America*   International Monetary Fund and International Labor Organization, "The Challenges of Growth, Employment and Social Cohesion," September 2010, 7, 44.

32   *it has come back down*   International Monetary Fund, World Economic Outlook Database, October 2010, http://www.imf.org/external/pubs/ft/weo/2010/ 02/weodata/index.aspx

32   *"I think [a middle-class life]"*   Michael Luo, "Months After Plant Closed, Many Still Struggling," *New York Times*, February 9, 2009.

33   more than half *of the nation's*   Analysis by Emmanuel Saez and Thomas Piketty in "Income Inequality in the United States, 1913–1998," *Quarterly Journal of Economics* 118, no. 1 (2003): 1–39, updated at http://www.econ.berkeley .edu/-saez/; updated tables and figures, "Table A6: Top Fractiles Income Levels

(Including Capital Gains) in the United States," July 2010, http://www.econ.berkeley.edu/~saez/.

33 *the rise of the super-elite* U.S. Bureau of Labor Statistics, "College Enrollment and Work Activity of 2002 High School Graduates," June 25, 2003.

34 *incomes for college graduates* David Leonhardt, "Education Still Pays," *Economy* (blog), *New York Times*, January 20, 2011, http://economix.blogs.nytimes.com/2011/01/20/education-still-pays/.

35 *college graduates make up* U.S. Census Bureau, "2005–2009 American Community Survey 5-Year Estimates: Educational Attainment," 2010.

35 *family income* U.S. Census Bureau, "Percent Distribution of Families, by Selected Characteristics Within Income Quintile and Top 5 Percent in 2009," *Current Population Survey 2010: Annual Social and Economic Supplement*, 2010.

35 *The share of the male population* Michael Greenstone and Adam Looney, "The Problem with Men: A Look at Long-Term Employment Trends," *Up Front* (blog), Brookings Institution, December 2, 2010, http://www.brookings.edu/opinions/2010/1203_jobs_greenstone_looney.aspx.

35 *for every two men* Rosin, "The End of Men."

36 *women earned more* Paul Wiseman, "Young, Single, Childless Women Out-Earn Male Counterparts," *USA Today*, September 2, 2010.

36 *It's the opposite trend* U.S. Bureau of Labor Statistics, "International Comparisons of Annual Labor Force Statistics, Adjusted to U.S. Concepts, 10 Countries, 1970–2009: Table 2-11. Employment-Population Ratios for Men," http://www.bls.gov/fls/flscomparelf/employment.htm#table2_11.

36 *more than 18 percent of men* U.S. Bureau of Labor Statistics, "Labor Force Statistics From the Current Population Survey: Employment-Population Ratio—Men," 2011.

37 *the urban theorist Richard Florida* Richard Florida, "Where the Brains Are," *Atlantic*, October 2006, http://www.theatlantic.com/magazine/print/2006/10/where-the-brains-are/5202/.

38 *A 2010 Brookings Institution report* Brookings Institution, "The State of Metropolitan America," May 2009, 107–8, 135.

38 *roughly as many college graduates* Aaron Renn, "College Degree Density Revisited," *The Urbanophile* (blog), December 5, 2010, http://www.urbanophile.com/2010/12/05/college-degree-density-revisited/.

38 *Powerful economic forces* Bill Bishop, *The Big Sort* (New York: Houghton Mifflin, 2008), 130–35.

39 *"superstar cities"* Joseph Gyourko, Christopher Mayer, and Todd Sinai, "Superstar Cities" (National Bureau of Economic Research Working Paper 12355, July 2006).

39 *The housing bust has revealed* James R. Follain, "A Study of Real Estate Markets in Declining Cities," Research Institute for Housing America, December 2010.

39 *In a Brookings Institution* "Bachelor's degree attainment, age 25 and over," State of Metropolitan America Indicator Map, Brookings Institution, http://

www.brookings.edu/metro/StateOfMetroAmerica/Map.aspx#/?subject=4&ind=
30&dist=1_0&data=Percent&year=2009&geo=metro&zoom=0&x=0&y=0.

3: TWO DEPRESSIONS AND A LONG MALAISE

42 *"the public features"* Alexander Keyssar, *Out of Work: The First Century of Unemployment in Massachusetts* (New York: Cambridge University Press, 1986), 57.

43 *Deflation was a fixture* Benjamin Friedman, *The Moral Consequences of Economic Growth* (New York: Knopf, 2005), 116.

43 *the availability of jobs* Robert Putnam, *Bowling Alone: The Collapse and Revival of American Community* (New York: Simon & Schuster, 2000), 360.

43 *Income inequality was* Friedman, *The Moral Consequences of Economic Growth*, 112.

43 *Charles Spaur estimated* Putnam, *Bowling Alone*, 370.

43 *perhaps half of America's families* Friedman, *The Moral Consequences of Economic Growth*, 117–18.

43 *Unemployment became* Keyssar, *Out of Work*, 9, 23–31.

44 *Some of these critics . . . Atlantic Monthly* December 1878, quoted in ibid., 19.

45 *To feed themselves* Ibid., 162.

45 *unemployment stood* Ibid., 308–11.

45 *job loss was hardest* Ibid., 95–96.

45 *"My oldest girl"* Ibid., 173–74.

46 *a group of white nativists* Putnam, *Bowling Alone*, 375; Friedman, *The Moral Consequences of Economic Growth*, 126.

46 *one person was lynched* Putnam, *Bowling Alone*, 375.

46 *"perfect cultural seedbed"* Friedman, *The Moral Consequences of Economic Growth*, 12.

46 *Like other forms* Ibid., 121–26.

47 *In nearly every aspect* Ibid., 124.

47 *"There is scarcely"* Keyssar, *Out of Work*, 76.

48 *The United States emerged* Friedman, *The Moral Consequences of Economic Growth*, 140–41.

49 *the nation's real output* Robert McElvaine, *The Great Depression: America, 1929–1941* (New York: Times Books, 1984), 75, 320.

49 *the 1920s stand out* Friedman, *The Moral Consequences of Economic Growth*, 147.

49 *Farmers still made up* McElvaine, *The Great Depression*, 11, 36.

49 *In America's towns* Ron Chernow, *The House of Morgan: An American Banking Dynasty and the Rise of Modern Finance* (New York: Atlantic Monthly Press, 1990), 302.

49 *disposable per capita income*   McElvaine, *The Great Depression*, 38–39.

50 *willingness of ordinary people*   Ibid., 40–41.

50 *Robert McElvaine wrote*   Ibid., 42.

50 *In Florida*   Ibid.

50 *The real-estate mania*   Robert Lynd and Helen Merrell Lynd, *Middletown in Transition: A Study in Cultural Conflicts* (New York: Harcourt, Brace, and Company, 1937), 190–91.

50 *Residential construction imploded*   Ibid., 190–93.

51 *The economic conditions*   Benjamin Schwarz, "Life In (and After) Our Great Recession," *Atlantic,* October 2009, http://www.theatlantic.com/magazine/archive/2009/10/life-in-and-after-our-great-recession/7651/.

51 *In her classic sociology*   Mirra Komarovsky, *The Unemployed Man and His Family* (1940; repr., Walnut Creek: AltaMira Press, 2004), esp. 23, 41.

51 *the stories paint a picture*   Komarovsky, *The Unemployed Man*, esp. 43, 94, 112.

52 *most people kept their jobs*   Lynd and Lynd, *Middletown*, 202.

52 *"In its relation to"*   Ibid., 443.

52 *Trust among strangers*   Ibid., 427–28.

53 *Disillusionment among*   Ibid., 482–84.

53 *The Lynds interviewed*   Ibid., 485.

53 *pronounced diffidence*   Glen Elder, *Children of the Great Depression* (Chicago: University of Chicago Press, 1974).

53 *the period's adolescents*   McElvaine, *The Great Depression*, 185.

54 *That's in fact*   Elder, *Children of the Great Depression*.

54 *extremism and rancor*   McElvaine, *The Great Depression*, 187.

54 *Father Charles Coughlin*   Ibid., 238–40.

55 *John Maynard Keynes wrote*   John Maynard Keynes, "Economic Possibilities for Our Grandchildren" (1930), published in *Essays in Persuasion* (New York: W. W. Norton & Co., 1963), 358–373.

56 *"more than Watergate"*   Edward Berkowitz, *Something Happened: A Political and Cultural Overview of the Seventies* (New York: Columbia University Press, 2006), 53.

56 *The seventies saw*   Ibid., 55, 67.

56 *A third recession*   For additional historical context, see Kevin Quealy, Gregory Roth, and R. M. Schneiderman, "How the Government Dealt with Past Recessions," *New York Times,* January 26, 2009, http://www.nytimes.com/interactive/2009/01/26/business/economy/20090126-recessions-graphic.html.

57 *"hopeful legacy began"*   Berkowitz, *Something Happened*, 4.

57 *Legal challenges*   Bruce Schulman, *The Seventies: The Great Shift in American Culture, Society, and Politics* (New York: The Free Press, 2001; Cambridge: Da Capo Press, 2002), 58, 70. Citations refer to the Da Capo edition.

57 *In previous decades*   Ibid., 80.

58 *Women entered the workforce*   Berkowitz, *Something Happened*, 68, 144.

58 *This revolution*   Schulman, *The Seventies*, 68.

59 *The young adults*   See, for example, ibid., xii.

59 *unemployment never neared*   U.S. Bureau of Labor Statistics, "Labor Force Statistics from the Current Population Survey: Unemployment Rate," 2011.

59 *Theodore White wrote*   Theodore White quoted in Joseph Nocera, *A Piece of the Action* (New York: Simon & Schuster, 1994), 178.

59 *houses, or at least those*   Ibid., 188–89.

60 *All of these developments*   Ibid., 193.

60 Newsweek *dubbed*   Jerry Adler, "The Year of the Yuppie," *Newsweek*, December 31, 1984.

61 *Recent academic research*   See, for example, the work of David Moss (Harvard) and Robert Frank (Cornell), summarized in Nicholas Kristof, "Our Banana Republic," *New York Times*, November 6, 2010; and Louise Story, "Income Inequality and Financial Crisis," *New York Times*, August 21, 2010.

4: GENERATION R: THE CHANGING FORTUNES OF AMERICA'S YOUTH

63 *"I'm definitely seeing"*   Steve Friess, "In Recession, Optimistic College Grads Turn Down Jobs," *New York Times*, July 24, 2009.

64 *In one recent study*   Lisa B. Kahn, "The Long-Term Labor Market Consequences of Graduating from College in a Bad Economy" (paper, Yale School of Management, 2009); Lisa Kahn, conversation with author, 2009.

65 *"Graduates' first jobs"*   Austan Goolsbee, "Hello Young Workers: One Way to Reach the Top Is to Start There," *New York Times*, May 25, 2006.

65 *This job environment*   National Association of Colleges and Employers, "Job Outlook 2011," 2011, http://www.naceweb.org/Research/Job_Outlook/Job _Outlook.aspx?referal=research&menuID=377.

66 *Strong evidence suggests*   Krysia Mossakowski, "The Influence of Past Unemployment Duration on Symptoms of Depression Among Young Women and Men in the United States," *American Journal of Public Health* 99: 1826–32; Krysia Mossakowski, conversation with author, 2009.

66 *Today in Japan*   Kenji Hall and Ian Rowley, "Japan's Lost Generation," *BusinessWeek*, May 28, 2007; additional data from the Productivity Center for Socio-Economic Development provided to author by Kenji Hall.

67 *poor health is prevalent*   Till Von Wachter and Daniel Sullivan, "Job Displacement and Mortality: An Analysis Using Administrative Data," *Quarterly Journal of Economics* 124, no. 3 (August 2009): 1265–1306; Till Von Wachter, conversation with author, 2009.

67 *various labels*   Steven Greenhouse, "As Plants Close, Teenagers Focus More on College," *New York Times*, June 25, 2009.

67 *today's young adults*   Jean Twenge, *Generation Me* (New York: Free Press, 2006); Jean Twenge, conversation with author, 2009.

68   *In her 2006 book*   Twenge, *Generation Me.*

69   *Ron Alsop, a former reporter*   Ron Alsop, "The 'Trophy Kids' Go to Work," *Wall Street Journal*, October 21, 2008; Ron Alsop, conversation with author, 2009.

69   *In his 2009 commencement*   Steve Friess, "In Recession, Optimistic."

70   *According to a recent Pew survey*   Sam Roberts, "Economy Is Forcing Young Adults Back Home in Big Numbers, Survey Finds," *New York Times*, November 24, 2009.

72   *Aubrey Howell, who'd tweeted*   Kimi Yoshino, "For the 'Funemployed,' Unemployment's Welcomed," *Los Angeles Times*, June 4, 2009; Aubrey Howell, conversation with author, 2009.

73   *rate the importance*   Allstate/*National Journal*, "Heartland Monitor Poll Topline: Generation Y," April 22–26, 2010, 8, 9.

73   *Overall, job tenure increased*   U.S. Bureau of Labor Statistics, "Employee Tenure in 2010," September 14, 2010, http://www.bls.gov/news.release/archives/tenure_09142010.htm.

73   *These trends are dispiriting*   Mike Mandel, "Where Young College Grads Are Finding Jobs: Government," *Mandel on Innovation and Growth* (blog), October 5, 2010, http://innovationandgrowth.wordpress.com/2010/10/05/where-young-college-grads-are-finding-jobs-government/.

76   *The relationship between*   "Heartland Monitor Poll," 14.

76   *Karen Fingerman indicates*   Karen Fingerman et al., "Giving to the Good and the Needy: Parental Support of Grown Children," *Journal of Marriage and Family* 71, no. 5 (December 2009): 1220–33.

76   *A May 2010 "Shouts & Murmurs"*   Simon Rich, "Your New College Graduate: A Parents' Guide" *New Yorker*, May 24, 2010, http://www.newyorker.com/humor/2010/05/24/100524sh_shouts_rich.

76   *family and financial consultants*   Alina Tugend, "Full Nest Syndrome," *National Journal*, May 8, 2010, http://nationaljournal.com/njmagazine/nj_20100508_2642.php.

76   *instead living at home*   For more on youth in Japan, see Michael Zielenziger, *Shutting Out the Sun: How Japan Created Its Own Lost Decade* (New York: Nan A. Talese, 2006); Kosugi Reiko, "Youth Employment in Japan's Economic Recovery: Freeters and NEETs," *Asia Pacific Journal: Japan Focus* (May 2006), http://japanfocus.org/-Kosugi-Reiko/2022; Peggy Orenstein, "Parasites in Prêt-à-Porter," *New York Times Magazine*, July 1, 2001; Kenji Hall and Ian Rowley, "Japan's Lost Generation," *Businessweek*, May 17, 2007; Maggie Jones, "Shutting Themselves In," *New York Times Magazine*, January 15, 2006.

77   *What often gets lost*   Pew Research Center, "Millennials: Confident. Connected. Open to Change," February 2010, 16, http://pewresearch.org/pubs/1501/millennials-new-survey-generational-personality-upbeat-open-new-ideas-technology-bound.

78   *But obligations*   "Heartland Monitor Poll," 12.

78   *12 percent of adults*   Wendy Wang and Rich Morin, "Home for the Holidays . . . and Every Other Day," Pew Research Center, November 24, 2009, http://pewresearch.org/pubs/1423/home-for-the-holidays-boomeranged-parents.

78   *Millennials entered*   "Millennials: Confident. Connected. Open to Change," 67–70.

79   *When asked whom*   "Heartland Monitor Poll," 4.

79   *A recent paper*   Paolo Giuliano and Antonio Spilimbergo, "Growing Up in a Recession" (working paper 15321, National Bureau of Economic Research, September 2009), http://www.nber.org/papers/w15321.

79   *The optimism*   "Millennials: Confident. Connected. Open to Change," 21–22.

80   *college attendance has risen*   Catherine Rampell, "College Enrollment Rate at Record High," *Economix* (blog), *New York Times*, April 28, 2010, http://econo mix.blogs.nytimes.com/2010/04/28/college-enrollment-rate-at-record-high/.

5: HOUSEBOUND: THE MIDDLE CLASS AFTER THE BUST

82   *Since the recession began*   Shannon Behken, "Homeowner Fees 'Like Extortion,' Homeowner Says," *Tampa Tribune*, September 5, 2010; Mark Spector, conversation with author, 2010.

85   *real home prices rose*   S&P/Case-Shiller Home Price Indices.

85   *Home buyers*   National Association of Realtors, conversation with author, 2010; U.S. Bureau of Labor Statistics, Consumer Expenditure Survey.

85   *nearly one in four*   Chris Arnold, "Economists Brace for Worsening Subprime Crisis," *All Things Considered*, National Public Radio, August 7, 2007, http://www.npr org/templates/story/story.php?storyId=12561184.

85   *20 percent of all new mortgages*   Ben Bernanke, "Fostering Sustainable Homeownership" (speech, National Community Reinvestment Coalition Annual Meeting, March 14, 2008), http://www.federalreserve.gov/newsevents/speech/bernanke20080314a.htm.

85   *this kind of appreciation*   Don Peck, "Pffffttt," *Atlantic*, July/August 2005, http://www.theatlantic.com/magazine/archive/2005/07/pffffttt/6751/.

85   *typical families saw*   U.S. Census Bureau, "American Housing Survey," http://www.census.gov/hhes/www/housing/ahs/ahs.html; S&P/Case-Shiller Home Price Indices.

85   *Many cashed out*   Federal Deposit Insurance Corporation, http://www2.fdic.gov/sdi/main.asp.

85   *more than 12 million*   U.S. Census Bureau, "American Housing Survey for the United States: 2007."

86   *Nationwide, housing values*   S&P/Case-Shiller Home Price Indices.

86   *the total housing vacancy rate*   Alex Tabarrok, "Why Are So Many Homes Unemployed?" *Marginal Revolution* (blog), July 29, 2010, http://www.margin alrevolution.com/marginalrevolution/2010/07/why-are-so-many-homes-unem ployed.html.

86   *roughly one in four*   CoreLogic, "New CoreLogic Data Shows 23 Percent of Borrowers Underwater With $750 Billion of Negative Equity," March 8, 2011, http://www.mbaa.org/ResearchandForecasts/ProductsandSurveys/NationalDelinquencySurvey.htm; Mortgage Bankers Association, "Delinquencies and Foreclosure Starts Decrease in Latest MBA National Delinquency Survey," August 26, 2010.

86   *But a larger number*   Joint Center for Housing Studies, Harvard University, "The State of the Nation's Housing 2010," June 2010, http://www.hks.harvard.edu/news-events/news/press-releases/sonh-2010.

86   *"Disillusionment is"*   Andrew Sullivan, "The View from Your Recession," *Daily Dish* (blog), *Atlantic*, April 23, 2009, http://andrewsullivan.theatlantic.com/the_daily_dish/2009/04/the-view-from-your-recession-13.html#more.

87   *This pattern*   Richard Florida, "How the Crash Will Reshape America," *Atlantic*, March 2009, http://www.theatlantic.com/magazine/archive/2009/03/how-the-crash-will-reshape-america/7293/.

88   *So, too, have recent immigrants*   Audrey Singer, "The State of Metropolitan America: Immigration," Brookings Institution, 2010, http://www.brookings.edu/metro/MetroAmericaChapters/immigration.aspx.

88   *Christopher Leinberger argued*   Christopher Leinberger, "The Next Slum?" *Atlantic*, March 2008, http://www.theatlantic.com/magazine/archive/2008/03/the-next-slum/6653/.

89   *difficult compromises*   Fannie Mae, "Fourth Quarter 2010," National Housing Survey Fact Sheet, http://www.fanniemae.com/about/housing-survey.html.

89   *roughly 3.5 million Americans*   Arianna Huffington, *Third World America: How Our Politicians Are Abandoning the Middle Class and Destroying the American Dream* (New York: Crown Publishers, 2010), 104.

89   *Related research shows*   Robert Frank, *Falling Behind: How Rising Inequality Harms the Middle Class* (Los Angeles: University of California Press, 2007), 88.

89   *Once suburban communities*   Leinberger, "The Next Slum?"

90   *A 2010 Brookings Institution study*   Singer, "The State of Metropolitan America," 114, 133.

90   *crime, too, has migrated*   Hanna Rosin, "American Murder Mystery," *Atlantic*, July/August 2008, http://www.theatlantic.com/magazine/archive/2008/07/american-murder-mystery/6872/; Leinberger, "The Next Slum?"

90   *Detroit remained*   Florida, "How the Crash Will Reshape America."

90   *Today, after years of rapid growth*   J. Patrick Coolican, "Las Vegas Population in Decline; Will It Reverse?" *Las Vegas Sun*, November 13, 2010.

90   *as Sin City beckoned*   Alex Tabarrok, "Leaving Las Vegas (If They Can)," *Marginal Revolution* (blog), October 4, 2010, http://www.marginalrevolution.com/marginalrevolution/2010/10/leaving-las-vegas-if-they-can.html.

90   *That's no surprise*   Adam Nagourney, "Las Vegas Faces Its Deepest Slide Since the 1940s," *New York Times*, October 2, 2010, http://www.nytimes.com/2010/10/03/us/03vegas.html.

91   *What's surprising is*   Jean Guerrero, "All Signs Point to Continuing Las Vegas Exodus," *Las Vegas Sun*, September 2, 2010, http://www.lasvegassun.com/news/2010/sep/02/moving-vegas-not-anymore/.

91   *Anchored by houses*   Haya El Nasser, "More Move, But Not Long Distance," *USA Today*, May 11, 2010.

91   *surely this recession*   Social & Demographic Trends Project, "How the Great Recession Has Changed Life in America," Pew Research Center (June 30, 2010), 7.

91   *the suburbs were never*   Kenneth Jackson, *Crabgrass Frontier: The Suburbanization of the United States* (New York: Oxford University Press, 1985), 272–76.

94   *In his 2008 book*   Bill Bishop, *The Big Sort* (New York: Houghton Mifflin; 2008), esp. 49–54.

96   *middle-class status anxiety*   Social & Demographic Trends Project, "How the Great Recession Has Changed Life in America," 36–51.

97   *But middle-class optimism*   Ibid.

97   *According to Fannie Mae's*   "National Housing Survey," Fannie Mae, http://www.fanniemae.com/media/pdf/2010/National-Housing-Survey-112310.pdf.

97   *In their analysis*   Carmen Reinhart and Kenneth Rogoff, "The Aftermath of Financial Crises" (paper prepared for presentation at American Economic Association meeting, San Francisco, January 3, 2009).

97   *In Japan*   Information provided to author by the Japan Real Estate Institute, 2010.

97   *the New York Times has taken*   For example, see Martin Fackler, "Take It from Japan: Bubbles Hurt," *New York Times*, December 25, 2005; Martin Fackler, "Japan Goes from Dynamic to Disheartened," *New York Times*, October, 16, 2010.

98   *Evidence of a growing*   U.S. Bureau of Economic Analysis, "Personal Savings Rate," http://www.bea.gov/briefrm/saving.htm.

98   *As it relates to housing*   Alex Kotlowitz, "All Boarded Up," *New York Times Magazine*, March 4, 2009, http://www.nytimes.com/2009/03/08/magazine/08Foreclosure-t.html.

98   *In Las Vegas and Phoenix*   David Streitfeld, "Building Is Booming in a City of Empty Houses," *New York Times*, May 15, 2010, http://www.nytimes.com/2010/05/16/business/16builder.html.

98   *under a pilot program*   Annie Lowrey, "The Return of the $1,000 Down Mortgage," *Washington Independent*, August 5, 2010, http://washingtonindependent.com/93795/the-return-of-the-1000-down-mortgage.

6: PLUTONOMY: THE VERY RICH IN
RECESSION AND RECOVERY

100 *three Citigroup analysts* Ajay Kapur, Niall Macleod, and Narendra Singh, "Plutonomy: Buying Luxury, Explaining Global Imbalances," Citigroup Research, Citigroup Global Markets, Inc., October 16, 2005.

101 *The report was a hit* Angela Barnes, "Want Wealth? Invest in the Uber-Rich," Scripps News, October 4, 2006; Ajay Kapur et al., "The Plutonomy Symposium—Rising Tides Lifting Yachts," Citigroup Research, Citigroup Global Markets, Inc., October 2006.

101 *on the eve of the recession* Analysis by Emmanuel Saez and Thomas Piketty in "Income Inequality in the United States, 1913–2002," *Quarterly Journal of Economics* 118, no. 1 (2003): 1–39, updated at http://www.econ.berkeley .edu/~saez/; Updated Tables and Figures, "Table A6: Top Fractiles Income Levels (Including Capital Gains) in the United States," July 2010, http://www.econ .berkeley.edu/~saez/.

102 *Income inequality usually shrinks* The Gini coefficient, perhaps the most widely used measure of income inequality, rose from 0.463 in 2007 to 0.468 in 2009, a small increase. See U.S. Census Bureau, "Selected Measures of Household Income Dispersion: 1967–2009," http://www.census.gov/hhes/www/income/ data/historical/inequality/taba2.pdf.

102 *The top 1 percent* Emmanuel Saez, "Striking It Richer: The Evolution of Top Incomes in the United States (Updated with 2008 Estimates)," July 17, 2010, http://www.econ.berkeley.edu/~saez/saez-UStopincomes-2008.pdf.

102 *Corporate profits have marched* Catherine Rampell, "Corporate Profits"; Wall Street Journal/Hay Group, "2009 CEO Compensation Study," *Wall Street Journal*/Hay Group, November 15, 2010, http://www.haygroup.com/ww/ services/index.aspx?ID=2589.

102 *According to* Forbes "The Forbes 400: The Richest People in America," *Forbes,* September 16, 2010.

102 *Even in the financial sector* Nelson D. Schwartz and Louise Story, "Pay of Hedge Fund Managers Roared Back Last Year," *New York Times*, March 31, 2010; Susanne Craig and Eric Dash, "Study Points to Windfall for Goldman Partners," *New York Times*, January 18, 2011, http://dealbook.nytimes.com/2011/01/18/ study-points-to-windfall-for-goldman-partners/?hp.

102 *The crisis may have begun* "Employment, Hours, and Earnings from the Current Employment Statistics Survey (National)," U.S. Bureau of Labor Statistics; Mike Mandel, "Why Financial Jobs Have Fared Relatively Well," Mandel on Innovation and Growth (blog), May 19, 2010, http://innovationand growth.wordpress.com/2010/05/19/financial-jobs/.

102 *"Finance Firms Rev Up Hiring"* Brett Philbin, "Finance Firms Rev Up Hiring," *Wall Street Journal,* June 28, 2010; U.S. Bureau of Labor Statistics, "Current Population Survey"; Patrick McGeehan, "New York Rebounds From Slump, Unevenly," *New York Times*, August 30, 2010.

103 *The recession, meanwhile* Emmanuel Saez, conversation with author, 2010.

103 *Anthony Atkinson, an economist* Anthony Atkinson, conversation with author, 2010.

104 *The Boston Consulting Group* Nathaniel Popper, "Millionaires Make a Comeback," *Los Angeles Times,* June 11, 2010.

104 *"The rich seem to be"* Saez, conversation.

104 *Since the crash* Gabriel Sherman, "The Wail of the 1%," *New York,* April 19, 2009, http://nymag.com/news/businessfinance/56151/?imw=Y&f=most-viewed -24h10.

105 *Treasury committed* Timothy Lavin, "The Fed's Cash Machine," *Atlantic,* May 2009, http://www.theatlantic.com/magazine/archive/2009/05/the-fed -apos-s-cash-machine/7386/.

105 *Because of these actions* Louise Story, "Wall Street Pay," *New York Times,* http://www.nytimes.com/info/wall-street-pay/?scp-2&sq=Louise%20Story%20 Wall%20Street%20Pay&st=Search.

106 *Wall Street's response* John Heilemann, "Obama Is From Mars, Wall Street Is From Venus," *New York,* May 22, 2010, http://nymag.com/print/?/news/ politics/66188/.

106 *The public-relations initiatives* John Arlidge, "I'm Doing 'God's Work.' Meet Mr. Goldman Sachs," *Times* (London), November 8, 2009, http://www.timeson line.co.uk/tol/news/world/us_and_americas/article6907681.ece; Simon Johnson and James Kwak, *13 Bankers: The Wall Street Takeover and the Next Financial Meltdown* (New York: Pantheon Books, 2010), 182; Reid Pillifant, "Lloyd Blankfein Is Taking Matters into His Own Hands," *New York Observer,* May 3, 2010, http://www.observer.com/2010/daily-transom/lloyd-blankfein-taking -matters-his-own-hands.

107 *J. P. Morgan took* Ron Chernow, *The House of Morgan: An American Banking Dynasty and the Rise of Modern Finance* (New York: Atlantic Monthly Press, 1990), 73–77, 122; Johnson and Kwak, *13 Bankers,* 26.

107 *the economic historian Richard Sylla* Richard Sylla, conversation with author, 2010.

108 *the actions of Wall Street's* Johnson and Kwak, *13 Bankers,* 159.

108 *Concerned with the optics* Heilemann, "Obama Is from Mars."

109 *elite attitudes seemed different* Barbara Kellerman, conversation with author, 2010; Barbara Kellerman, "Chief Executive Pay Needs to Get Real," *Harvard Business Review* blog, May 13, 2008, http://blogs.hbr.org/kellerman/2008/05/ chief_executive_pay_needs_to_g.html.

110 *Even David Brooks* David Brooks, *Bobos in Paradise: The New Upper Class and How They Got There* (New York: Touchstone, 2000), 271–73.

111 *the defining characteristic* For more on the rise of the meritocracy, see Chrystia Freeland, "The Rise of the New Global Elite," *Atlantic,* January/February 2011, http://www.theatlantic.com/magazine/print/2011/01/the-rise-of-the-new -global-elite/8343/.

111 *In his final book* Christopher Lasch, *The Revolt of the Elites and the Betrayal of Democracy* (1995; repr., New York: W. W. Norton, 1996), 4, 40.

112 *modern elites tend to* Ibid., 41.

113 *Bill Gates was one of* Bill Gates, interview by Walter Isaacson, "Conversation With Bill Gates," Aspen Ideas Festival 2010, http://www.aifestival.org/audio -video-library.php?menu=3&title=667&action=full_info.

113 *In a recent essay* Freeland, "The Rise of the New Global Elite."

114 *But in Aspen* Michael Splinter, interview by David Bradley, "Turning Innovation Into Industry," Aspen Ideas Festival 2010, http://www.aifestival.org/audio-video -library.php?menu=3&title=581&action=full_info; Tom Wilson, panel moderated by Ronald Brownstein, "Is America Still the Land of Opportunity? Taking a Hard Look at the Middle Class," Aspen Ideas Festival 2010, http://www.aifestival.org/ audio-video-library.php?menu=3&title=634&action=full_info.

114 *David Hale* David Hale, panel discussion, "Views on America's Economy: At Home and Abroad," Aspen Ideas Festival 2010.

116 *Onstage, Bill Gates* Bill Gates interview.

116 *The Bill & Melinda Gates Foundation* Bill & Melinda Gates Foundation, "2009 Annual Report: Grants Paid Summary," http://www.gatesfoundation.org/ annualreport/2009/Pages/grants-paid-summary.aspx; "More U.S. Billionaires Pledge to Give Away Wealth," Reuters, December 9, 2010.

117 *But the town has not escaped* Diane Tegmeyer, "Madoff Scandal Hits Aspen," CNNMoney, December 22, 2008, http://money.cnn.com/2008/12/22/ news/companies/madoff_aspen.fortune/index.htm; David Streitfeld, "Biggest Defaulters on Mortgages Are the Rich," *New York Times*, July 8, 2010.

118 *She showed me* Brent Gardner-Smith, "Banks Seek to Foreclose on Base Village," *Aspen Daily News*, July 9, 2010, http://www.aspendailynews.com/ section/home/141390.

7: UNDERCLASS: MEN AND FAMILY IN A JOBLESS AGE

119 *In his 1996 book* William Julius Wilson, *When Work Disappears: The World of the New Urban Poor* (1996; repr., New York: Vintage Books, 1997), xiii. Citations refer to the Vintage edition.

119 *most urban black men* Ibid., 31.

119 *As inner cities shed* Ibid., 27.

119 *Wilson's research shows* Ibid., 140–42.

120 *death rate of young black men* Samuel H. Preston and Emily Buzzell, "Service in Iraq: Just How Risky?" *Washington Post*, August 26, 2006, http://www.wash ingtonpost.com/wp-dyn/content/article/2006/08/25/AR2006082500940.html.

120 *Many of those row houses* Maria Kefalas, conversation with author, 2010.

120 *These sorts of problems* Bill Bishop, *The Big Sort* (New York: Houghton Mifflin, 2008), 136–41.

121 *Appalachia has long been* Lawrence E. Wood and Gregory A. Bischak,

"Progress and Challenges in Reducing Economic Distress in Appalachia: An Analysis of National and Regional Trends Since 1960," Appalachian Regional Commission, January 2000, 19; Lawrence E. Wood, "Trends in National and Regional Economic Distress: 1960–2000," Appalachian Regional Commission, April 2005, 27, 43. Also, see "West Virginia: State Profile" in *Almanac of American Politics*, http://nationaljournal.com/almanac/2008/states/wv/wv_profile.php.

121 *It has since come down* Bishop, *The Big Sort*, 137.

121 *In McDowell County* U.S. Census Bureau, "American Community Survey, 2005–2009: Educational Attainment."

121 *That's less often the case* Mark Mather, "Households and Families in Appalachia," Population Reference Bureau, May 2004.

121 *Abuse of drugs* Bishop, *The Big Sort*, 136–41.

122 *The weight of this recession* Anna Turner, "Jobs Crisis Fact Sheet," Economic Policy Institute, 2010; Hanna Rosin, "The End of Men," *Atlantic*, July/August 2010, http://www.theatlantic.com/magazine/archive/2010/07/the-end-of-men/8135/.

122 *In January 2011* U.S. Bureau of Labor Statistics, 2011, "Labor Force Statistics From the Current Population Survey: Employment-Population Ratio," U.S. Bureau of Labor Statistics, 2011.

123 *The proportion of young men* Michael Greenstone and Adam Looney, "The Problem with Men: A Look at Long-Term Employment Trends," Brookings Institution, December 2, 2010, http://www.brookings.edu/2010/1203_jobs_greenstone_looney.aspx.

123 *And as the sociologists* Maria Charles and David Grusky, *Occupational Ghettos: The Worldwide Segregation of Women and Men* (Stanford: Stanford University Press, 2004), 312.

123 *the ratio of women to men* U.S. Bureau of Labor Statistics, e-mail message to author, December 27, 2010. Findings are based on unpublished data from the Current Population Survey.

123 *U.S. manufacturing still employed* U.S. Bureau of Labor Statistics, "Employment, Hours, and Earnings from the Current Employment Statistics Survey (National)," 2011.

124 *"Forty years ago"* Rosin, "The End of Men."

124 *And men have yet to adjust* Greenstone and Looney, "The Problem with Men."

124 *In her 2010 Atlantic essay* Rosin, "The End of Men."

124 *"I'm deeply concerned"* Bruce Weinberg, conversation with author, 2010; Lex Borghans, Bas ter Weel, and Bruce A. Weinberg, "People People: Social Capital and the Labor-Market Outcomes of Underrepresented Groups" (NBER Working Paper 11985, January 2006).

125 *women are more likely than men* Borghans et al., "People People."

125 *women are also struggling* U.S. Bureau of Labor Statistics, "Household Data; Table A-10. Selected Unemployment Indicators, Seasonally Adjusted," http://www.bls.gov/news.release/empsit.t10.htm.

125 *while employment among women*   Greenstone and Looney, "The Problem with Men."

125 *"I like it outside"*   Frank Massoli (pseudonym), conversation with author, December 2010.

128 *Between 2007 and 2010*   Information provided by e-mail to author by the National Domestic Violence Hotline, January 14, 2011.

128 *More common than violence*   George Akerloff and Rachel Kranton, *Identity Economics: How Our Identities Shape Our Work, Wages, and Well-Being* (Princeton, NJ: Princeton University Press, 2010).

128 *Many working women*   Kathryn Edin, conversation with author, 2009.

128 *The national divorce rate*   Brad Wilcox, conversation with author, 2009; National Marriage Project, "The Great Recession and Marriage," University of Virginia, February 2011, 4; National Marriage Project, "State of Our Unions 2009," University of Virginia, 2009.

129 *Among couples without*   Edin, conversation.

130 *For both men and women*   Christina Gibson-Davis, "Did Marriage and Fertility Get a Divorce? The Differential Association of Earnings on Marriages and Births" (presentation to Department of Human Development and Family Studies, University of North Carolina–Greensboro, February 2010).

130 *Many children are already*   John Irons, "Economic Scarring: The Long-Term Impacts of the Recession," Economic Policy Institute, September 2009, 4, http://www.epi.org/publications/entry/bp243/; Michael Luo, "Job Woes Exacting a Toll on Family Life," *New York Times*, November 12, 2009, http://www.nytimes.com/2009/11/12/us/12families.html.

130 *But a large body of research*   Sara McLanahan, "Children in Fragile Families" (working paper 09-16-FF, Center for Research on Child Wellbeing, Princeton University, 2009); W. Bradford Wilcox, "The Evolution of Divorce," *National Affairs*, no. 1 (Fall 2009), http://www.nationalaffairs.com/publications/detail/the-evolution-of-divorce; Edin, conversation.

131 *One 2005 study*   Avner Ahituv and Robert Lerman, "How Do Marital Status, Work Effort, and Wage Rates Interact?" (IZA Discussion Paper 1688, July 2005), 7, 30.

131 *jobless men take on*   Edin, conversation.

132 *Even as weak job prospects*   Algernon Austin, "Three Lessons About Black Poverty," Economic Policy Institute, September 18, 2009, http://www.epi.org/analysis_and_opinion/entry/the_lessons_of_black_poverty/; Algernon Austin, conversation with author, 2009; "Labor Force Statistics From the Current Population Survey," U.S. Bureau of Labor Statistics.

132 *Ellis Cose wrote*   Ellis Cose, "The Good News About Black America," *Newsweek*, June 7, 1999, http://www.newsweek.com/1999/06/06/the-good-news-about-black-america.html.

132 *But many of those gains*   Michael Powell, "Blacks in Memphis Lose Decades

of Economic Gains," *New York Times,* May 30, 2010, http://www.nytimes.com/2010/05/31/business/economy/31memphis.html.

132 *unemployment among black teens* U.S. Bureau of Labor Statistics, "Labor Force Statistics From the Current Population Survey."

133 *With so few jobs available* William Julius Wilson, conversation with author, 2009.

133 *The sociologist Glen Elder* Glen Elder, conversation with author, 2009.

133 *In New York City* Community Service Society, "The Unheard Third Survey," Community Service Society, 2010, http://www.cssny.org/research/unheard_third/survey_findings/.

133 *Wilson argues that* Wilson, conversation.

134 *Bad social norms spread* Bruce A. Weinberg, Patricia B. Reagan, and Jeffrey J. Yankow, "Do Neighborhoods Affect Hours Worked: Evidence From Longitudinal Data," Department of Economics and Center for Human Resource Research, Ohio State University, August 2002.

134 *When a couple divorces* Rose McDermott, James H. Fowler, and Nicholas A. Christakis, "Breaking Up Is Hard to Do, Unless Everyone Else Is Doing It Too: Social Network Effects on Divorce in a Longitudinal Sample Followed for 32 Years" (working paper, October 2009).

134 *"The newest and perhaps"* National Marriage Project, "State of Our Unions 2010," University of Virginia, 2010, ix–xi, 19–37, http://www.stateofourunions.org/2010/SOOU2010.php.

135 *The same pattern emerges* Ibid.

135 *attendance at religious services* Thomas H. Sander and Robert Putnam, "Still Bowling Alone?" *Journal of Democracy* 21, no. 1 (January 2010): 9–16; National Marriage Project, "State of Our Unions 2010," 45–50.

136 *Wilcox has tried* W. Bradford Wilcox, e-mail to author, February 10, 2011.

136 *The number of couples* U.S. Census Bureau, "Current Population Survey Reports: Families and Living Arrangements," 2010; Rose M. Kreider, "Increase in Opposite-Sex Cohabiting Couples from 2009 to 2010 in the Annual Social and Economic Supplement to the Current Population Survey" (working paper, Housing and Household Economic Statistics Division, U.S. Bureau of the Census, September 15, 2010).

136 *In their 2009 book* Ron Haskins and Isabel Sawhill, *Creating an Opportunity Society* (Washington, DC: Brookings Institution, 2009), 65.

137 *one indication of the degree* Bishop, *The Big Sort,* 137–38.

8: THE POLITICS OF THE NEXT TEN YEARS

139 *On the eve of the Great Recession* Thomas H. Sander and Robert Putnam, "Still Bowling Alone?" *Journal of Democracy* 21, no. 1 (January 2010): 9–16.

140 *Economic hardship clearly* National Conference on Citizenship, "2009 America's Civic Health Index," 5–6, August 27, 2009, http://www.ncoc.net/index.php?tray=content&tid=top5&cid=2gp54.

140 *Public views toward* Pew Research Center for the People & the Press, "Independents Take Center Stage in the Obama Era," May 21, 2009, http://people-press.org/report/517/political-values-and-core-attitudes.

140 *Mistrust of all things foreign* Sara Murray and Douglas Belkin, "Americans Sour on Trade," *Wall Street Journal*, October 12, 2010, http://online.wsj.com/article/SB10001424052748703466104575529753735783116.html.

140 *the state of Arizona passed* Randal C. Archibold, "Arizona Enacts Stringent Law on Immigration," *New York Times*, April 23, 2010, http://www.nytimes.com/2010/04/24/us/politics/24immig.html?_r=1&ref=us.

140 *According to a poll* Wall Street Journal/NBC News survey, conducted by Hart/McInturff, May 6–10, 2010, http://online.wsj.com/article/SB100014240527487042479045752408126721 73820.html, cited in Peter Wallsten, Naftali Bendavid, and Jean Spencer, "Republican Party Wins Back Supporters, Poll Finds," *Wall Street Journal*, May 13, 2010, 21.

140 *Deportations have risen* Peter Slevin, "Deportations of Illegal Immigrants Increase Under Obama Administration," *Washington Post*, July 26, 2010; Bill Ong Hing, "Babies 'R' Us," *Slate*, August 4, 2010, http://www.slate.com/id/2262791/.

141 *The percentage of Hispanics* Pew Research Center for the People & the Press, "Racial Attitudes in America II," December 2009, 15.

141 *Anti-Muslim sentiment* Bobby Ghosh, "Does America Have a Muslim Problem?" *Time*, August 19, 2010; Pew Research Center for the People & the Press, "Public Remains Conflicted Over Islam," August 24, 2010, http://people-press.org/report/647/.

141 *Martin Peretz, then the editor* Martin Peretz, "The New York Times Laments 'A Sadly Wary Misunderstanding of Muslim-Americans.' But Really Is It 'Sadly Wary' or a 'Misunderstanding' At All?" *New Republic*, September 4, 2010, http://www.tnr.com/blog/77475/the-new-york-times-laments-sadly-wary-misunderstanding-muslim-americans-really-it-sadly-w?page=1.

141 *an "emergency summit"* Laurie Goodstein, "Concern Is Voiced Over Religious Intolerance," *New York Times*, September 7, 2010.

141 *Middle-class discontent* Joshua Green, "The Tea Party Takes On Washington," *Atlantic*, November 4, 2010, http://www.theatlantic.com/politics/archive/2010/11/the-tea-party-takes-on-washington/66104/; Pew Research Center for the People and the Press, "A Clear Rejection of the Status Quo," Pew Research Center for the People & the Press, November 3, 2010, http://pewresearch.org/pubs/1789/2010-midterm-elections-exit-poll-analysis.

142 *The Tea Party's active supporters* "Polling the Tea Party," *New York*

Times, April 14, 2010, http://www.nytimes.com/interactive/2010/04/14/us/
politics/20100414-tea-party-poll-graphic.html?ref=politics.

142 *An analysis of Tea Party events*   Dante Chinni, "Has the Tea Party's Influence
Slowed?" *Rundown* (blog), *PBS NewsHour*, October 18, 2010, http://www.pbs
.org/newshour/rundown/2010/10/has-tea-party-influence-crested-ahead-of-elec
tions.html.

142 *many of the Tea Party's supporters*   "Polling the Tea Party," *New York Times*.

143 *At Rand Paul's*   Kate Zernike, "Paul Vows to Remain True to the Tea Party,"
New York Times, May 19, 2010; Sarah Palin, keynote speech, National Tea Party
Convention, Nashville, Tennessee, February 6, 2010, http://www.americanrhetoric
.com/speeches/sarahpalin2010teapartykeynote.htm.

143 *At a Utah GOP convention*   Carl Hulse and David M. Herszenhorn, "Bank
Bailouts Potent Issue for Fall Elections," *New York Times*, July 10, 2010.

143 *According to a survey*   Robert P. Jones and Daniel Cox, "Old Alignments,
Emerging Fault Lines: Religion in the 2010 Election and Beyond," Pew Public
Religion Research Institute, November 2010, 15.

143 *Tea Party supporters generally favor*   Supported by "Polling the Tea Party,"
New York Times.

143 *The ideal of market freedom*   Pew Research Center for the People & the Press,
"Public Support for Increased Trade, Except With South Korea and China,"
November 9, 2010, http://people-press.org/report/673/.

143 *If you squint hard enough*   Lawrence Goodwyn, *The Populist Movement* (New
York: Oxford University Press, 1978), vii.

144 *David Frum has noted*   David Frum, "Post-Tea-Party Nation," *New York
Times Magazine*, November 12, 2010, http://www.nytimes.com/2010/11/14/
magazine/14FOB-idealab-t.html.

144 *In his 1951 book*   Eric Hoffer, *The True Believer: Thoughts on the Nature of Mass
Movements* (New York: Harper & Row, 1951; Perennial Classics, 2002), xi, 26.
Citations refer to the Perennial edition.

146 *a Penn Schoen Berland poll*   Andy Barr, "Poll: D.C. Elites a World Apart,"
Politico, July 18, 2010, http://www.politico.com/polls/power-and-the-people.
(Full results available as a PDF at this URL.)

146 *Washington's political elites*   Francesca Levy, "America's 25 Richest Counties,"
Forbes, March 4, 2010, http://www.forbes.com/2010/03/04/america-richest
-counties-lifestyle-real-estate-wealthy-suburbs.html.

147 *In his 2005 paper*   Martin Gilens, "Inequality and Democratic Responsiveness,"
Public Opinion Quarterly 69, no. 5 (special issue, 2005): 778–896; Martin Gilens,
conversation with author, 2010.

148 *A new free-trade agreement*   "U.S.–South Korea Trade Deal Largest Since
NAFTA," Associated Press, December 3, 2010.

149 *the state of the economy*   Miller Center of Public Affairs, University of
Virginia, "George Herbert Walker Bush, American President: An Online
Reference Resource," http://millercenter.org/president/bush/essays/biography/3.

Democrats who decided not to run against George Bush in 1996 included Senator Bill Bradley and Governor Mario Cuomo.

149 *But economic conditions*   Larry Bartels, *Unequal Democracy: The Political Economy of the New Gilded Age* (Princeton, NJ: Princeton University Press, 2008), 100–104; John B. Judis, "Job One," *New Republic,* September 22, 2009, http://www.tnr.com/article/job-one.

150 *unemployment doesn't matter*   Bartels, *Unequal Democracy*, 100–120; Seth Masket, conversation with author, December 2010.

151 *polling in early 2011*   "Romney, Huckabee Even With Obama, Other GOP Hopefuls Trail," Rasmussen Reports, February 6, 2011; Lydia Saad, "Nameless Republican Ties Obama in 2010 Election Preferences," Gallup, February 16, 2011.

151 *After the 2010 midterms*   David M. Kennedy, "Throwing the Bums Out for 140 Years," *New York Times,* November 6, 2010, http://www.nytimes.com/2010/11/07/opinion/07kennedy.html.

152 *Japan's economy since*   John B. Judis, "A Lost Generation," *New Republic,* November 13, 2010, http://www.tnr.com/article/politics/78890/a-lost-generation.

9: A WAY FORWARD

157 *In 1937, as Franklin*   U.S. Census Bureau, "Historical Statistics of the United States, Colonial Times to 1957," 1960, 70; Robert McElvaine, *The Great Depression: America, 1929–1941* (New York: New York Times Books, 1984), 298.

157 *after years of deficits*   Jodie T. Allen, "How a Different America Responded to the Great Depression," Pew Research Center, December 14, 2010, http://pewresearch.org/pubs/1810/public-opinion-great-depression-compared-with-now.

157 *And so, in 1937*   Ibid.; McElvaine, *The Great Depression,* 297–98, 307.

157 *Deficit spending intuitively*   U.S. Office of Management and Budget, Historical Tables, "Federal Debt at the End of the Year: 1940–2016," http://www.whitehouse.gov/omb/budget/Historicals.

157 *Debt kept rising*   Richard Auxier, "Reagan's Recession," Pew Research Center, December 14, 2010, http://pewresearch.org/pubs/1818/reagan-recession-public-opinion-very-negative.

157 *The size of the debt*   U.S. Office of Management and Budget, Historical Tables, "Federal Debt at the End of the Year: 1940-2016."

158 *Many observers believe*   Debt Reduction Task Force, "Restoring America's Future," Bipartisan Policy Center, November 2010.

158 *Yet concerns over*   Data and analysis provided to author by Marc Goldwein, Policy Director, Committee for a Responsible Federal Budget, by e-mail on March 24, 2011.

158 *Jobs are scarce*   U.S. Bureau of Labor Statistics, "Labor Force Statistics from the Current Population Survey," accessed March 2011, http://www.bls.gov/cps/.

158 *The unemployment rate* U.S. Bureau of Labor Statistics, data provided to the author.

159 *fears are driven* See, for instance, Congressional Budget Office, "The Budget and Economic Outlook: Fiscal Years 2008 to 2018," January 2008, figure 1-4 ("Projected Federal Spending Over the Long Term"), showing rapid increases in federal spending over the next several decades, driven exclusively by growth in Medicare and Medicaid spending, http://cbo.gov/ftpdocs/89xx/doc8917/Chapter1.5.1.shtml#1070080.

160 *we should also focus* The economists Ezekiel J. Emanuel and Victor R. Fuchs have described a much broader version of such a plan. See, for example, "Health Care Vouchers—A Proposal for Universal Coverage," *New England Journal of Medicine* 352, no. 12 (March 24, 2005), http://www.robert-h-frank.com/PDFs/Emanuel-Fuchs.NEJM.3-24-05.pdf.

160 *the city of Camden, New Jersey* Christopher Beam, "Officers Down," *Slate*, January 19, 2011, http://www.slate.com/id/2281694/.

161 *One of the best targets* Michael Mandel, "Our Aging Capital Stock," *Mandel on Innovation and Growth* (blog), December 14, 2010, http://innovationand growth.wordpress.com/2010/12/14/our-aging-capital-stock/.

161 *The American Society of Civil Engineers* American Society of Civil Engineers, "Report Card for America's Infrastructure," 2009, http://www.infrastructure reportcard.org/.

161 *Over the past decade* McKinsey Global Institute, "Growth and Competitiveness in the United States: The Role of Its Multinational Companies," June 2010, 45, http://www.mckinsey.com/mgi/publications/role_of_us_multinational_companies/index.asp.

161 *China spends about 9 percent* "The Cracks Are Showing," *Economist*, June 26, 2008, http://www.economist.com/node/11636517.

161 *Not all of this investment* Christopher Leinberger, "Here Comes the Neighborhood," *Atlantic*, June 2010, http://www.theatlantic.com/magazine/archive/2010/06/here-comes-the-neighborhood/8093/.

162 *And targeted expansion* The CBO estimates full-time equivalent job savings of between 1.8 and 5 million, and a boost to real GDP of between 1.1 and 3.5 percent. See Congressional Budget Office, "Estimated Impact of ARRA on Employment and Economic Output from October 2010 Through December 2010," *Director's Blog*, Congressional Budget Office, February, 2011, http://cboblog.cbo.gov/?p=1852; Adam Posen, *Restoring Japan's Economic Growth* (Washington, DC: Institute for International Economics, 1998).

163 *Economic woes are not* U.S. Bureau of Labor Statistics, "Local Area Unemployment Statistics: Unemployment Rates for Metropolitan Areas," December 2010, http://www.bls.gov/web/metro/laummtrk.htm.

163 *the ratio of unemployed people* Juju.com, "Job Search Difficulty Index," February 2011, http://www.job-search-engine.com/press/Juju-Releases-Job-Search-Difficulty-Index-for-Major-Cities-February-2011.

163 *the rate of migration*   William Frey, "Migration Declines Further: Stalling Brain Gains and Ambitions," Brookings Institution, January 2011, http://www .brookings.edu/opinions/2011/0112_migration_frey.aspx.

163 *a 2010 Rutgers University survey*   Debbie Borie-Holtz, Carl Van Horn, and Cliff Zukin, "No End in Sight: The Agony of Prolonged Unemployment" (paper, Rutgers University, May 2010), available at http://www.scribd.com/doc/ 32165839/Work-Trends-May-2010-No-End-in-Sight-The-Agony-of-Prolonged -Unemployment.

164 *The Internet has made it much easier*   Jens Ludwig and Steven Raphael, "The Mobility Bank: Increasing Residential Mobility to Boost Economic Mobility," Hamilton Project, October 2010.

164 *Under the Trade Adjustment Assistance Program*   Howard Rosen, conversation with author, 2010; see also U.S. Department of Labor, "Trade Adjustment Assistance Fact Sheet," http://www.doleta.gov/programs/factsht/taa.htm.

164 *As a lower-cost alternative*   Ludwig and Raphael, "The Mobility Bank."

165 *In a 2010 survey by the National Association of Manufacturers*   Motoko Rich, "Factory Jobs Return, but Employers Find Skills Shortage," *New York Times,* July 2, 2010.

165 *In some places, what employers need*   Ibid.

165 *many people who lost their job*   Borie-Holtz, Van Horn, and Zukin, "No End in Sight."

166 *time limits on unemployment benefits*   Mai Dao and Prakash Loungani, "The Human Cost of Recessions: Assessing It, Reducing It" (IMF Staff Position Note, November 11, 2010), http://www.imf.org/external/pubs/ft/spn/2010/spn1017 .pdf, see p. 18 in particular; http://www.politiquessociales.net/IMG/pdf/dp3667 .pdf.

166 *the comparatively short duration*   Walter Nicholson and Karen Needels, "Optimal Extended Unemployment Benefits," Mathematica Policy Research, Inc., October 2004, www3.amherst.edu/~wenicholson/Optimal_UI.APPAM .pdf.

167 *Wage insurance wouldn't*   Lael Brainard, "Meeting the Challenge of Income Instability," Testimony to the Joint Economic Committee of the U.S. Congress, February 28, 2007, http://www.brookings.edu/testimony/2007/0228labor_brain ard.aspx.

168 *the McKinsey Global Institute*   McKinsey Global Institute, "Growth and Competitiveness."

168 *Yet for all their outsized presence*   Hearing on the Current Federal Income Tax and the Need for Reform Before the Committee on Ways and Means, U.S. House of Representatives (January 20, 2011; testimony of Martin Sullivan), http://ways andmeans.house.gov/UploadedFiles/sullivan_written_testimony_WM_Jan_20 .pdf.

169 *"The value of knowledge capital"*   Michael Mandel, "A Massive Writedown of U.S. Knowledge Capital," *Mandel on Innovation and Growth* (blog), December

13, 2010, http://innovationandgrowth.wordpress.com/2010/12/13/a-massive
-writedown-of-u-s-knowledge-capital/.

170 *The product cycle* Michael Mandel, "Why Isn't the Innovation Economy
Creating More Jobs? Part I," *Mandel on Innovation and Growth* (blog), February
22, 2010, http://innovationandgrowth.wordpress.com/2010/02/22/why-isnt
-the-innovation-economy-creating-more-jobs-part-i/.

170 *Yet in the aughts* See, for example, Michael Mandel, "The Failed Promise of
Innovation in the U.S.," *Bloomberg Businessweek*, June 3, 2009; Edmund Phelps
and Leo Tilman, "Wanted: A First National Bank of Innovation," *Harvard
Business Review*, January/February 2010; Tyler Cowen, *The Great Stagnation*
(New York: Penguin, 2010).

171 *Foreign students still flock* McKinsey Global Institute, "Growth and
Competitiveness," 40, 41.

172 *the Sarbanes-Oxley accounting reforms* Phelps and Tilman, "Wanted."

173 *The growth of the Internet* Michael Mandel, "The Coming Communications
Boom? Jobs, Innovation and Countercyclical Regulatory Policy" (policy memo,
Progressive Policy Institute, July 20, 2010), http://www.progressivefix.com/the
-coming-communications-boom-jobs-innovation-and-countercyclical-regula
tory-policy.

173 *In periods of strong growth* Ibid.

173 *Only about 65,000 H-1B visas* McKinsey Global Institute, "Growth and
Competitiveness," 56.

173 *One group of venture* The StartUp Visa Act is available to view at www
.startupvisa.com.

174 *A special focus on improving* Ron Haskins and Isabel Sawhill, *Creating an
Opportunity Society* (Washington, DC: Brookings Institution, 2009), 149.

175 *In* The Race Between Education and Technology Claudia Goldin and
Lawrence Katz, *The Race Between Education and Technology* (Cambridge: Belknap
Press, 2008), 5, 27, 43, 244, 324.

175 *Meanwhile, with remarkable speed* Ibid., 43.

176 *Over the past thirty years* CPS Historical Time Series Tables, "Percent of
People 25 Years and Over Who Have Completed High School or College, by
Race, Hispanic Origin, and Sex, Selected Years: 1940 to 2009," U.S. Census
Bureau, September 22, 2010.

177 *Grants, loans, and tax credits* Haskins and Sawhill, *Creating an Opportunity
Society,* 186–87.

178 *One recent major study* Ibid., 188.

179 *Analysis by David Autor* David Autor, "The Polarization of Job Opportunities
in the U.S. Labor Market," Center for American Progress, the Hamilton Project,
April 2010.

179 *While the lion's share of jobs* National Employment Law Project cited by
Harold Meyerson in "Business Is Booming," *American Prospect*, January 28, 2011,
http://prospect.org/cs/articles?article=business_is_booming.

179 *As Richard Florida writes*   Richard Florida, *The Great Reset* (New York: HarperCollins, 2010), 121–22.

179 *Whole Foods Markets*   Elizabeth Flock, "Whole Foods' Organic Capitalism," *Forbes*, October 20, 2010.

180 *American economists on both*   Edmund S. Phelps, *Rewarding Work* (Cambridge: Harvard University Press, 2007); Robert Reich, *Aftershock: The Next Economy and America's Future* (New York: Knopf, 2010); among others.

180 *The Earned Income Tax Credit*   U.S. Internal Revenue Service, Earned Income Tax Credit Home Page, http://www.irs.gov/individuals/article/0,,id=96406,00 .html; Tax Policy Center, "Earned Income Tax Credit Parameters, 1975–2011," Tax Policy Center, http://www.taxpolicycenter.org/taxfacts/displayafact.cfm?Doc ID=36&Topic2id=40&Topic3id=42.

182 *The panic of 1893*   Louise Story, "Income Inequality and Financial Crises," *New York Times*, August 21, 2010; David Moss, "Chart: Bank Failures, Regulation, and Inequality in the United States," Harvard Business School, http://www.tobin project.org/conference_economic/papers/BankFailures_ChartwithComments _Moss.pdf.

183 *Over time, the United States*   Tax Foundation, "U.S. Federal Individual Income Tax Rates History, 1913–2011," January 1, 2011, http://www.tax foundation.org/publications/show/151.html.

184 *Soaking the rich*   Rosanne Altshuler, Katherine Lim, and Roberton Williams, "Desperately Seeking Revenue" (Tax Policy Center; paper presented January 15, 2010).

186 *The former labor secretary*   Reich, *Aftershock*, 140.

188 *The journalist James Fallows*   James Fallows, "How America Can Rise Again," *Atlantic*, January/February 2010.

ACKNOWLEDGMENTS

In 2010 I wrote a cover story for *The Atlantic* exploring how high unemployment might change American society if it continued to persist. Soon after it was published, I received a phone call from John Glusman at Crown, suggesting a broader inquiry into the enduring impact that the recession and its aftermath would have on American life. John's enthusiasm, to a large degree, convinced me to write this book. I am grateful to him for his encouragement and ideas throughout this process, and for his skillful editing.

James Bennet, the editor of *The Atlantic,* made this book possible by generously granting me several months off to write it, despite the staffing complexities that decision entailed. Special thanks go to James and to all my colleagues at *The Atlantic,* who helped me in too many ways to count with this book and the magazine article that preceded it. It is a pleasure and an honor to work with such gracious, curious, and committed professionals.

The Woodrow Wilson Center for International Scholars gave me valuable support and a quiet office in which to write. Hallie Detrick, Aleschia Hyde, and Cale Salih provided careful research assistance. Rachael Brown diligently checked thousands of facts contained in the book, conducted invaluable ad hoc research, and helped assemble the endnotes. Janice Cane's excellent copyediting improved the book's flow. Patrick Appel and Zoe Pollock, of *The Daily Dish,* kindly compiled scores of blog entries written by readers in the blog's recurring feature, "The View from Your Recession," and helped me follow up with some of those readers. The professional staff at the

U.S. Bureau of Labor Statistics was unfailingly helpful in my many requests for assistance in finding employment data.

Dozens of economists, sociologists, historians, and other scholars graciously agreed to speak with me about this book, sharing their research and ideas, and I am grateful to all of them. David Autor, Gary Burtless, Kathryn Edin, Maria Kefalas, Edmund Phelps, Heidi Shierholz, and Bradford Wilcox were especially generous with their time. I owe a special intellectual debt to Benjamin Friedman, whose 2005 book, *The Moral Consequences of Economic Growth,* first opened my eyes to how dramatically—and in some respects, how predictably—societies can change when the economy is anemic for an extended period of time.

I leaned on many friends and associates for advice as I researched and wrote this book. Shannon Brownlee, William Cohan, Clive Crook, James Fallows, Richard Florida, James Gibney, Joshua Green, Simon Johnson, Christopher Leinberger, Christopher Orr, Hanna Rosin, Benjamin Schwarz, and Bradford Wilcox kindly read draft sections or chapters, and the book is better for their comments and critiques. My agent, Raphael Sagalyn, was also an attentive reader, in addition to all the other help he provided.

At its heart, this book is about the millions of people whose lives have gone off course since the crash. In my research and reporting, many people shared painful experiences of unemployment or foreclosure or downward mobility. I am grateful to all of them for their openness. In the main, their stories remind me daily of the pragmatism, flexibility, and personal dignity—even in hardship—that continue to define the American character.

My deepest gratitude goes to my wife, Meghan, for her patience and support throughout the writing of this book; for her many sacrifices (not least at the dinner table, where she endured far too much talk of the recession and its consequences); for her good advice; and for her energy, exuberance, and companionship, which make every day a joy.

INDEX

About the Author

DON PECK is a national-award-winning writer and a features editor at *The Atlantic*, where he covers the economy and American society, among other subjects. He lives with his wife, Meghan, in Washington, DC.